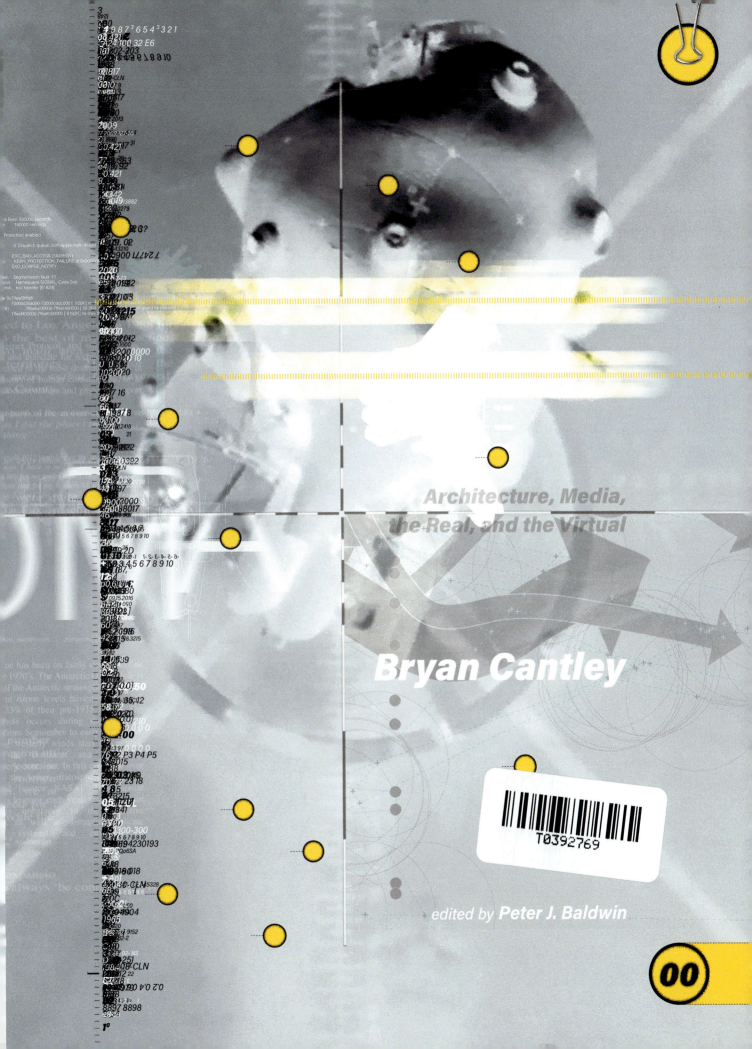

Architecture, Media, the Real, and the Virtual

Bryan Cantley

edited by Peter J. Baldwin

Image by Kevin F. O'Donnell

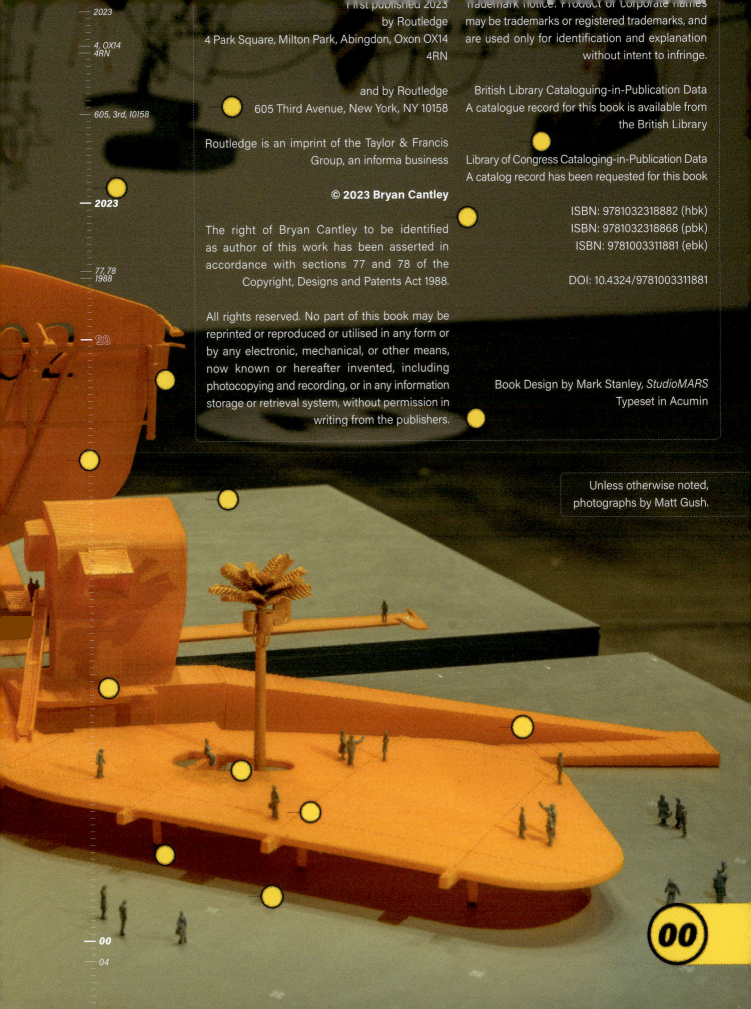

First published 2023
by Routledge
4 Park Square, Milton Park, Abingdon, Oxon OX14 4RN

and by Routledge
605 Third Avenue, New York, NY 10158

Routledge is an imprint of the Taylor & Francis Group, an informa business

© 2023 Bryan Cantley

The right of Bryan Cantley to be identified as author of this work has been asserted in accordance with sections 77 and 78 of the Copyright, Designs and Patents Act 1988.

All rights reserved. No part of this book may be reprinted or reproduced or utilised in any form or by any electronic, mechanical, or other means, now known or hereafter invented, including photocopying and recording, or in any information storage or retrieval system, without permission in writing from the publishers.

Trademark notice: Product or corporate names may be trademarks or registered trademarks, and are used only for identification and explanation without intent to infringe.

British Library Cataloguing-in-Publication Data
A catalogue record for this book is available from the British Library

Library of Congress Cataloging-in-Publication Data
A catalog record has been requested for this book

ISBN: 9781032318882 (hbk)
ISBN: 9781032318868 (pbk)
ISBN: 9781003311881 (ebk)

DOI: 10.4324/9781003311881

Book Design by Mark Stanley, *StudioMARS*
Typeset in Acumin

Unless otherwise noted, photographs by Matt Gush.

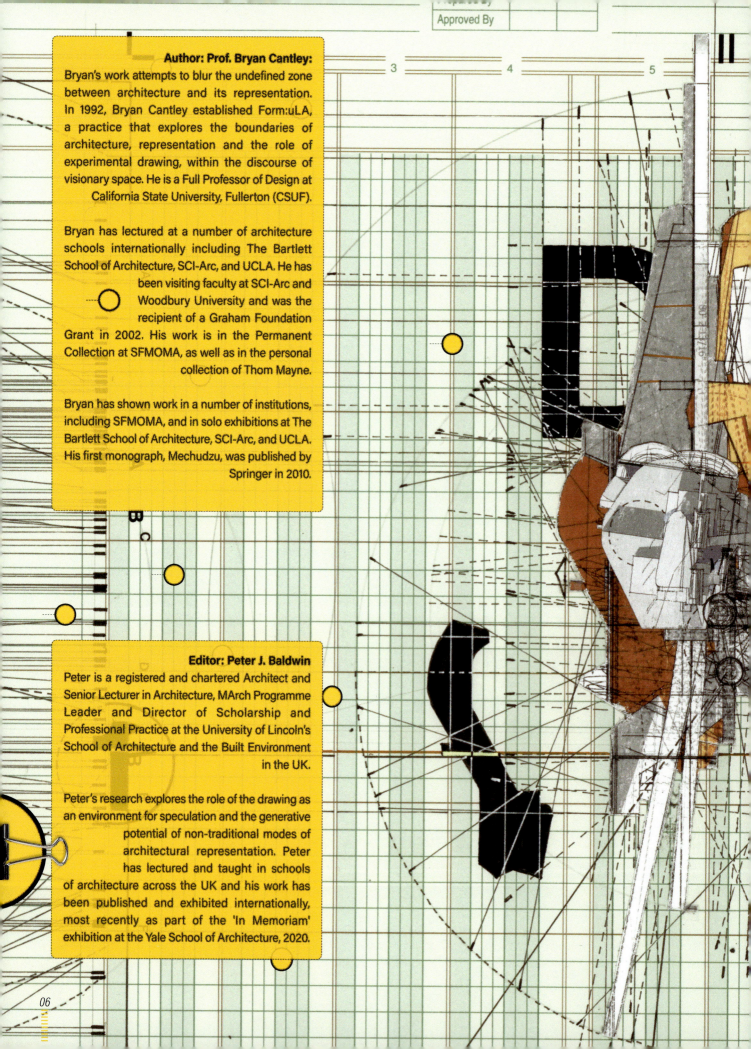

Author: Prof. Bryan Cantley:

Bryan's work attempts to blur the undefined zone between architecture and its representation. In 1992, Bryan Cantley established Form:uLA, a practice that explores the boundaries of architecture, representation and the role of experimental drawing, within the discourse of visionary space. He is a Full Professor of Design at California State University, Fullerton (CSUF).

Bryan has lectured at a number of architecture schools internationally including The Bartlett School of Architecture, SCI-Arc, and UCLA. He has been visiting faculty at SCI-Arc and Woodbury University and was the recipient of a Graham Foundation Grant in 2002. His work is in the Permanent Collection at SFMOMA, as well as in the personal collection of Thom Mayne.

Bryan has shown work in a number of institutions, including SFMOMA, and in solo exhibitions at The Bartlett School of Architecture, SCI-Arc, and UCLA. His first monograph, Mechudzu, was published by Springer in 2010.

Editor: Peter J. Baldwin

Peter is a registered and chartered Architect and Senior Lecturer in Architecture, MArch Programme Leader and Director of Scholarship and Professional Practice at the University of Lincoln's School of Architecture and the Built Environment in the UK.

Peter's research explores the role of the drawing as an environment for speculation and the generative potential of non-traditional modes of architectural representation. Peter has lectured and taught in schools of architecture across the UK and his work has been published and exhibited internationally, most recently as part of the 'In Memoriam' exhibition at the Yale School of Architecture, 2020.

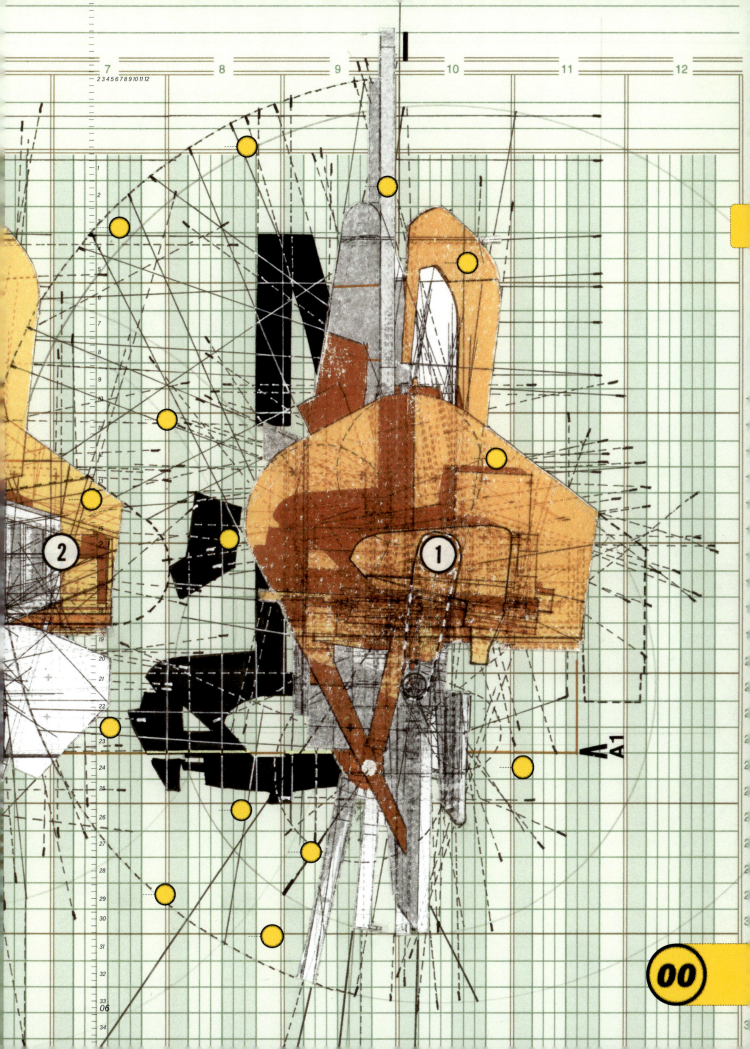

Dedicated to my father,
Walter N. Cantley, 1938–2015

[Acknowledgments]

Kim — My darling wife, my muse, my confidant, my partner in crime. You have always believed, even when I didn't, and for that I can never thank you enough. Thank you for being the other half of Team Cantley. LF+LF ...

Talia — My inspiration, my legacy. All this will be yours someday ... haha. You help me understand the future as more than a conceptual entity. Make this world a better place, ok?

Mom — Without whom I would not be writing any of this. My lifelong gratitude for your humor, your insights, your advice, and your loving spirit. "The only thing I can draw is flies ..."

Thom Mayne — Thank you for your gracious mentorship, belief in and encouragement of the project, and your friendship. I have jokingly blamed you for the way I draw, but to say that your work has been a critical inspiration in my work would be the understatement of the century. Gratitude.

Neil Spiller — Thank you for your continued unwavering support of my work. Its an honor to have someone of your caliber find an interest in my musings.

Matt Gush — This book would not be, either without your brilliant photography or your kind encouragement and pushing me to publish again. You make my work look good. I cannot thank you enough my friend. I look forward to your professional journey.

Peter Baldwin — Editor extreme. My gratitude for your insight, enriching conversations, critical eye, and humo[u]r. I am very proud of this project, and thank you greatly for your time, effort, and energy in getting this thing off the ground. Looking forward to seeing how much damage we do! WEAA!

Mark Stanley — Graphic designer extraordinaire. Much appreciation for the sculpting and transmission of this graphic dissemination ... no small task. An artifact for the ages.

Fran Ford — My salute to your vision, guidance, and patience during the proposal and construction of the book. You believed when many others did not.

CSUF + Lincoln — A large thank you to California State University Fullerton and the University of Lincoln for granting time to diligently work on this project. The support is greatly appreciated.

Essayists — A large thank you to the essayists who frame my work in a much better way than I might. Your words and observations are truly critical to this book and its delivery.

Rana Abudayyeh
Peter J. Baldwin
Helen Castle
Nat Chard
Dora Epstein-Jones
Wes Jones
Thom Mayne
Bob Sheil
Neil Spiller
Martin Summers

1938–2015

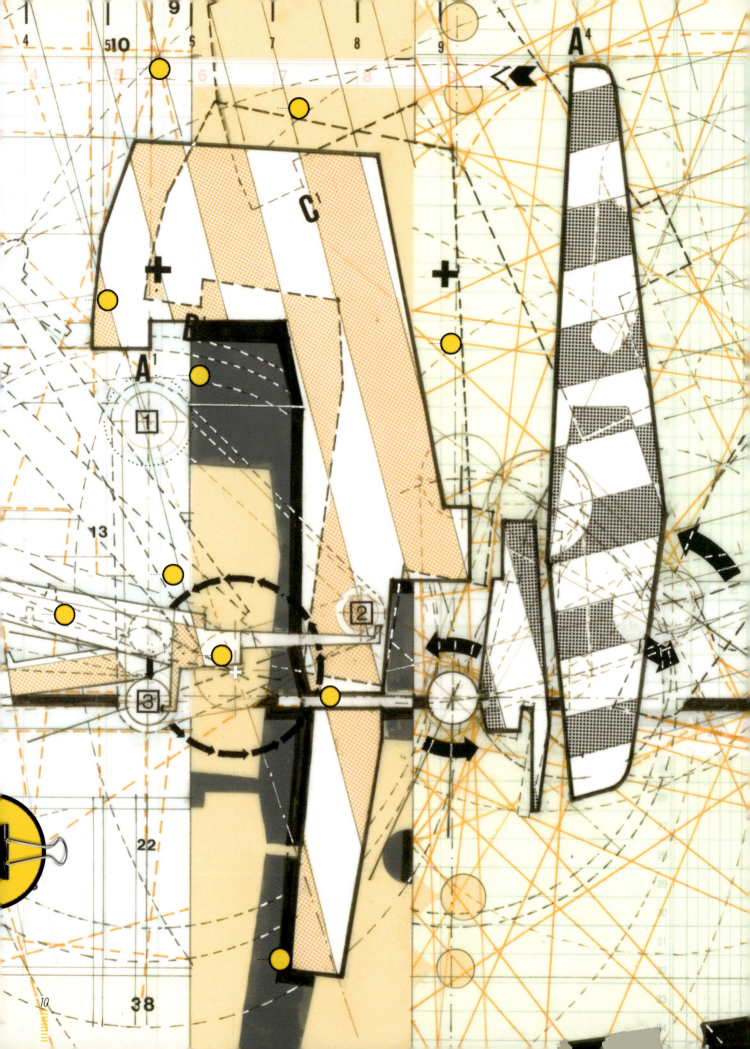

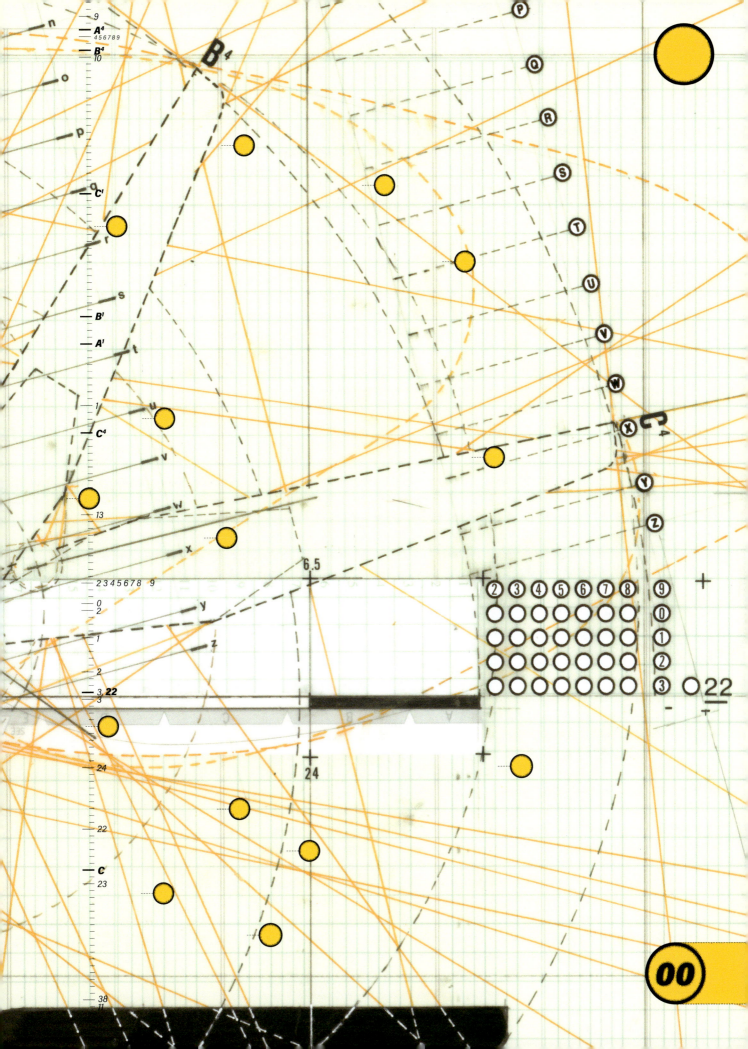

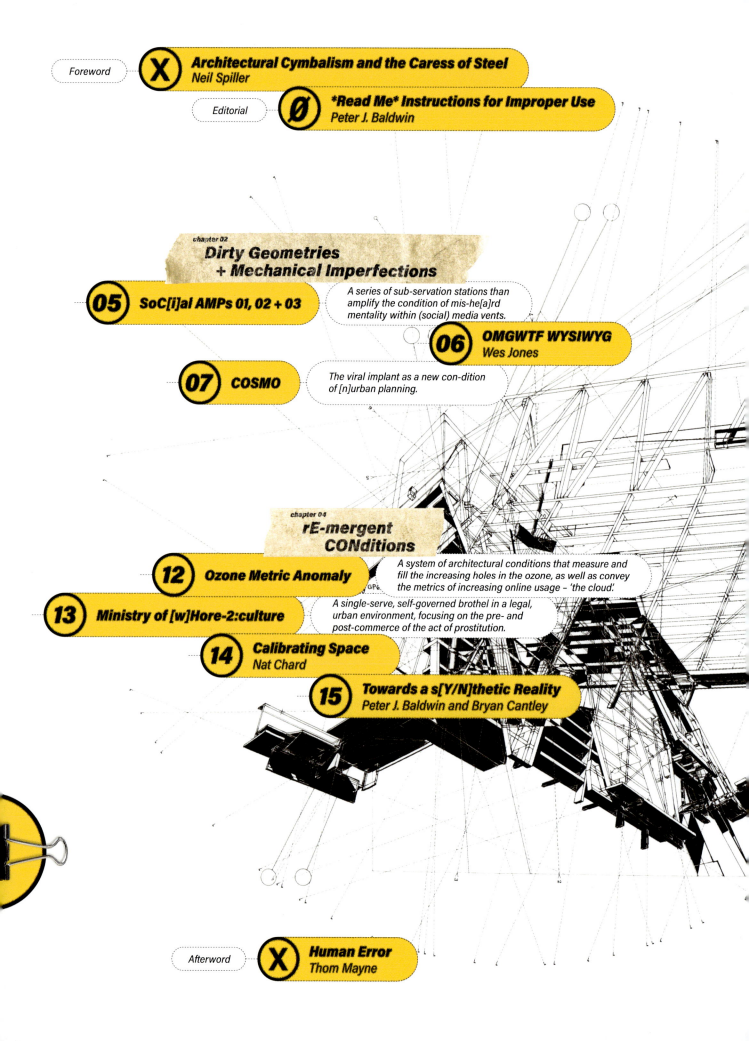

Foreword	**X**	**Architectural Cymbalism and the Caress of Steel** Neil Spiller
Editorial	**Ø**	***Read Me* Instructions for Improper Use** Peter J. Baldwin

chapter 02
Dirty Geometries + Mechanical Imperfections

05 **SoC[i]al AMPs 01, 02 + 03**

A series of sub-servation stations than amplify the condition of mis-he[a]rd mentality within (social) media vents.

06 **OMGWTF WYSIWYG**
Wes Jones

07 **COSMO**

The viral implant as a new con-dition of [n]urban planning.

chapter 04
rE-mergent CONditions

12 **Ozone Metric Anomaly**

A system of architectural conditions that measure and fill the increasing holes in the ozone, as well as convey the metrics of increasing online usage – 'the cloud'.

13 **Ministry of [w]Hore-2:culture**

A single-serve, self-governed brothel in a legal, urban environment, focusing on the pre- and post-commerce of the act of prostitution.

14 **Calibrating Space**
Nat Chard

15 **Towards a s[Y/N]thetic Reality**
Peter J. Baldwin and Bryan Cantley

Afterword	**X**	**Human Error** Thom Mayne

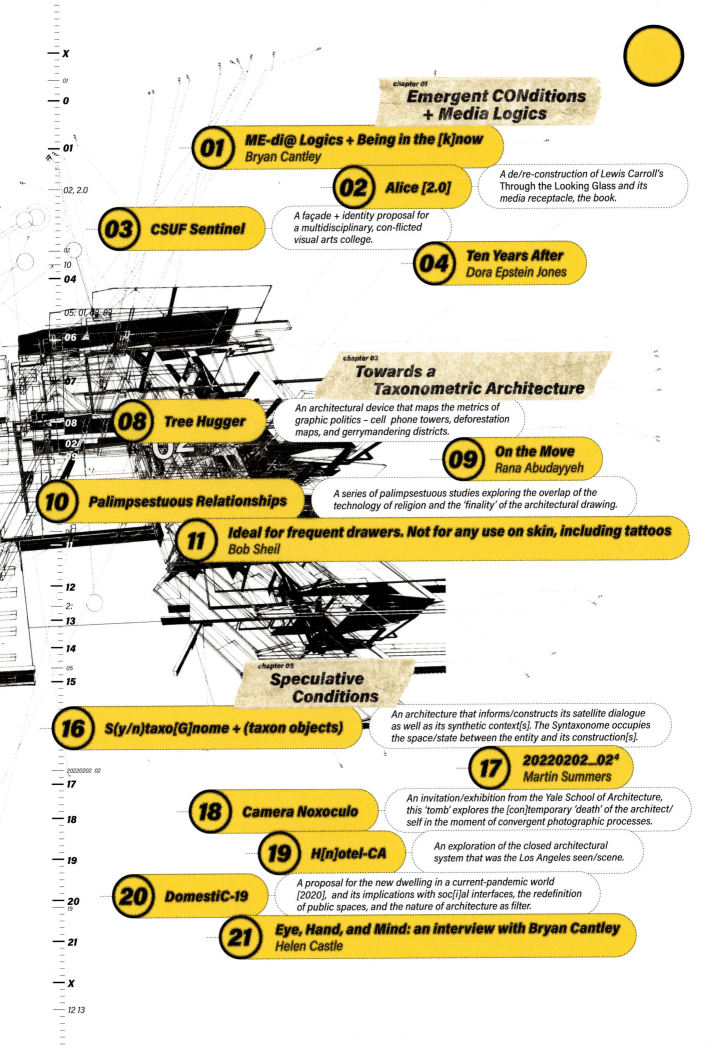

chapter 01
Emergent CONditions + Media Logics

01 ME-di@ Logics + Being in the [k]now
Bryan Cantley

02 Alice [2.0]
A de/re-construction of Lewis Carroll's *Through the Looking Glass* and its media receptacle, the book.

03 CSUF Sentinel
A façade + identity proposal for a multidisciplinary, con-flicted visual arts college.

04 Ten Years After
Dora Epstein Jones

chapter 03
Towards a Taxonometric Architecture

08 Tree Hugger
An architectural device that maps the metrics of graphic politics – cell phone towers, deforestation maps, and gerrymandering districts.

09 On the Move
Rana Abudayyeh

10 Palimpsestuous Relationships
A series of palimpsestuous studies exploring the overlap of the technology of religion and the 'finality' of the architectural drawing.

11 Ideal for frequent drawers. Not for any use on skin, including tattoos
Bob Sheil

chapter 05
Speculative Conditions

16 S(y/n)taxo[G]nome + (taxon objects)
An architecture that informs/constructs its satellite dialogue as well as its synthetic context[s]. The Syntaxonome occupies the space/state between the entity and its construction[s].

17 20220202_02[4]
Martin Summers

18 Camera Noxoculo
An invitation/exhibition from the Yale School of Architecture, this 'tomb' explores the [con]temporary 'death' of the architect/self in the moment of convergent photographic processes.

19 H[n]otel-CA
An exploration of the closed architectural system that was the Los Angeles seen/scene.

20 DomestiC-19
A proposal for the new dwelling in a current-pandemic world [2020], and its implications with soc[i]al interfaces, the redefinition of public spaces, and the nature of architecture as filter.

21 Eye, Hand, and Mind: an interview with Bryan Cantley
Helen Castle

Architectural Cymbalism and the Caress of Steel

Neil Spiller

Professor Emeritus, University of Greenwich, London;
Editor, Architectural Design

This short introduction will explain some of the precedent and influences for Cantley's work, its conceptual architectural preoccupations and its graphic dexterities and their implications for the future of architectural discourse, and usher you, dear reader, into its powerful embrace, so you can be no stranger to its mechanical love.

But first, we must talk about purely theoretical architectural practice. In Raymond Roussel's 1914 novel *Locus Solus*, a group of visitors are given a guided tour by a famous scientist, Canterel, of his estate. Central to the novel is a description of eight curious *tableaux vivants*. We learn that the actors are actually dead people whom Canterel has revived with 'resurrectine', a fluid of his invention, which if injected into a fresh corpse causes it continually to act out the most important incident of its life.

Resurrecting the Interstitial

So why do certain architects still draw? In a world of the shiny digital render, where images can be made quickly and flipped to view from any angle, are such 'drawing' architects no more than Canterel's animated cadavers – continuously acting out a personally important scene from previous decades – irrelevant to others? No, they are, in fact, spatial astronauts traveling to and exploring new architectural terrain. Such architects are finding new architectures inconceivable to the binary logics of computers and often creating works of interstitial beauty – between art and architecture. Such pursuits expand architectural discourse, re-examine what constitutes architecture and pulls the turgid, everyday, normative world of building into new universes. The theoretical drawn project is about this thrill of architectural discovery and developing new methodologies. In fact, the corpse being resurrected by drawing is architecture itself, not to repeat itself, but to become exquisite.

Bryan Cantley's work is inspired by the machinic yet drenched in pixel juice. This intermediate, and highly contemporary space of the 21st century, is one driven by digital media with shifting coalitions of forms and technologies and how they appear to human perception at different moments of time. Cantley has developed a series of architectural concepts, graphic protocols, and notations that explore the fecundity of this space of architectural potential.

Cantley's world is filled with snaky conduits, cylindrical canisters, organic-looking bladders, hydraulic armatures, compass-like scribers and mediated mechanical ground planes that hug trees, attach to the walls of the city, perch Batman-like atop buildings, or inhabit more abstract terrains that exist between the sides of drafting paper.

Cantley is a master draughtsman, collager and modeler. His delicate line work tender and precise, sometimes barely perceptible to the viewer, at other times confident and powerful. An often-used tactic in some visionary architecture, is the establishment of gridded regimes that interfere with each other. In Cantley's work these grids harbor machine-like but organic forms that mediate or ignore the orthogonal, geometric, Mercators and contrast with them.

Like the late rock musician, Neil Peart, whom we both admire for the fluent, inventive and innovative imaginative rhythms of his drumming and the beauty of his lyric writing with the band Rush, Cantley's syncopated, drawn and modeled progressions, innovative graphic paradiddles and nested, often a-scalar, spaces bring a verve and a personal, detectable, indelible imprint to anything he touches.

Planes of Detonation

Recently, Cantley has started to talk of his work, particularly the drawings, as 'Planes of Detonation.' Whilst they are certainly explosive, I prefer to think of them as black holes, in a good way. They are areas of space, not fully understandable but where the traditionally useful protocols of architectural representation are compacted together, where scale is monstrously large or minuscule, forms are distorted and their machinic semiotics coagulated into aggregations of registrations, words, numbers forming palimpsestual constellations of universes of discourse.

The drawings and models have an iconoclastic beauty to them, individually. However, the attainment of one-off beauty is secondary to the self-appointed task of redesigning architectural language that gives Cantley an instantly recognizable lexicon of spatial and formal moves and a way of describing and mapping the contemporary architectural condition. One gets the same feeling as when one initially dipped into William Gibson's now iconic cyberspatial novel *Neuromancer* with its unfamiliar mixed reality terrains and its invented techno-languages and slang and its jump-cut and partial expositions and denouements. One is also reminded, when reading the prose or titles of works, of James Joyce's *Finnegans Wake* and the feeling of language breaking down into schizoid dualities, familiar characters and phrases recognizable but in a new context; within this book's pages *The Matrix*, The Eagles and multiple Alices are also amongst a menagerie of references.

> *"... the same feeling as when one initially dipped into... Neuromancer, with its unfamiliar mixed reality terrains and its invented techno-languages and slang and its jump-cut and partial expositions and denouements."*

Heavy Metal Hotel California

Cantley's iconography is the iconography of the everyday writ large extracting from the mundane to make the sublime. Industrial warning symbols, for example, assume duties of architectural notation in a symphony of calibrations, movements, and trajectories.

Equally, Cantley fits into the visionary architectural tradition of machinic extreme dreams. A tradition that can be mapped back to the genesis of the Industrial Revolution in Coalbrookdale in the UK with the first Iron Bridge, the Crystal Palace of 1851, the Wright brothers, Barnes Wallace, Archigram, Norman Foster and Richard Rogers and the bygone days of Hi-Tech architecture and the architectures of Neil Denari and Wes Jones; nowadays these preoccupations have their epicenter in SoCaL.

Architects and their students must take from somewhere in order to start a process of design, the so-called 'blank canvas' is never there, influences and aspirant ambitions are there to be reached into. I have seen Cantley's influence on others, his social media follower numbers bear testament to this fact. This book will be another influential weapon in his armory and will become another bible for those interested in exploring our contemporary world and reinventing architectural language through newfound graphic cross hairs.

Welcome to Cantley's Odyssey, one has to speculate to accumulate! ✢

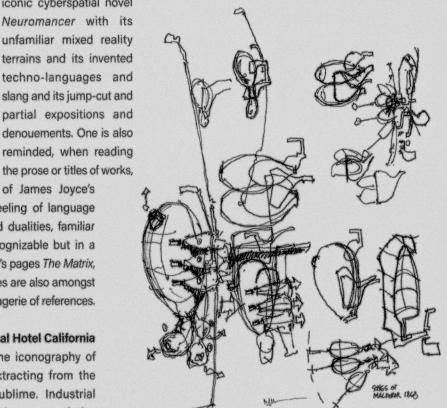

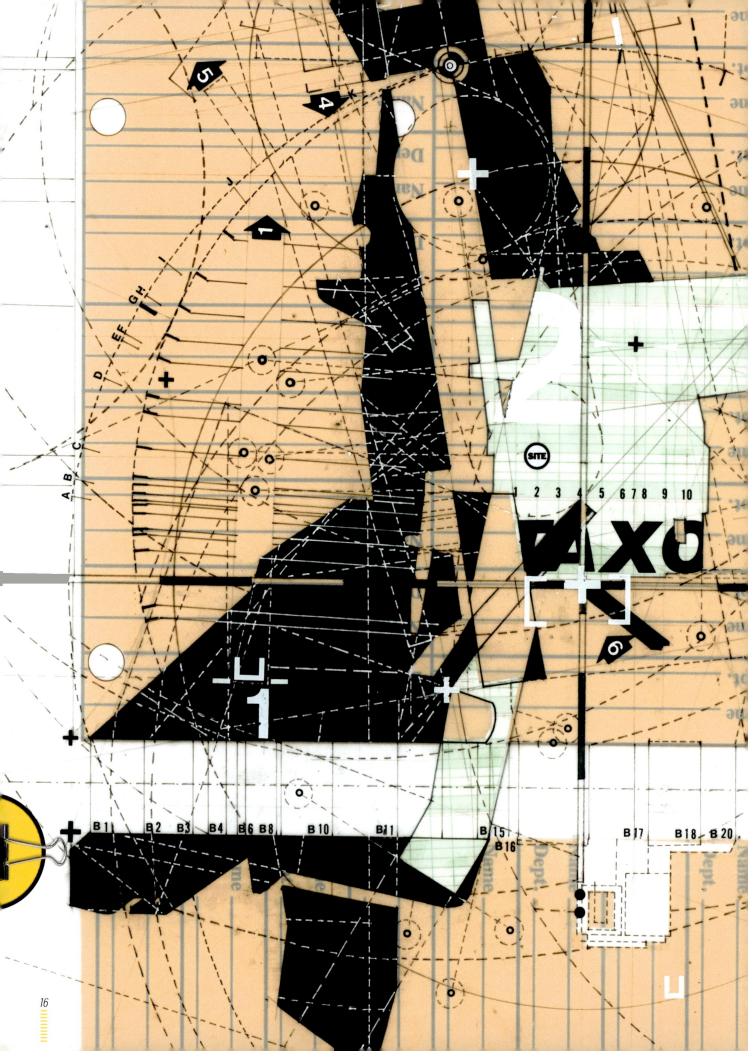

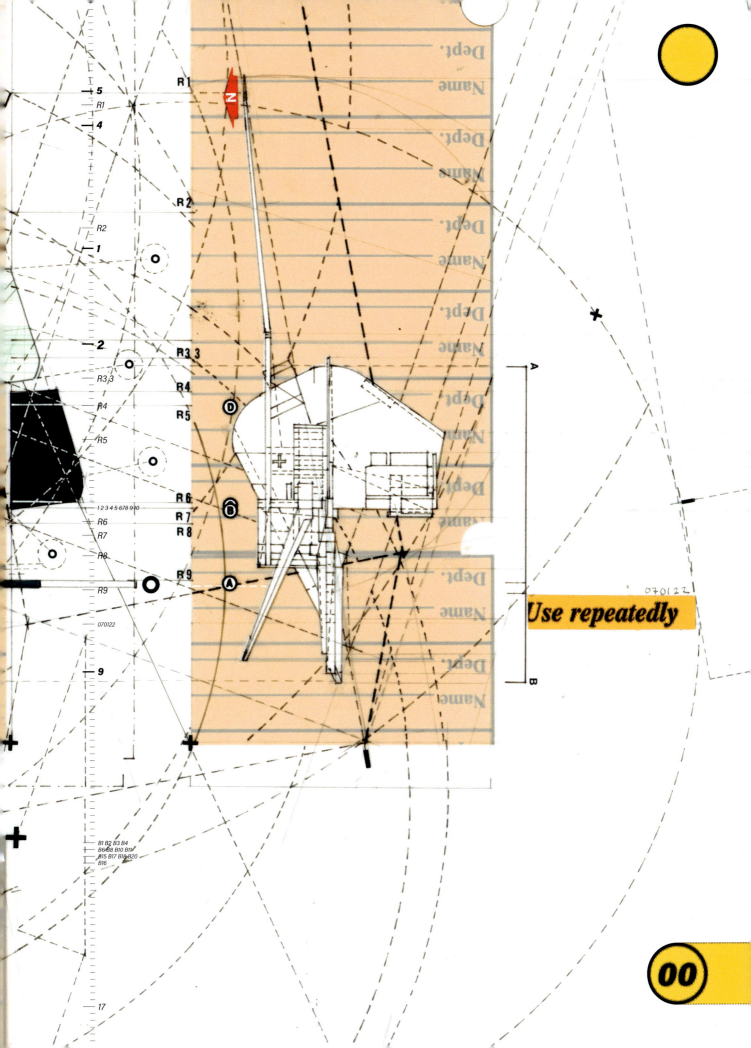

Read Me

Peter J. Baldwin
Senior Lecturer in Architecture,
University of Lincoln, UK

Instructions for Improper Use

At this juncture, it is often customary for an editor to foreshadow what is to come, outlining the content of each chapter, or perhaps heaping platitudes upon the creator of the work. Whilst my admiration for Bryan's capacity for critical, humorous, and achingly beautiful work knows no bounds, I believe that it might serve the reader better if I take a slightly different tack. Whilst many of the types of information that will be found in the following pages are likely to be familiar to the reader, some of the structural idiosyncrasies and methods of framing and communicating the work might be less familiar to those not well versed in the speculative corners of the architectural page and will therefore likely require a little more grounding.

This editorial-come-essay is comprised of two parts, the first addresses 'The story so far', setting out the conditions which have led to a critical need for work of this type and the inception of this book. The second offers set of 'rules for engagement,' introducing three key concepts/methods that frame the work presented: 'The Discursive Formation,' 'Media Logics,' and the 'Portmant[yp]eau.' These rules are not intended to prescribe a reading, but to offer the reader a means of accessing the complexities of the work. They are intended as geodetic datum set at [0⁰, 0⁰, 0⁰,] to aid your navigation through these [un]charted lands ...

Disclosing New Conceptual Horizons, or 'The Story so Far' ...

> """Begin at the Beginning' the king said very gravely ..."[1]
> [1] L. Carroll, *Alice in Wonderland* (London: Macmillan and Co. Limited, 1871).

The 21st-century city has already been described as a place of simultaneous experience (Dunn and Brook, 2011).[2] Whilst the city, and indeed, its individual architectural components are still, undeniably, places of physical interaction it is becoming increasingly apparent that within the palimpsest of centuries of development, demolition, and decay, new and often intangible influences are emerging. Invisible to the un-augmented eye, the siren songs of pervasive marketing, social media and technological saturation compete with more traditional public and private narratives, increasingly influencing our behaviors and patterns of (spatial) occupation. No longer confined to geographical certainties of the television set, the high-street, or motorway billboard, the media has transcended the physical, becoming a metaverse,[3] an ever-present digital dreamscape which can invade the waking mind through the merest swipe of a screen. The media has become the medium; a pervasive soup through which sensory impressions are conveyed, the Medi(a/um) has become the Mass-Age.

[2] N. Dunn and R. Brook, *Urban Maps: Instruments of Narrative and Interpretation in the City* (London: Routledge, 2011).

[3] The term 'metaverse' was first used by American science fiction writer Neal Stephenson, in his book *Snow Crash* (New York: Bantam Press, 1992).

This exponential expansion of (social) media has been facilitated and enabled through the rapid proliferation of a technological infrastructure of emitters, receivers, and relays, altering not just the way we occupy our time, but the very fabric of our environment. In his seminal text, *The Archaeology of Knowledge*, French philosopher Michel Foucault asserts that for a discipline to exist there must not only be the possibility of formulating fresh propositions, new ideas, new ways of thinking and doing, but also, more importantly, that a discipline must be cognizant of the borders of its world and the world that borders it (Foucault, 1972).[4] Yet despite the jubilant celebrations heralding the arrival of these new – virtual – territories in the 1990s and 2000s,[5] the architectural discipline has, for the most part, been curiously reticent to explore our new synthetic reality.

[4] M. Foucault, *The Archaeology of Knowledge* (New York: Pantheon, 1972).

[5] Championed in particular by Professor Neil Spiller through the titles *Architects in Cyberspace, I and II, Integrating Architecture* (1996), and his own *Digital Dreams: Architecture and the New Alchemic Technologies* (1998).

Conceived through a series of conversations that centered on our shared concerns about a lack of contemporary disciplinary engagement with these urgent matters, *Speculative Coolness* is intended to serve as both record of an emerging discourse, and something that attempts to provoke (and I use that word advisedly) a greater disciplinary awareness of a set of contextual changes, challenges, and possibilities that it may have, thus far, preferred to ignore ...

> **"Speculative Coolness is intended to serve as both record of an emerging discourse, and something that attempts to provoke a greater disciplinary awareness of a set of contextual changes, challenges, and possibilities that it may have, thus far, preferred to ignore..."**

Discursive Formations and Relational Entanglements

Featuring both resolved projects and work(s) that are still in progress, a conscious decision has been made to present the work in its discursive state. The book is framed through Foucault's model of the 'Discursive Formation' (Foucault, 1972),[6] in the hope that the openness of interpretation that this structure permits will encourage a broader engagement and the emergence of new perspectives, interpretations, and understandings.

[6] Foucault, *Archaeology of Knowledge*.

Our intention here is to avoid the dual pitfalls of premature reduction and homogeneity; the Discursive Formation permits the simultaneity of multiple relational entanglements between the various thematic devices, including architecture, media, technology, and representation, that run throughout these explorations and investigations.

Many of the categories of information included within the book will be familiar to the reader, and as such I will attempt to be brief in my summary, before delving further into Media Logics and Portmant(yp)eaus ...

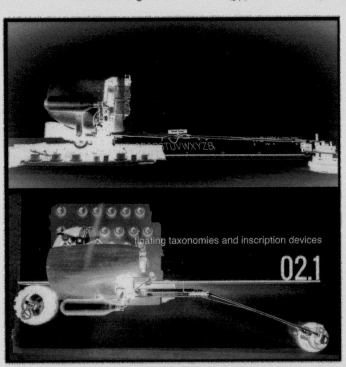

floating taxonomies and inscription devices
02.1

Projects [DRAWING and TEXT]

This category of information will, perhaps, be most familiar to the reader, composed of drawings, photographs, sketches and text-based descriptions. Each project description might be thought of as comprising three parts, the premise – the condition which the project explores; the project – the programmatic or typological response, and the object(s) – the documentation of that response.

Essays [Contributed]

The projects are presented alongside a series of critical essays written by eminent architectural practitioners and theorists. The contributed essays form a vital link, contextualizing the work presented within a broader disciplinary context. Ranging from engagements with method through to explorations of the socio-cultural context and applications of Bryan's work, they serve to underscore the importance of these explorations to the expansion of disciplinary knowledge.

Myth Quotations

Taking as its base assumption that architecture is a product of the culture that creates it, the work makes frequent references to pop culture. Of the many qualities of the mediascape is a blurring of reality and fiction. In this text you will find quotations from people and places real and imagined. From Morpheus to Alice, a range of fictional protagonists and antagonists are quoted directly; this is not an attempt to take credit from the author, but perhaps an observation that one is as likely to be familiar with a character's speech, a quote, a reference, or a meme as they are with the author of those works. It is a move which asks a question of the context of delivery.

> "Follow the white rabbit. Knock, Knock, Neo" (Trinity, 1999).[7]

[7] Trinity, "The Matrix Has You," *The Matrix*, 11 June 1999.

Media Logics

As with any discipline, architecture has, over the centuries, evolved its own set of design methods. Yet for all their sophistication, these practices do not necessarily have the capacity to adequately articulate the spatial relationships, occupational behaviors and functions that are characteristic of the emerging liminality between the real and the virtual.

Often seen as a way of overcoming the shortfalls or perceived limitations of current working methods, the adoption of extra-disciplinary thinking and methods has a long history within architectural thinking. From Abbot Suger's advent of the Gothic to the various '-ists' and '-isms' begat by postmodernism, the assimilation and interpretation of theoretical models from linguistic or literary theory is well known.

Originally developed as part of Studio C's conceptual toolkit of Diegetic Design Methods, the 'Media Logic' is an extension of an earlier set of design projects that explored a set of ideas set out in Jerome Bruner's "The Narrative Construction of Reality" (Bruner, 1991).[8]

[8] J. Bruner, "The Narrative Construction of Reality," *Critical Inquiry* 18, no. 1 (Autumn 1991): 1–21.

Coined by David Altheide and Robert Snow, the term 'Media Logic' refers to the dominant processes, established routines and standardized formats which frame and shape the production of mass-media content, especially its representation or construction of reality. Seeing architecture as a cultural product itself, it was proposed that architectural responses might be influenced by other forms of cultural production, including new and emerging media types.

Seeing within Bryan's work a similar approach to systematic and creative appropriation of technologies, typologies and systems, often inspired by contemporary(ish) forms of production, we began to discuss projects in light of the media that they took inspiration from. This allowed a common understanding of the often complex analogically driven designs. Unpacking the media type allowed for a ready appreciation of the underlying design intention, and ultimately generated the organizational structure of this book, moving from the physicality of the book, through to the birth of the solid state, through to more contemporary virtual territories.

This is a case of parallel evolution and the projects presented here differ in the breadth of interpretation of the 'mass media.' Perhaps due to Bryan's obsession with gadgetry and technology (in particular, a certain fruit-themed brand), the work shown here begins to regard not only the media itself, but also the mechanics of its creation and devices of its dissemination as sources of inspiration for its programmatic logics and typological functions.

Portmant[yp]ography –
'The Art of the Constructing Terminology'

In the same way that it has become necessary to cast our net outside the boundaries of the discipline to find methods, concepts, and programmatic logics better suited to our emerging context, it has also become necessary to broaden our linguistic frames of reference to find terminology to adequately articulate the moves, concepts, and intentions within each project. Some of these terms are taken directly and applied to an architectural context, others analogously, harvested from music, biology, engineering, and other more esoteric sources. Yet there are times when even the most ardent logophile comes up short, when even the most widely cast nets turn out empty. In these situations, it has become necessary to construct terms more appropriate to the subject of discussion.

Portmanteau
/pɔːtˈmantəʊ/
noun

1. a word blending the sounds and combining the meanings of two others, for example, motel or brunch ..."*podcast is a portmanteau, a made-up word coined from a combination of the words iPod and broadcast.*"[9]

[9] Second definition of portmanteau in the *Oxford Concise English Dictionary*.

The term or concept of portmanteau will be familiar to many a seductive practice that is, in essence, a blending of word sounds and combination of their meanings. But there are places where even these methods fail, often this occurs in situations where rather than a combinatory meaning being the desired outcome, the desire is to sustain two (or more) separate readings in parallel, to acknowledge the multiplicity of a given scenario.

> "Seeing architecture as a cultural product itself... architectural responses might be influenced by other forms of cultural production, including new and emerging media types."

In these situations, it has been necessary to use typographical devices, parenthesis, superscript, capitalization to allow multiple words to occupy the same paper space. These Portmant(yp)eaus contain perhaps two or three alternative words, and multiple valid readings and interpretations.

Let us take for example, 'he[a]rd mentality'. This could be read as Herd Mentality if one ignores the supplemental information – a term used to describe how people can be influenced by their peers to adopt certain behaviors on a largely emotional, rather than rational, basis.

If one includes the information contained within the brackets 'a' then He[a]rd can be read as Heard – to be told or informed of. This term then could also be seen to describe the tendency for people's behavior or beliefs to conform to those that they hear loudest and most frequently.

[Foot]Notes: Fragments and Traces
Woven throughout other categories of information, the reader will encounter conversational fragments, notes, and questions, and pop culture references that so often pepper our exchanges.

These reveal a level of uncertainty, the drivers for the work, the questions that we have asked of each other. Through the inclusion of interjections and provocations (elements that would normally be erased or hidden) we are laying our cards on the metaphorical table ...

There you have it: a set of instructions for (im)proper use, a body of work guided as much by the search for questions as by the quest for answers, playing off the hunch that as a discipline we must develop practices that allow us to design for technology and media culture, rather than reworking existing conditions and paradigms to allow for it. It is for you, dear reader, to interpret this book as you will, to construct your own questions, and perhaps to find your own answers ...

"and go on till you come to the end: then stop."[10] ✚
[10] Carroll, *Alice in Wonderland*.

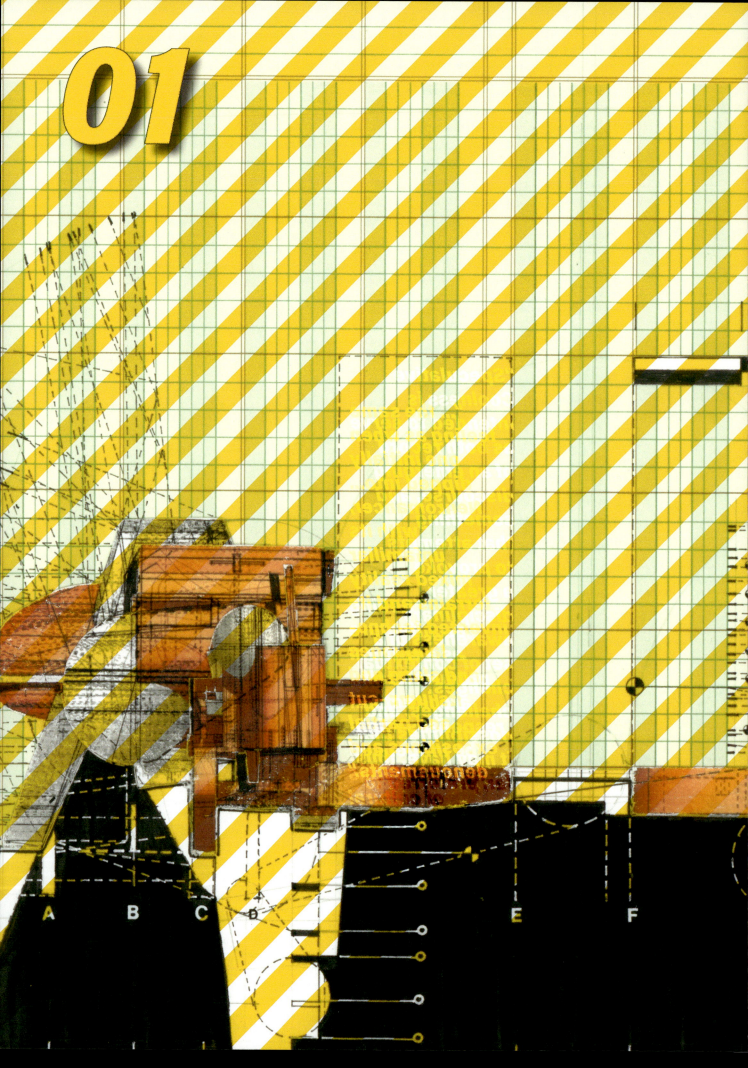

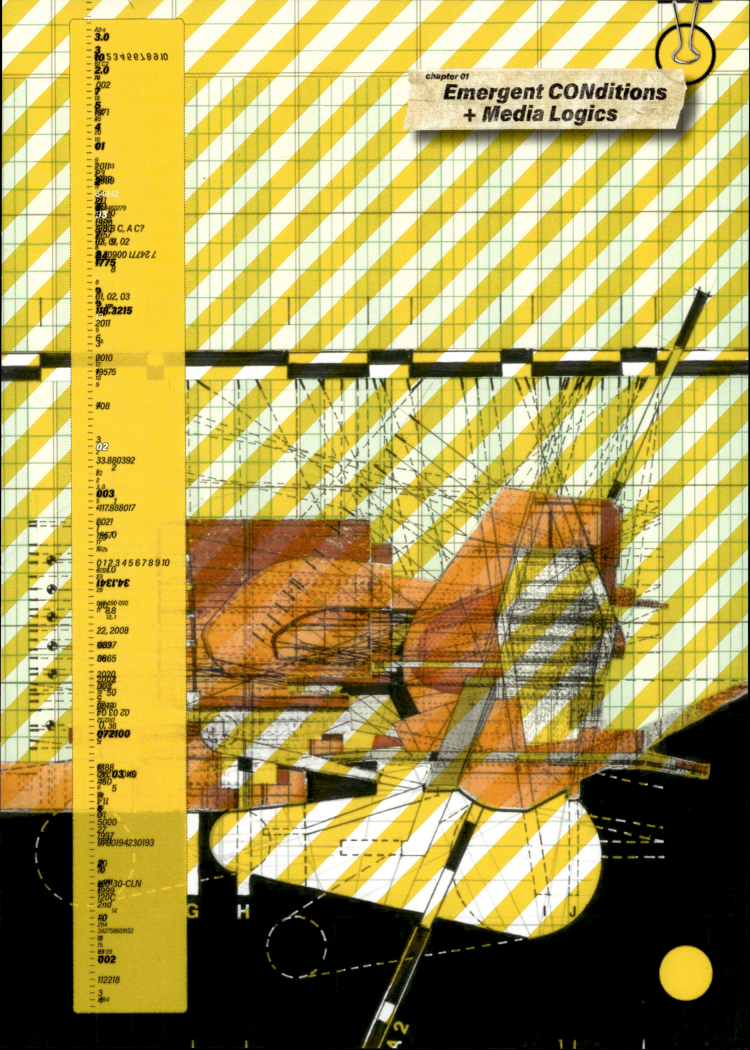

chapter 01
**Emergent CONditions
+ Media Logics**

> "'The time has come,' the walrus said, 'to talk of many things: Of shoes and ships – and sealing wax – of cabbages and kings."[1]
>
> [1] Lewis Carroll, *Through the Looking-Glass and What Alice Found There* (London: Macmillan and Co., (1871).

ME-di@ Logics + Being in the [k]now

Bryan Cantley

① ✚ K[now]ing – the convergence of a chronological and intellectual cognizance. A spatial hybrid construct of time and informational awareness.

This book is an anthology of projects that assemble in theoretical context, trapped within synthetic chronologies, obscured by fictitious parameters and hypothetical physics. The work is not concerned with constructability or existing praxis. Collectively it represents an inquiry into the conditions created by the media, technology, social and political space, fiscal and pharmaceutical informants – all asking how architecture might influence, and in turn be influenced by, these uniquely human constructs/constraints.

It is also a manifesto of constructed un-realities, fabricated orthographies, and synthetic syntax[es] (a *synt(h)ax*?). The text is a parallel to the nature of the work – these fabricated histories, projections, and rogue inquiries are the sites, conceptual and physical, of both the projects and the book itself. It is a self-referential proto-typology; an experiment in the curation, articulation, and dissemination of the author's work and *work-ing*. It fumbles and missteps as much as it finds its mark. It invites inquiry, interpretation, and relishes divergence. Construction of new vocabularies may initially confuse the casual reader, but it is hoped that with an understanding of the reasoning behind the de/re-constructed text, these constructs will read no differently from the architectural proposals that populate the manuscript. They are shifts from the norm, in pursuit of a different type of implicit knowledge. Might we speak of diverse ideas in/with alternative mediums?

Playing off inherent oppositions and contradictions – conflict versus compatibility, unquestioned answers versus rigorous problem solving, *when* versus *now* – the projects within this compilation occupy the realm (and planes) of paper architecture, an increasingly ironic term, once used to describe visionary projects of fantastical ut/dystopic propositions, now increasingly used in an incongruous sense. It seeks questions as much as answers. More so, it seeks the *nature* of inquiry. The book as a whole questions conventional, reductive epistemologies in a time of unprecedented, distorted, rampant, and non-verifiable (social) media atmospheres. It asks, "Are we ready for the questions that will surely come our way once the page is turned/swiped?"

② of Artificial References

In much the same way that the creation of a book is an exercise in artificial construction, so too is the work, punctuated, bracketed and [in]formed with a set of artificial references. They don many guises from *Myth-placed chronologies* (÷), anachronisms, conscripted calibrations, registration marks, and [mis]quotations. Amongst the most prominent contingencies, the synthetic interval stamps are perhaps one of the most prevalent.

Artifacts are presented alongside purposefully distorted chronological identifiers. Although these referents often contradict each other [*please play nice*] these artificial chronicles allow the concatenation of the work to be founded in the questionable, while simultaneously providing an external framework for [non]verification. 'Social ME-di@' and the emergence of 'fake news',[2] [perhaps the most artificially biased of all transmitted information], is a perfect term for this synthetic congress. Perhaps then, the architecture and its annotations [the writing about/of/*from* it] is the most natural environment in which to discuss the creation and broadcast of such un-real events. This leads to the evolution of the 'con-text' as a viable receiver of the discussion of the *[k]now*. Never has architecture had both the opportunity and responsibility to reflect [on] the condition of fake(d) news, [anti]social media, and the tech[k]no[w]legies of their distributions and broadcasts as physical manifestations.

[2] B. Stelter, *Hoax: Donald Trump, Fox News, and the Dangerous Distortion of the Truth* (New York: One Signal Publishers/Simon & Schuster, 2020).

③ The Medi@-ᵘʰᵐ > [medium]

The completeness of a (collective) body of work cannot be recognized unless we examine the broader sub/contextual relationships between elements of the work presented and its wider operational context of 'media', in all forms and manifestations. The attempt will be to initiate this recognition through the filter of **ME-di@**, as a means of communication reaching a wide range audience and their spatial awareness, or *Architectural [k]nowledge* > (now + knowledge]).

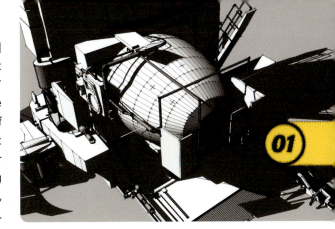

> **+ ME** – the ultimate, singular self-referential personal pronoun, the common physical qualifier in the age of the selfie *(me versus us)*.
>
> **+ di@** – referring to the specificity of place[ment] and the 'atmark', a media protocol for individual virtual-geographic position. One's internet qualifier. Your *@vitar* *(Here versus ... where's here?)*
>
> **MEDIA LOGICS**

The communication of an architectural intention requires various levels of comprehension, many of which require proper tools to validate an investigation or interpretation. The work here attempts to offer and embody such riggings. The projects serve as broadcast devices / conditions that reach two groups of non-exclusive audiences – *users* and *observers*:

₁**The users** read the performance of the architecture – they observe a typical architectural performance of a specific spatial configuration, ranging from the minor (self-adjusting fenestration) to the major (the self-relocation of an entire spatial configuration).

In the case of the **[W]horologe**, the entirety of the construct reforms are based on the specificities of function in an exchange between the resident/vendor and the visitor/customer. The **Social AMPs** engage the occupant with destabilizing technology on both ends of their progression – multiple recording strategies at the entry procession, and immersive playback auditoria at the termination of the user's journey. The **H[n]o-tell California** assembly adjusts its observer platform to both suggest entry as well as to adjust the parallax between the spectator and its blurred focal point.

This is the media used by + filtered through the device[s] itself.

Users experience the technology of the *media*, as well as the media of the *technology* – both required to [k]now the *project*.

₂**The observers/read-ors** engage with the media of the project, a meta-condition, perhaps the 'ME[t]DIA'. They additionally project the umbrellaed modes of technology, here an amplified performance of architectural expression. This is the act that the reader commits at a one-to-one scale, the interpretation of architectural data. The expressed graphic notation of a project contains self-referencing meta data. The project is intended to be understood more fully through the divulgence of this graphic evidence. This information will contain both the user and the observer states. This is the media projected to the read-or of the *project* (referring to the media), not the architecture.

Read-ors experience the media of the broadcast through the medium of the representation of the *project*, as a simulacrum.

[K]nowing then is a result of the revealing of an entity and its relation to itself and its contexts – discovered and produced expressing interior[ity] and exterior[ity]. The notation system is one way of knowing a single type of architectural condition, drawn upon the project, manifested by the model. The second type of knowing is the ME-di@ logics of the collective body of work, the projection and manifestation of the logics onto/into architectural form.

> *"Why, sometimes I've **believed** as many as six impossible things **before** breakfast."* [3]
>
> [3] The White Queen, "Wool and Water," *Wonderland*, 27 December 1871.

In the [k]Now – a recognition of the *now* visible layer of data, equipment, conditions, and capabilities of the *obj.ect* (object). The [k]now is the recognition of the currently known, the previously unknown, and the spatial position and indications of each.

 of [OO].O_{BJ-etc[s]}

Etymologically unpacked >

"The keyboard recedes into the background and is inconspicuous while in use ... one does not notice its aesthetic properties or other qualities. However, if it ceases to function, it becomes visible to one's attention as an object, no longer mentally processed as background equipment. This extends Heidegger's observation on tools and broken tools to illustrate the invisibility of most of our human experience ... The objects of our explicit consciousness seem to form a thin and volatile film atop a heavy layer of invisible equipment that is not usually seen. The idea that we live our lives on a layer of invisible equipment has a significant ramification for architecture, a discipline that produces the equipment on and in which we exist."4

⁴ M. Foster Gage, "Killing Simplicity: Object-Oriented Philosophy in Architecture", Log, 33 (Winter 2015), pp. 95–106.

[OO]O – a derelict homage to Object Oriented Ontology, here replaced by *Ocular Object Ontology* – a system assumes that the graphic revelation is animate; a dynamic condition of the architectural object. The previously unperceived plane of denotation has become acknowledged and amplified and detonated. The 'Emperor's New Clothes' narrative extrapolated and translocated; pluralistic ignorance is no longer a function of architectural ME-di@.

Might then the Taxonometric condition (an entity that constructs its own notation and graphical interface system, evolved *at the time* of its construction) be considered, in this context, a *broken* tool? If we can accept this, it brings into question the description of broken. If we assume that (a) tool is the non-visible aggregate of architectural drawing within a design, operating in stealth mode, its notations, taxonomies, and implications hidden from view, perhaps then the malfunctioning tool is the drawing, [non]evidenced in the final construction? Perhaps the damaged construct (the indiscernibility of drawing) is the reduction of information? Perhaps it *is* broken, and it certainly *needs* fixing ... ⁵

⁵ B. Lance, "Bert Lance Seeks Business Help" *Nation's Business*, May 1977, https://digital.hagley.org/Nationbiz_197705#page/24/mode/2up

.OBJ – an organized machine code file with the '*.obj*' file extension. The file typically contains a reference to a two- or three-dimensional body, as well as its coordinates and qualifiers, spatial conditions, texture mappings, polygonal face[s], notations, residues and other objective evidence. It is suggestive of a simulative manifestation of an architectural *project*, a clarification and/or totality of an entity's constraints.

This supposes that, in this curation of work, the invisible layer is not so invisible, thus the evolution and recognition of the

[OO].OBJ-etc. ...

-etc. ... – pointing towards the suffix of the word '*object*' (ect/etc.), as well as a play on the term 'etc.', which here references the scenario of the repetitious dataset, an all-inclusive body that becomes a familiar tolerance. This suffix modifies the nomenclature to a mimic misfire that does not affect its translational projection. "Ones sees what one wants to see." ⁶

⁶ M. Serullaz, *L'Univers de Degas* (Paris: H. Screpel, 1979), p. 13.

This new [OO]Ontology seeks to amplify the comprehension of the equalized expression of reconnaissance. Here we see the emergence of *Ontolography*, or an ontological orthography.

⑤ of Fabricated timestamps

In a 'post-architectural' condition, the drawing, as an active tool, no longer carries the mark of a *pre-cursor*. It is also a *post-cursor*. It is a con-current resident, as this recognition removes the 'linearity of chronology' in the realm of architectural ME di@. All conditions of speculation, experimentation, analysis, and conclusion within the media of discourse are sublet to this new phase classification.

The 'post-', formerly a non-active reflective condition, becomes a situation of analysis only, even if it is active. It is a back-shifter, where reverse is forward, and forward is sideways ... *or are they?*

If the timestamp is synthetic, whe[n]re are you?

Are you in the [k]now?

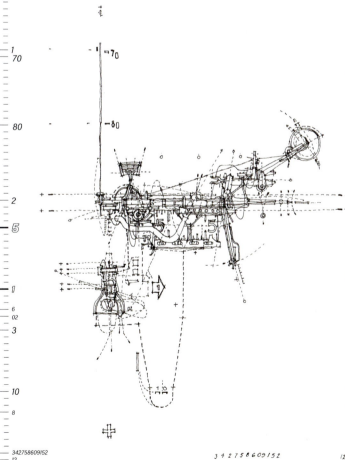

COSMOLOGY DEVICE ⑧

⑥ The [k]no[w]tation system > (know + notation)

This is a combination of both found and synthetic simultaneous con-texts. An entity may of course project its own [k]no[w]tation system, in both real time and as an atypical post-operative condition. The graphic notation structure is considered an integral component of the entity reconceptualized as the **[k]no[w]bject** > (know + now + object). The constructed terms attempt to deal with normally segregated entities of time, space, and awareness as coinciding events.

This graphic evolution addresses all three terms of the [k]now/ME:di@ Logics. In the world of creative production, or the 'bringing forth,'[7] we might then look at the following lexica to explore the ideas of objects, their creation, and their knowledge/knowledge of them:

[1]**Poiesis** – the activity of making something into being that did not exist before. Here, the creation of the[k]no[w]tation, after *and* during the [f]act. It might be argued that these configurations are inherent in the media itself. The act of extraction that is needed to visualize/accept itself. A condition of who knowing who, what, and through which mechanism?

[2]**Autopoiesis** – the ability of a system to recreate itself. These objects create (their) notation, a part of the integral and total self. The graphic [k]no[w]tation re/creates itself and its graphic offspring – a perpetual feedback loop of intrinsic data fields. Fractal descendants are constant in this realm. 'Itself' here being a dualistic reference.

[3]**Sympoiesis** – collectively producing systems that do not have self-defined spatial or temporal boundaries. The object and its live notation are without fixed external edges with specious timestamps. Lacking constraint they expand freely, creating their own adaptive micro verse. Here the drawing and the model of a project are considered the same epigenetic entity.[8]

The Taxonometric condition is the occurrence of exactly this acknowledgment, and its simultaneous occurrence with a viewing of the object. The graphic structures and notational fields of an object are considered as 'solid' as the thing itself. There is no separation, no division, no curation of the metadata. The data is the object. Background events become foreground objects. This is a distortion perhaps overdue in the evolution of architectural Me-di@.

⑦ of OOOBjects

"An entity in its reality is determined by the shifting, capricious storm of references and assignments in which it is enveloped."[9] ... These references are both internalized and externalized, with the representation of technology being paramount. The conditions, ramifications and artifacts of technology are communicated through an internal dialogue between the mechanisms. They are conveyed as an external conversation between the entity and the sub-site/con-text. The synthetic position of the ME-di@ Logics and their corresponding adjacencies (the 'site' of an architecture, the physical surface of drawing occupancy, the realm of communicative vessels) effected by distortion, transmission, and reception of data. Such negotiations are the condition of this new OOO.

[9] G. Harman, *Towards Speculative Realism: Essays and Lectures* (Winchester, UK and Washington, USA: Zero Books, 2010).

> "I know who I WAS when I got up this morning, but I think I must have been changed several times since then."[10]
> [10] Carroll, *Through the Looking-Glass*.

"When equipment is most equipment(-like), it is concealed from view, as something relied upon."?[11] The **[OO].OBJ-etc.** ... states an alternative reading, where the act concealment does not take place, but rather the equipment becomes as much a part of the foreground as of the activity of which such equipment speaks. Viewing, and therefore acknowledgment, must occur. A Machine Architecture therefore is the manifestation of the [OO].obj-etc.

[11] Harman, *Towards Speculative Realism*.

> "The key is that it shows us that descriptions of the object as solid material and descriptions of it as functionally useful are derivative."[12]
> [12] Ibid.

The portmanteau structural tablature is at play here, *in terms – of* the terms, the drawings, and the project vessels themselves. This publication ratifies these synthetic authenticities, in all properties and applications.

Con-text is expressed throughout, both by the creation of the artificial site, but additionally by the fabrication of constructed vocabularies. The term is used as a method of invited investigation ... it is hoped that the reader will suspend standards and exchange proper alignments for a new reading of these architectural inquiries. Context is additionally understood as an individualized chronological reference point, here thought of as more of an intellectual construct rather than an accepted metric of categorization.

This becomes an exercise of invented thinking. It becomes practice in fictitious instances.

Space, time, and language are relieved, provisionally, of their over-burdened segregated obligations, in hopes of opening a threshold to experimentation.

(k)now you [k]now... ✦

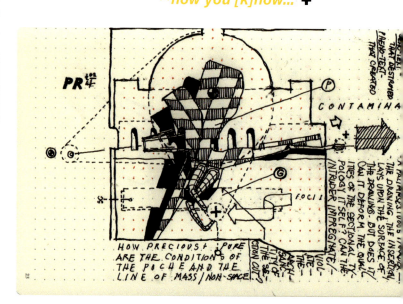

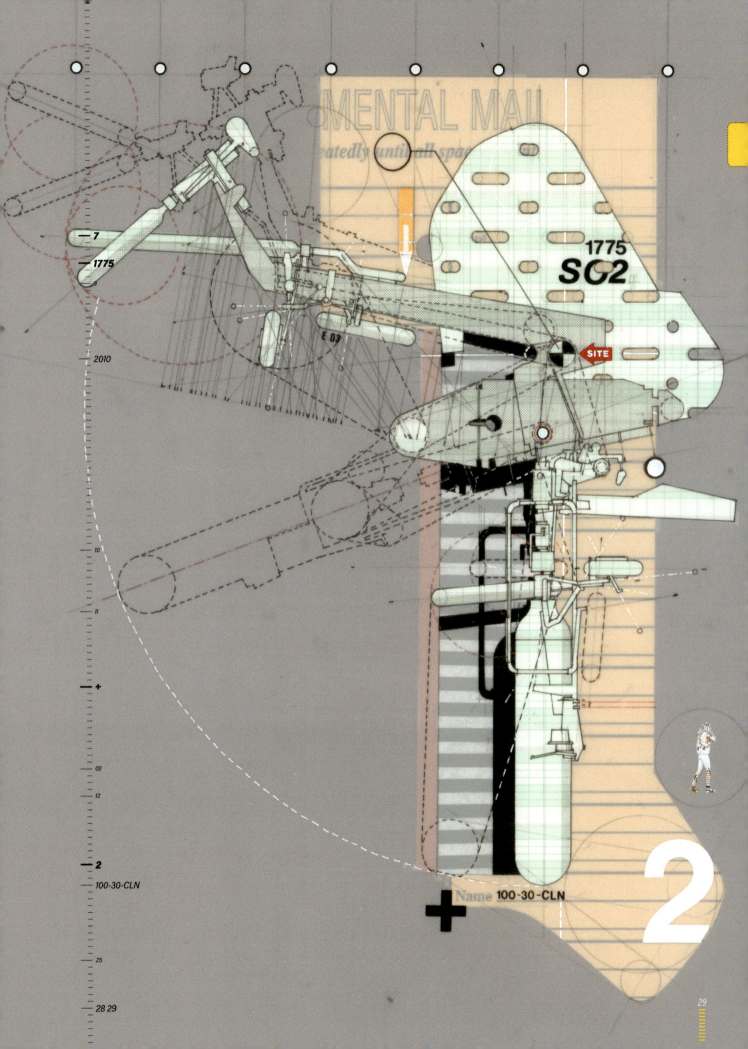

Alice [2.0]

A de/re-construction of Lewis Carroll's Through the Looking Glass *and its media receptacle, the book.*

Originally commissioned as part of an exhibition, the 'Open Book' at California State Polytechnic University, the brief was to design a structure (or structures) that expressed an architectural interpretation of [a/the]'BOOK.' The final artifact(s) are an interpretation of the narrative, constructed without the baggage of thematic or period set design. The project is an attempt to embody the mechanics, the spirit of movement, and the physical interactions with a *book* – in the creation of the formal proposition. Since architecture is a physical, man-made act, we began by examining fundamental components of an archetypal book, COVER, PAGE, and TEXT as a progression from physical to metaphysical.

TYPE 1 **Books**

MEDIA LOGICS

02

Symbolically Speaking the:
₁**COVER** is viewed as the protector, organizer, advertiser, a vessel for page and text. It represents the most physical component and the first level of communication.

₂**PAGE** is viewed as a datum providing a transparent consistency, a regulator, and a device ensuring consistent meter. It represents a union between physical and metaphysical realms.

₃**TEXT** is viewed as the syntax, morphology, ruling system or mechanism that gives birth to the desired mood, denotation, and pattern. It represents the most cerebral component.

Architecturally Speaking the:
₁**COVER** is viewed as wall(s), floor(s), ceiling(s), the apparatuses of enclosure, the material/form that announces and insulates the information to be communicated from exterior circumstances.

₂**PAGE** is viewed as the system(s) that physically represents information. It is the force of direction of size, margin, orientation, and attitude. It becomes the component that allows pedestrian interaction and union with the project, a primarily physically interactive component.

₃**TEXT**, including sentences, words, letters, and numbers, are viewed as the data itself. A highly structured system of rules and methods that convey messages and thoughts (architextural concepts and organizing principles).

We describe the *open book* as an interactive experience where the reader plays an integral role in the exchange between the author's intentions and the reader's perception. This interaction between human and [printed] media can be revealed dimensionally through an architectural intervention. The reader of a book becomes the activator of the architecture. These interactions occur in varying degrees through three primary dimensional components of 'book' – *cover page, and text.*

The author floats in a mechanical landscape of text

COVER is to PAGE, as PAGE is to TEXT. Each of these groupings deals directly with its corresponding structural organizations. Each serve as a datum for the latter, while providing a format for the former [in the case of the Cover, it collects the readers' hands/situation of interaction as well as the page]. The Text then organizes the thoughts of the reader.

The Hypothetical Syllogism: *If A then B, and if B then C, therefore, if A then C?*

Maybe a better way of attempting to understand this might be to say that the relationship that exists between A + B is identical to the relationship that connects B + C. Is there a direct line between A + C, or is it implied? Taking the cliché of not judging the character of the content by the appearance of the outside, one might think the connection to be non-existent. This is where the magic of this type of a project lies, analyzing a literary device, using the function of the subject itself to derive a paradoxical situation. This situation may be explored and expressed through the very discipline that unites symbolic content with the structural organization. The reason for spending time with understanding the relationships is to pursue a direction and parti for the architecture. Architecturally – is this a machine, a machine architecture, or an abstract installation/space that uses the external referent to suggest a programmatic strategy [i.e., the Red Sea Separator from the Bible].

The techno-monk and the temple of transformation

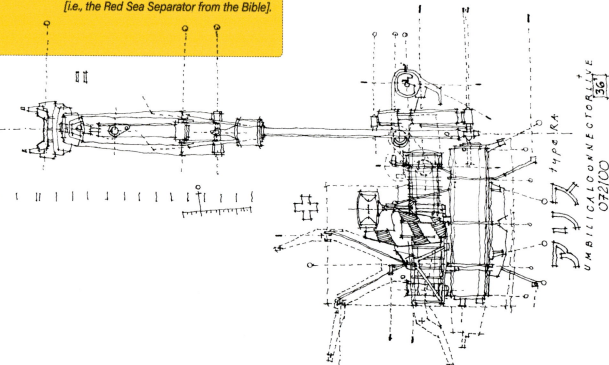

Umbilical Connector/Projection Core

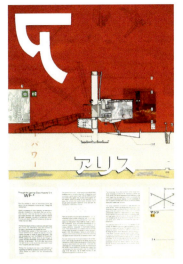
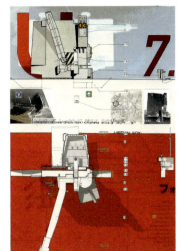

Analog Panels 01, 02, and 03

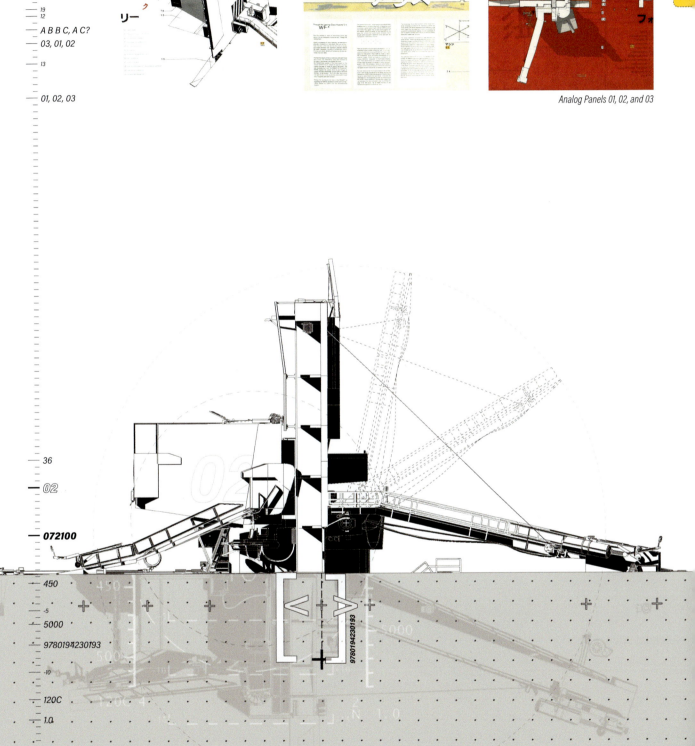

Sec[nota]tional Operations

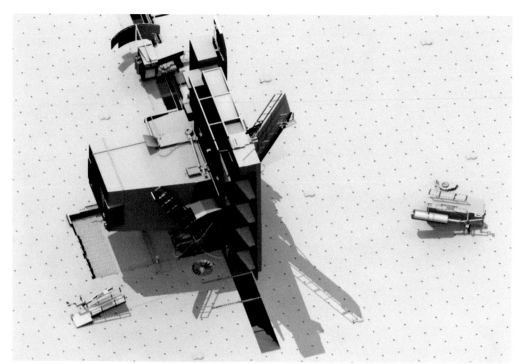

Occupied – a closed system once the reader is engaged

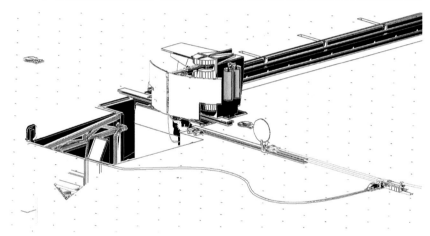

Authorship Device

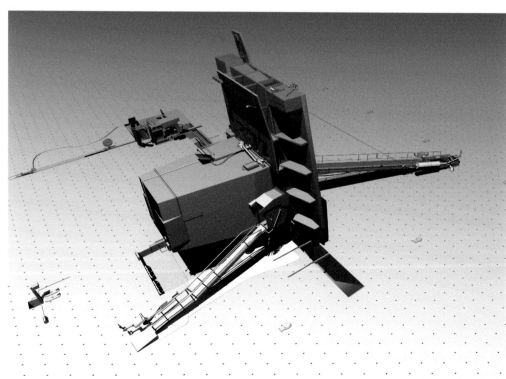

Entry/exit sequential unfolding

Committed in collaboration with Kevin Foster O'Donnell, Alice (in her increasingly pluralistic guises) was one of a pair of projects based upon the books *Alice's Adventures in Wonderland* and *Through the Looking Glass*. This project equivocates the physical landscape, the narrative landscape, and the components of the physical artifact, the book. This pairing was originally intended as a 'bookend' series, inspired by the tendency of publishers to present the two narratives as a single artifact, though they were written approximately four years apart.

The project explores the condition of the Enantiomorphic Inversion. The Enantiomorph [Tweedledum and Tweedledee] is a pair of entities that are mirror images of each other in structure, but that have different internal characteristics [for example, each of the twins has a different personality]. The Inversion Factor defines a set of entities that have an identical conceptual and subject base [in this case, Alice and her path through an imaginary landscape], but that are unique on the surface. The **DNA** is transfigured to the **AND**.

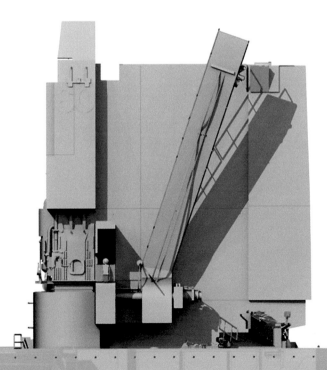

System in use: read-or engaged

Alice 3.0; "a www.ONderland of sorts"

Based on a sequence of chess maneuvers, physically the landscape is conceived as a chessboard. The main architectural factor in the book becomes the series of brooks and hedges that Alice must negotiate. They become a boundary of architectural regions. Precincts are clearly defined and bordered by the two elements (the brooks and hedges) on all four sides.

Whereas the integrity of Alice's relations with each brook deals directly with horizontal motion [the movement of the water in the channel], labeled as the x-axis, the transformative qualities of each brook are dependent on the residual Cartesian axis. One must traverse the water to initiate its layering mechanism. This constitutes the y-axis. The process of transformation requires the catalyst [Alice] to pass through an implied vertical membrane to activate the z-axis and trigger the affect/restructuring of the context. After Alice passes over each brook into a new square, her environments morph into a completely different situation.

The question then arises: *Is the transformative membrane [brook] a function of the edge of the precinct so much as it is a primary spatial system in and of itself, with the square becoming the interstitial space?*

The narrative taken in isolation suggests not, but attention should be placed to the importance of the space that contains the **transformative membrane.** Carroll actually gives typographic dimension to this area with the manipulation of asterisks in the text [a key architectural clue/signifier]:

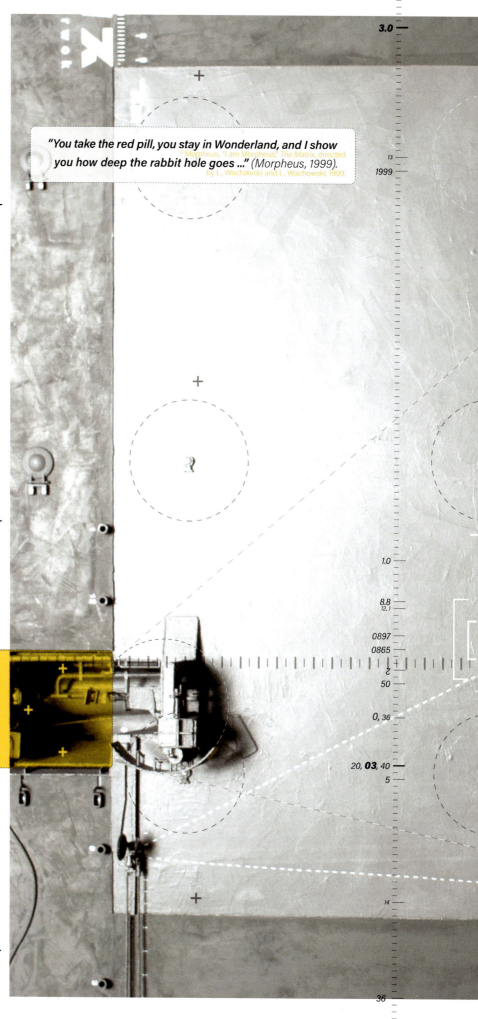

"You take the red pill, you stay in Wonderland, and I show you how deep the rabbit hole goes ..." (Morpheus, 1999).
    [13] Morpheus, "I am Morpheus," *The Matrix,* directed by L. Wachowski and L. Wachowski, 1999.

"'But oh!' thought Alice, suddenly jumping up, 'if I don't make haste, I shall have to go back through the Looking-glass, before I've seen what the rest of the house is like! Let's have a look at the garden first!'"[14]

[14] Carroll, *Through the Looking-Glass*.

Drone[ye view] – "Precinct of transformation"

The Components: The project intends that 12 structures should be dotting the landscape – each corresponding to a chapter of the book. Though identical in form, each folly plays host to a very different type of spatial experience. Once inside the virtual membrane, the occupant is presented with visual and spatial interpretations of that particular chapter. Artists are asked to contribute to the rotating interactive 'installation' of multi-media/spatial presentations. These productions are unique in that they physically engulf the viewer, as opposed to merely being projected in front of them. *Inhabitant/participant vs. voyeur.* This provides a vehicle for artist teams to conceive work in a truly dimensional nature, enhancing potential fluctuations in the spatial characteristics of the architectural medium itself.

COVER: The exterior layer of a book serves as the containment vessel, the protective membrane. It additionally acts as an advertising or broadcasting element, a billboard, to promote the representations of the inner workings. This was translated into the façade element, the entry layer or skin. Within each reading/occupancy, the user must interact with this component each time a sequence begins or ends. The *cover* is the metaphorical and physical gateway to accessing the printed [or architectural] experience of the text. It houses/frames the other [internal] components and serves as an information broadcasting surface. It is both sentinel and advertising agency. It is the transmitter of the physical connection required for access, as well as a hint toward the content.

The main tower, the structural casings of the architecture, as well as the arrangement of the structures within the landscape become the metaphorical COVER. They become the plane of transformation that is the space directly over each brook. They separate the unknowing from the enlightened, as well as referencing the duality of worlds in Alice's adventure. The tower also suggests the mirrored plane that Alice activated in order to penetrate the edge of her new world. The air intake channels are mechanized suggestions of the brook cavity/trough.

PAGE: The next sequential physical component is the *page* – the most physically interactive of all the components. The reader must turn each page in order to progress the narrative. The page is an information container and shaper. This notion was translated into the interactive component of each building, the components that house the *program* to be experienced, and the portion that the occupant must interact with at a physical level – the reservoir of kinetics. The page holds the text, and the page component hosts the source of all information – it serves as a distribution/transmission device.

The drawbridge and the virtual membrane enclosure become interactive systems that move and allow one to experience the architecture, the PAGE. Sheets must be viewed and turned in sequence for the successful transference of meaning, thus the progression of each occupant is carefully controlled via the removal of entry during the 'closed book' scenario.

TEXT: The final 'physical' component is *text*, the actual information that lodged within the pages' formatting, between the protective layers of the covers. The text is the entity that gives the book/building its meaning, and its conceptual structuring. The script can change over time. The format of the text remains constant – i.e, the characters [in this case] are the standard English alphabet, but the form is reordered for any given book, any unique scenario.

The Holocube and the Holochamber are the text elements. Each half of the project has a reprogrammable holographic representation of every chapter of the narrative. Here holographic images are projected on each of the five exposed planes of the distorted box, thus enabling the occupant to experience immersive manifestations of each chapter. Being inside the enclosure might be analogous to inhabiting a high-tech soap bubble. One is focused on the oils that appear on the sphere's surface, yet one is also faintly aware of the outer environmental signals as a background! It becomes the dwelling of enlightenment.

Author/Reader: The authorship device is the key in the operation of the building. An observer must be present to initiate the interaction with the folly. This satellite assembly represents the condition of the author: without someone to read her work, the author has no vehicle with which to discuss or convey ideas. This active witness plays the role of a participatory voyeur, carefully monitoring all phases of movement and sequence through a series of optical tracking cameras. Through observation of not only the experience of the occupant, but the dance of the mechanism themselves, they may understand better not only the chapter in question, but the unspoken, yet necessary, relationship that exists between author and reader – they are the embodiment of that most unique dance …

"Your appearance now is what we call residual self-image. It is the mental projection of your digital self."

—Morpheus, "You wanted to know what the Matrix is," *The Matrix*, 11 June 1999.

Relationship of the Authorship device to the read-or

CSUF Sentinel

A façade + identity proposal for a multidisciplinary, conflicted visual arts college.

"I prefer drawing to talking. Drawing is faster and leaves less room for lies" (Le Corbusier, n.d).
  ⁸ Le Corbusier, "Quotes About Drawing" (n.d.),
  https://www.azquotes.com/quote/64342

Emerging from a desire to denote the observer and the observed on the same (viewing) plane, this project is composed of two primary elements, the sheet and monocle. The CSFU sentinel project explores the *m[y]dentity* of the School of the Arts. The school is comprised of twelve different disciplinary threads, each falling under the umbrella of the department, and all fighting for identity within the mass. The project was charged to create a strong visual bacon to guests exiting a new mega-parking structure. Visitors emerged directly in front of the chosen site, so a bold welcoming gesture was of paramount importance.

The challenge was to devise a design strategy that stated the significance of all the arts disciplines without creating bias by focusing on any one of the 'competing' disciplinary areas.

The Sheet, Monocle, and the Registration Mark. Transmission + Reception

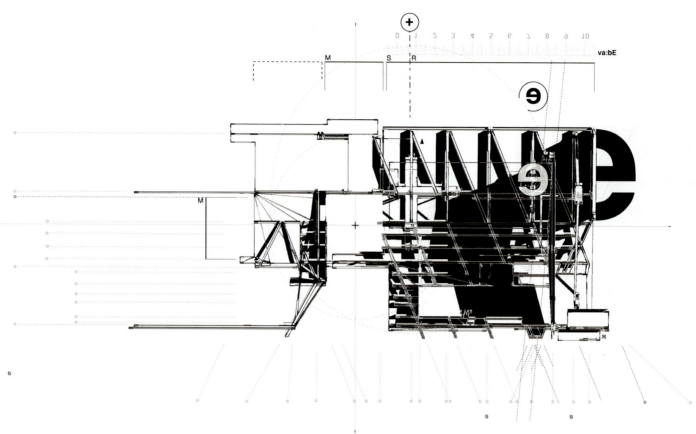

Rear projections. The anti-façade

The Sheet:

The façade embodies the logic of the media/um. A proposition for a measured, fiscally responsive, buildable solution [logic], a means of mass communication – a broadcast system. Its only function, thought multilayered, is to transmit. It does not collect nor curate [that is done by its operators], nor does it interact with its audience [that too is dictated/choreographed by its operators]. It is a surface of transmission, projection, and diffusion.

> "It means buckle your seatbelt Dorothy, 'cause Kansas is going bye-bye" (Cypher, 1999).[17]
> Cypher, "The Pill You Took Is Part of a Trace Programme," *The Matrix*,
> https://www.youtube.com/watch?v=HK2enP8IVhM

> "Architecture is a negotiated art, and it's highly political ... and if you want to make buildings, there is diplomacy required" (Mayne, 2008).[18]
> T. Mayne, interviewed by R. Pobrebin, "I'm the Designer, My Client's the Autocrat," *The New York Times*, 22 June 2008,
> https://www.nytimes.com/2008/06/22/arts/design/22pogr.html

The sheet offers the potentiality of a blank canvas ... the unmarked page ... the un-scored music staff ... the virgin site ... *[insert your own art 'base-layer' here]*. It is the surface on which we, as artists, construct our vision and locate our voice. The registration mark [+] represents the simple proposition that as artists, we 'make marks,' it acknowledges the importance of the mark, without nodding to any particular discipline. A form of equity, a gesture of mediation, a non-political statement in perhaps one of the more ego-based, political user-group atmospheres. This mark on the page is an act of diplomacy and discretion. It is a placeholder, a variable, an analogous participant.

Marks.
Symbols.
Cyphers.

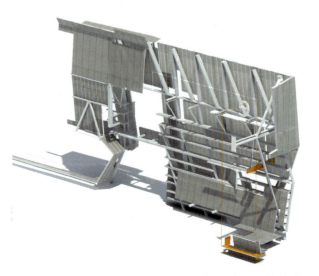

Connective Tissue/Faculty Bonds

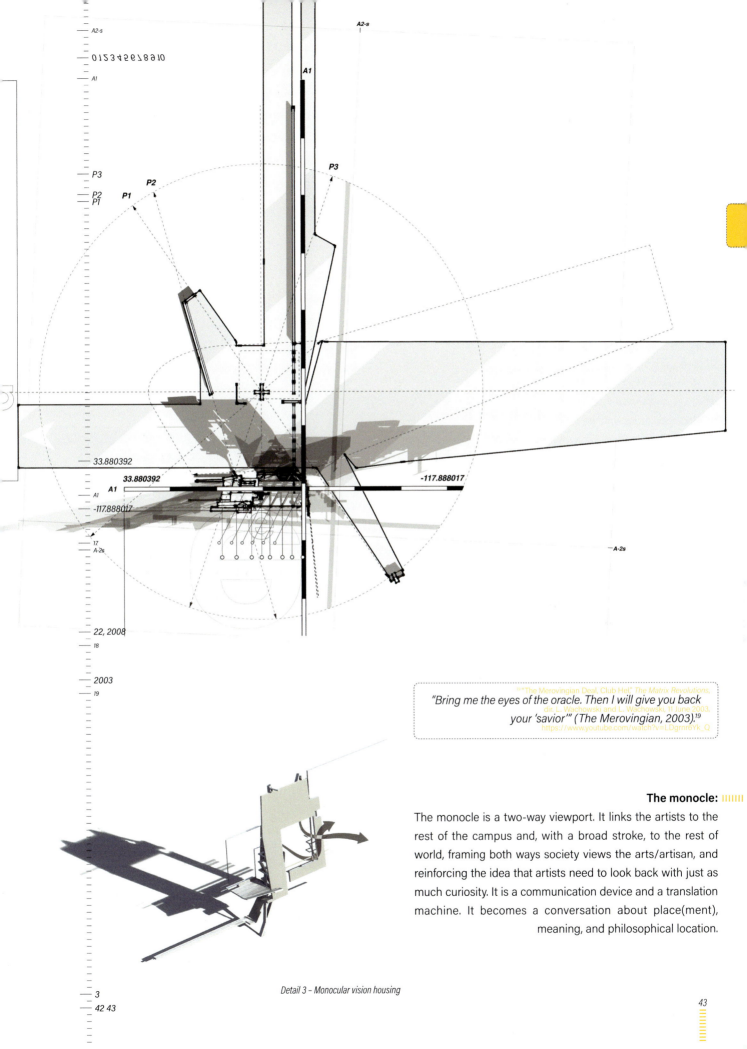

"*Bring me the eyes of the oracle. Then I will give you back your 'savior'*" (The Merovingian, 2003).[19]

The monocle:

The monocle is a two-way viewport. It links the artists to the rest of the campus and, with a broad stroke, to the rest of world, framing both ways society views the arts/artisan, and reinforcing the idea that artists need to look back with just as much curiosity. It is a communication device and a translation machine. It becomes a conversation about place(ment), meaning, and philosophical location.

Detail 3 - Monocular vision housing

The façade serves a second function as a multi-media projection screen, to display current work of the faculty and students back toward the campus and wider community. Its media typology might be closer to the now ancient slide projector than other types of projection systems. The slide carousel allowed for the on-the-fly adaptation and evolution of content that is inherent in any of that era's visual communication devices. One could add/delete/reorient any content at any time, as needed, as opposed to the attempt to foresee that need and pre-edit a captured presentation. Serving as a distribution system for the entire visual arts college, the need for the diversity of subject matter the same as the needs of 'now' versus 'then'. The adaptability of the media of the slide projector becomes 'in focus', additionally remarking on the not-so-distant past of academic dissemination, the darkened room with the hum of the projection unit, and the polyrhythmic click clack of slide advancement.

The projector had the ability to phase-shift, to become a flipper, the dual citizen of background and foreground media, at once the unbroken tool in its invisible world, and the sole source of engagement at the point of reception [the geography of the audience bodies], as opposed to the point of delivery [the screen itself]. It is a mirror of discovery and observation, in which we may all find ourselves daydreaming.

> *"This mirror will give us neither knowledge nor truth. Men have wasted away before it, entranced by what they have seen, or have been driven mad, not knowing if what it shows is real or even possible"* (Dumbledore, 1997).[20]

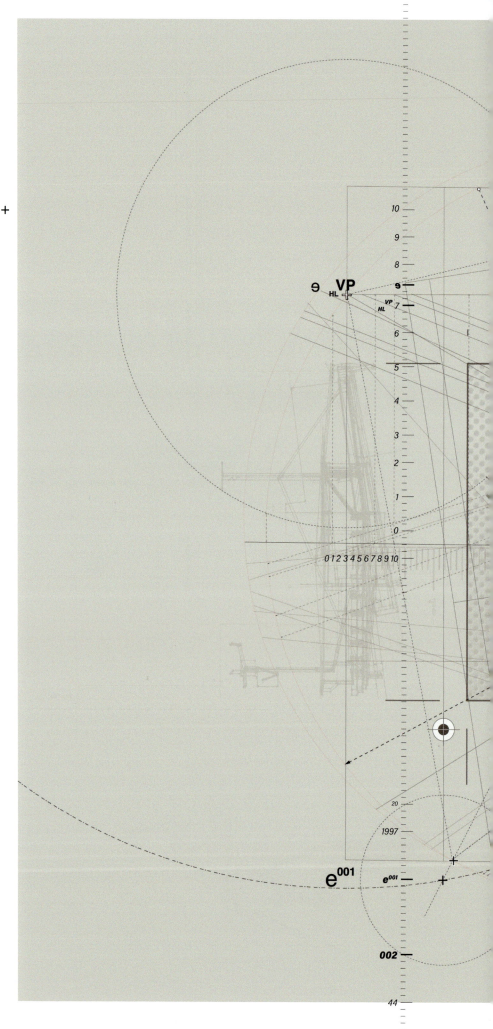

*Facadesignations.
Reskinning as re:identity*

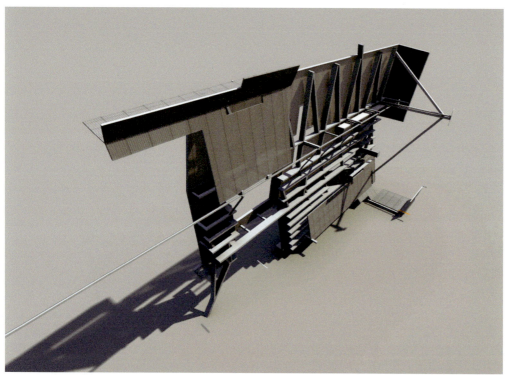

Rear projections. The anti-façade

*[RE]Framing the narrative –
occupying the space [be]tween*

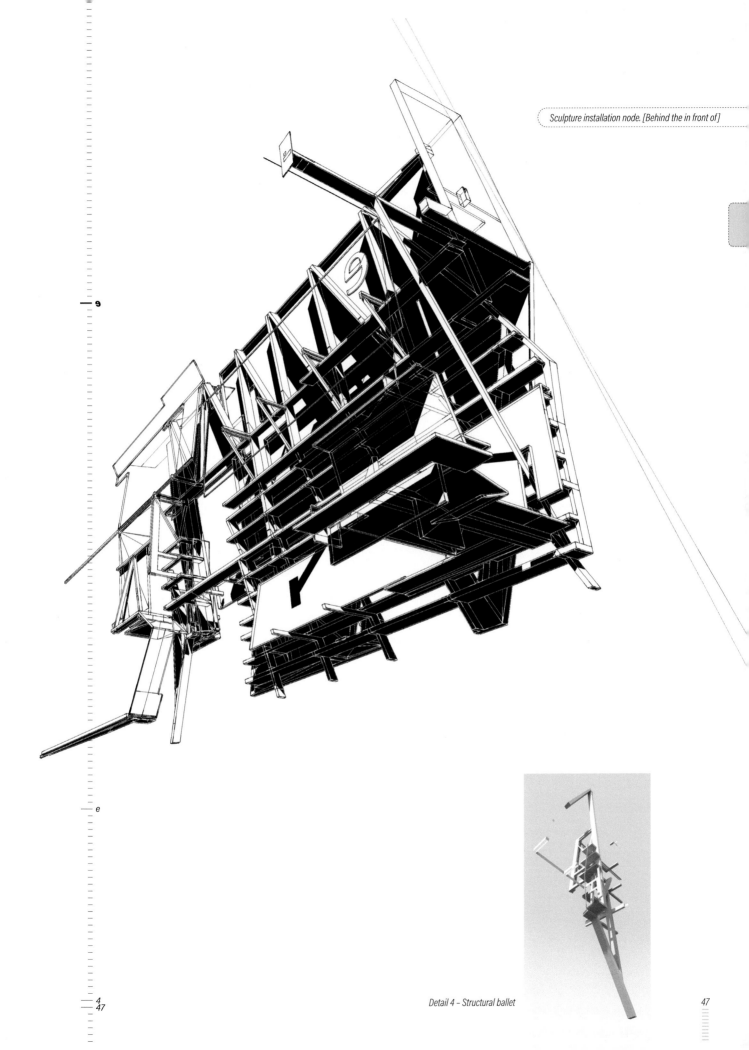

Sculpture installation node. [Behind the in front of]

Detail 4 – Structural ballet

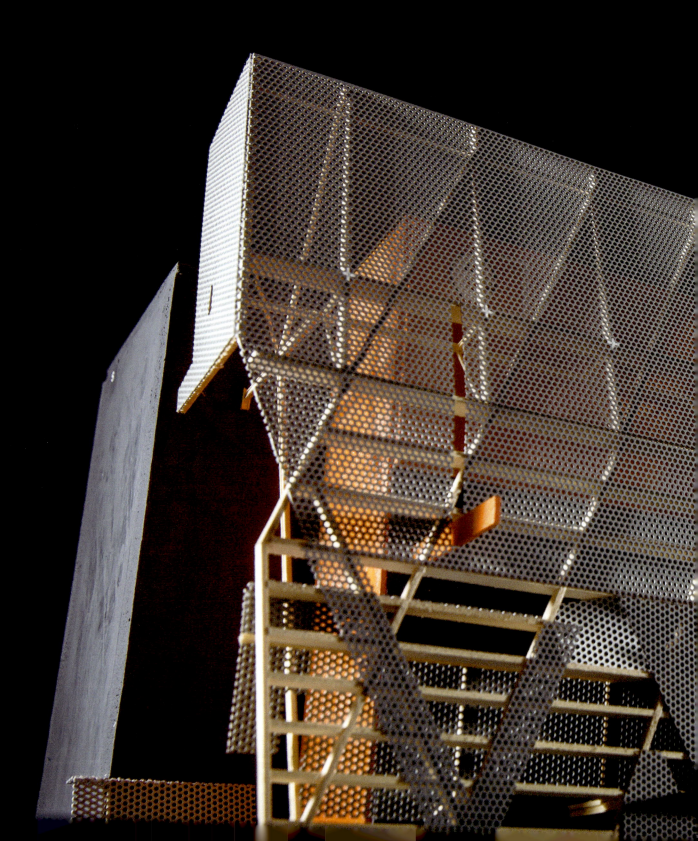

The fine, bold line between theory and application, the academy and its public constituents

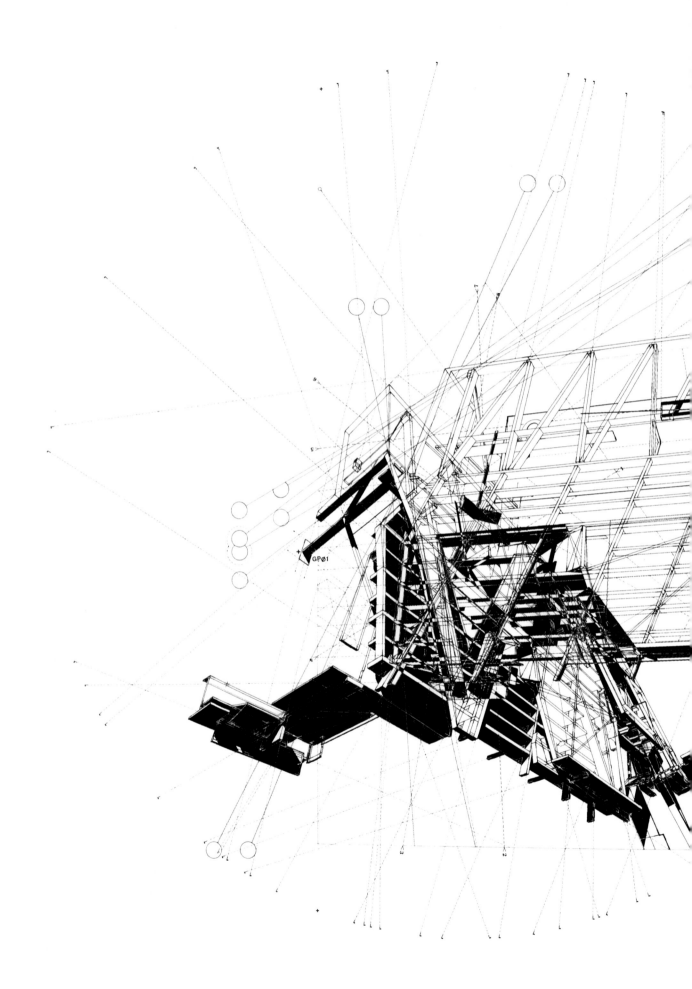

Multiplicities of chronological structuring. Where is the when of your world?

Ten Years After
Dora Epstein Jones

Chair of Architecture, Texas Tech University

It's been a while, and a lot has changed.

In 2011, when *Mechudzu* was but an apple in the Cantley eye, there was little space for transformative and experimental architectural drawing. Yes, there was a history: the daring collages and cartoonish grooviness of Archigram; and the so-called 'paper architecture' of the 1970s and 1980s. A few giants strode the Earth – Thom, Lebbeus, Daniel, Zaha, Peter – and later joining them, a cohort of radical assemblers – Jones and Denari, building machines, and then, everyone who copied them. But, even as late as 2011, experimental drawing was either personal (an indulgence) or a step in a process on the way to 'real architecture.' Despite the attempts to argue for an alternate form of architecture, experimental drawings remained a wild branch, a weed in a well-cultivated garden, an imprint on the sand, a doodle in the margins.

Enter now into the days of an experimental drawing that stands as is, per se, well within the discipline of architecture. Even the title change from *Mechudzu* (a mechanized and wild weed) to *Speculative Coolness* suggests a new moseying, a patient walk through each drawing. Coolness proposes a newfound ambivalence. Coolness also brings Marshall McLuhan's formulation of hot and cold media to mind.[21] For McLuhan, a 'hot medium' would be printed, like *Mechudzu*, with high-resolution and a content that only looks 'cool.' *Speculative Coolness*, however, encourages a sense of media that has cooled down. In McLuhan's terms, coolness would also invite greater participation, and this does seem to hold up analogous to this book – there are more participants, the audience is wider, the publisher is well-regarded. What is especially intriguing is that, in McLuhan's terms, cool media requires that the participant be familiar with the conventions of the genre. In other words, the work is not just slowing down or cooling off; it's entering into the conventions of architecture.

In 1957, Buddy Guy took his guitar to Chicago. Despite being hungry and weak from lack of employment, Guy joined a jam session in the 708 Club. He played so well that someone called Muddy Waters came to listen. Muddy Waters gave Buddy Guy a salami sandwich; a salami sandwich that convinced Guy to stay in Chicago and keep playing.[22] From that platform in Chicago, Guy influenced an entire generation of guitarists – Stevie Ray Vaughan, Eric Clapton, and Jimmy Page, to name just a few. Ten years later, in 1967, Jimi Hendrix, who emulated Guy in both technique and style, debuted *Are You Experienced*.[23] And, no, we were not yet experienced, but five million copies later, it sure seems like we were willing to try. In 2013, *Rolling Stone* named *Are You Experienced* as the third 'Greatest Debut Album' of all time, thanks, perhaps, to salami.

From this rock story, we could begin to ask ourselves a discipline-level 'big question': how long does it take for any act to go from wild and original to widely accepted or copied? The answer: at least ten years.

It took some time to accept experimental drawing as an architectural convention. James Ackerman only speaks of conventions in terms of architectural drawing, and then only in terms of its effectiveness as a communicative tool: "[The convention of architectural drawing] is an arbitrary invention, but once established it works only when it means the same thing to an observer as it does to the maker; it is a tool of communication."[24]

Convention is defined most broadly as a regularity. While not every regularity is a convention (e.g., eating), conventions tend to creep into verity through enforced social,

[21] M. McLuhan, *Understanding Media: The Extensions of Man* (New York: McGraw Hill, 1964).

[22] Buddy Guy in "Buddy Guy: The Blues Chase the Blues Away," *PBS* "American Masters" (2021).

[23] This story was related to me by Todd Roth, blues guitarist and historian (Bastrop, Texas, 2021).

[24] J. Ackerman, "The Conventions and Rhetoric of Architectural Drawing," reprinted in *Origins, Imitations, Conventions: Representation in the Visual Arts* (Boston, MA: MIT Press, 2002), p. 294.

political, economic, and cultural measures (e.g., dining etiquette). Some conventions are explicitly stipulated (i.e., rules) but most are apparent only through the implicit multiple acts of practice (i.e., tradition, custom, ritual).25 Thus, while Ackerman makes an initial claim that "once an architectural convention is established, it maintains an astonishing consistency through time," he also concedes (and eventually concludes) that "visionary or temporarily unrealizable" architectural drawings were beginning to leak into consideration.

[25 D. Lewis, *Convention: A Philosophical Study* (Cambridge, MA: Wiley-Blackwell, 1969).]

Like traditions, customs, and rituals, then, conventions are gradual. Ackerman prescribes that we think of architectural conventions like a language, or elements of a language, making conventions therefore both arbitrary and lasting. They are also, as Ackerman states, "invented or arrived at by mutual agreement." Conventions are collective. One person does not a convention make.

Following the idea of a more widespread acceptance or mutual agreement, conventions must also actively defeat bias. This seems like an odd statement because mostly, we think of conventions as bias. Nonetheless, every convention was at one time a revolution or an evolution; and on its journey to becoming a bias, it had to defeat at least a few standing biases. In part, the defeat of bias is what takes so long for any implicit practice to become a convention, much less be stated explicitly as a stipulation. As Jennifer Eberhardt states: "Bias is not something we exhibit and act on all the time. It is conditional, and the battle begins by understanding the conditions under which it is most likely to come alive."26

[26 One of the most important books of the last few years is Jennifer L. Eberhardt's *Biased: Uncovering the Hidden Prejudices that Shape Our Lives* (New York: Penguin, 2019), which definitively connects cognitive psychology to racial bias and injustice. Quote is from p. 285.]

So, if experimental drawing is closing in on becoming a convention, and if the ten-year timing trope holds true for cultural production,27 then we can also begin to uncover the biases that may have kept experimental drawing 'in the margins' for at least 40 years, if not, reaching all the way to Soane and Boullée.

[27 As it most certainly and tragically does not in the case of racial bias.]

First, there is the bias of purpose. For more than 40 years, architects were working intently and seriously on experimental drawings, with very little room to speak of them, very little space within the discipline. Experimental drawings were chalked up to 'process,' an artifact produced on the way to produce the actual architecture. As process, the drawings were considered as leftovers, curiosities of the eye but not much else. There was no real market for these drawings, except maybe for Libeskind's *Chamber Works*. Some, most, were spun into the books and monographs, vestiges, remnants of a creative journey. The bias of purpose concludes that the labor and information of drawings is intended towards a final goal, and that for the architect, the final goal is a building. An example might be a plan-ish drawing – lines on a page or sheet that are recognizable as a geometric or non-geometric figure. The plan-ish drawing is then perceived as a parti, a sketch, or some other as-yet-unformed idea of a final plan. The presumption is that the architect would not 'waste their time' on 'mere art.' Instead, the architect is imagined as working with intention. Ackerman aligns with the bias of purpose almost entirely in speaking of the convention of architectural drawing as primarily a "means for communicating architectural form." Any other reference, therefore, to the legibility of a drawing, or to the discernment of the figures or the lines, is also feeding the bias of purpose.

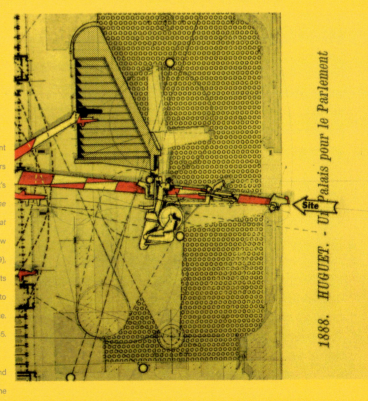

1888. HUGUET. *Un Palais pour le Parlement*

Second, there is the bias of innovation. When today we read Carpo's *Digital Turn*, and the *Second Digital Turn*, we follow a narrative of a permeating but unmistakable mythos that the computer would replace the hand as the primary means of drawing. Similarly, in Eisenman's *Diagram Diaries*, R.E. Somol asserts that the process of innovation that initiated the experimental drawing would necessarily be sped up by the computer. The bias of innovation imagines that the computational process can do what the experimental drawing of the 1970s or 1980s did, but faster, more efficiently, or more completely. Working in Maya or other animation software was intended to allow the computer to do the digesting, and the use of algorithms in parametric software such as Grasshopper, was intended to bypass the slow iterations of the hand and the (worse) limitations of the human brain. Computation is thought to lead the architect into the woods of the illegible and the incomprehensible to more easily forage for the morels that would eventually become the building. The bias of innovation therefore asks about the 'experimental' portion of experimental drawing, or the 'exploratory' of exploratory drawing. It insists that ink and zipatone are dead tech in achieving the true dimensional depth of the diagram and its complexities, and dismisses the hand drawing, or the partial hand drawing, or even the drawing in pixels, as quickly as we dismiss the rotary phone.

Third, but not probably finally, there is the bias of neatness. One of the most frustrating aspects of the early experimental drawings were their absolute precision. The issue with neatness is that neatness and legibility are aligned in our collective consciousness. Often, when we speak of architect's drawings, we speak of their 'graphical' nature; and it is this graphical aspect that connects the bias of neatness ultimately to an inscribed language – to words rather than nonsense. Of course, visual culture outside of architecture has not had to conform in this way – Surrealism, for example, nor really has film, or music, or even literature, which really should be the end-all when it comes to language. The bias of neatness in architecture is ultimately what cleans up the sketch. It does not tolerate well the chalky line, or the smear, or the palimpsest, all of which are welcomed into the experimental drawing. In fact, the experimental drawing eschews all of the above: purpose, computational innovation, and graphical clarity in favor of new traditions, customs and rituals based on the messiness of process, the undecidability that leads to new feelings and forms, and the illegibility that turns meaning into humor.

One person can make a statement that is hard to ignore (Buddy Guy in Chicago 1957) but the adoption and normalization of a convention, ten years after, implies that many of the biases have been defeated or overcome.

Perhaps now, we can see the soul of an experimental drawing, or enjoy the speculations brought on by a set of shadows, an intersection of lines, a collision of meanings, or a callout with nothing indexed. Architecture is perhaps loosening up, letting go of purpose, machine-driven innovation, and graphical clarity, in favor of a coolness that has a lot more cowbell, and that is, most importantly, becoming widely accessible and available in its own right. Let's give it another ten years, at least. ✚

> "Perhaps now, we can see the soul of an experimental drawing, or enjoy the speculations brought on by a set of shadows, an intersection of lines, a collision of meanings, or a callout with nothing indexed. Architecture is perhaps loosening up, letting go of purpose, machine-driven innovation, and graphical clarity, in favor of a coolness..."

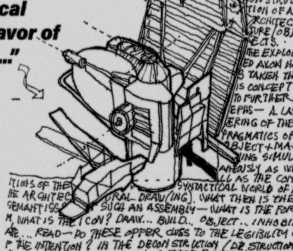

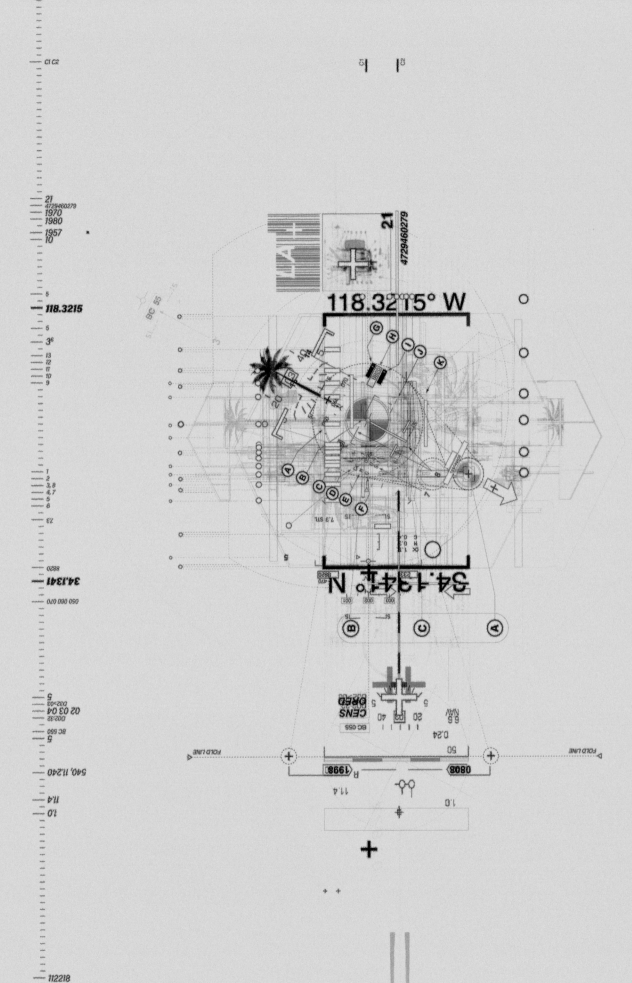

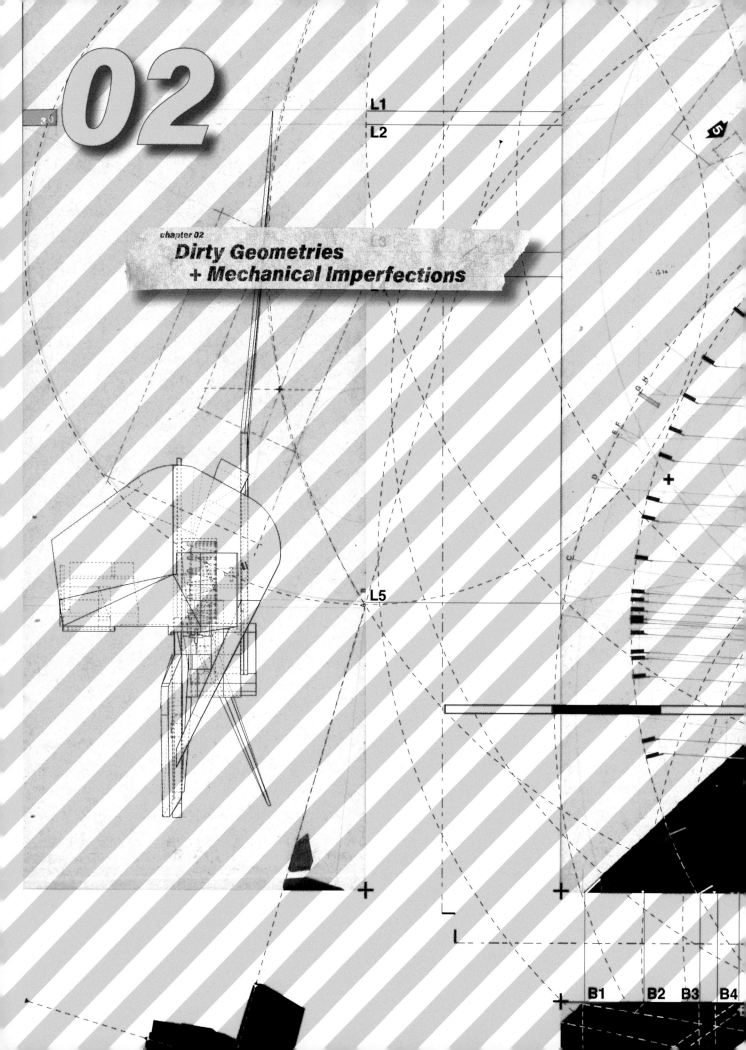

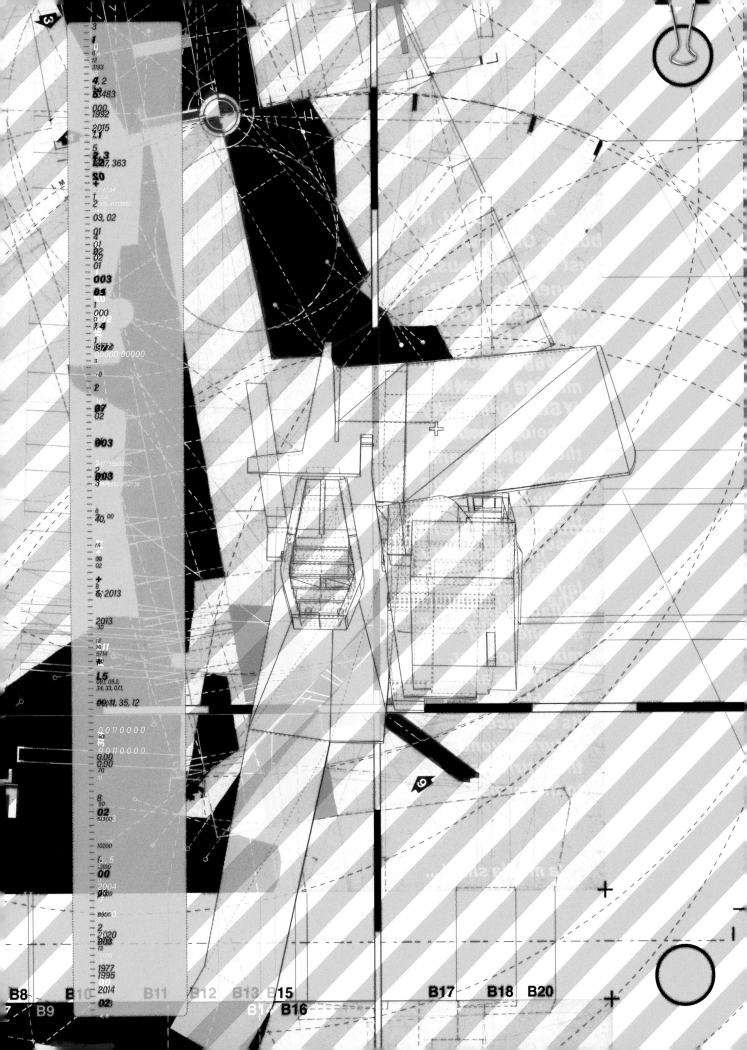

SoC[i]al AMPs +

A series of sub-servation stations than amplify the condition of mis-he[a]rd mentality within (social) media vents.

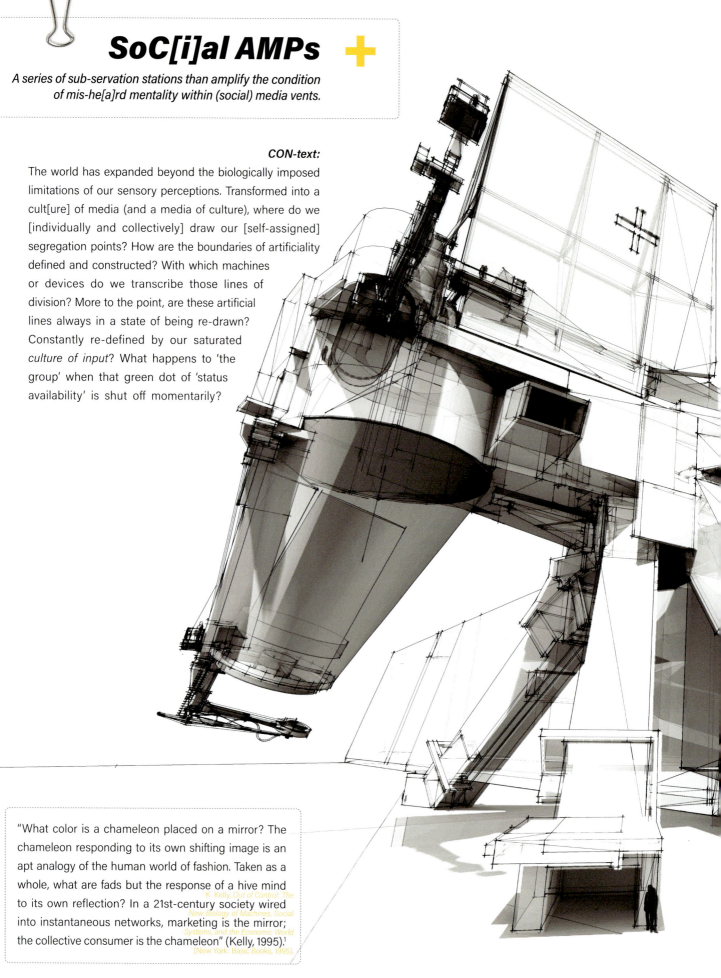

CON-text:

The world has expanded beyond the biologically imposed limitations of our sensory perceptions. Transformed into a cult[ure] of media (and a media of culture), where do we [individually and collectively] draw our [self-assigned] segregation points? How are the boundaries of artificiality defined and constructed? With which machines or devices do we transcribe those lines of division? More to the point, are these artificial lines always in a state of being re-drawn? Constantly re-defined by our saturated *culture of input*? What happens to 'the group' when that green dot of 'status availability' is shut off momentarily?

"What color is a chameleon placed on a mirror? The chameleon responding to its own shifting image is an apt analogy of the human world of fashion. Taken as a whole, what are fads but the response of a hive mind to its own reflection? In a 21st-century society wired into instantaneous networks, marketing is the mirror; the collective consumer is the chameleon" (Kelly, 1995).[1]

K. Kelly, *Out of Control: The New Biology of Machines, Social Systems, and the Economic World* (New York: Basic Books, 1995).

MEDIA LOGICS

TYPE 2 Drones

Drones are unmanned aerial vehicles, used to observe, record, and often edit the surface that they view, by means of air to surface (data) weaponry, or through information transfer effecting change(s) on the *(social) topography*. Through this surface altering invasion drones can observe from a vantage point that an un-augmented human being cannot, from **above**. They offer the operator the opportunity to observe from an offsite, mechanically induced safe haven. In relation to exploratory drawing, we sometimes have an opportunity to reveal scenarios that we cannot see whilst occupying the **locale** of the *drawn/observed object*. Through these media, we can suggest political change, social impact, and physical surfacing.

(05)

"Owning a drone does not a pilot make" (Morritt, n.d.).[2]

[2] A. Morritt (n.d.), "Quotes About UAV," https://www.goodreads.com/quotes/tag/uav

TYPE 3 Fracking

Fracking is a slang term for hydraulic fracturing, a process of injecting fluid (often salt water) into rocks to create fractures in order to release natural gas deposits that are otherwise unreachable. This is an invasion from **underneath** the surface. Again, in the act of the exploratory drawing, we have the opportunity to edit and record data and events that we cannot locate on the conceptual surface of the paper.

"If more young people are talking about fracking instead of twerking, we're heading in the right direction" (Brand, 2013).[3]

[3] R. Brand, "We Deserve More from our Democratic System," *The Guardian*, 5 November 2013, https://www.theguardian.com/commentisfree/2013/nov/05/russell-brand-democratic-system-newsnight

These opposing conditions deal with the implications of the relational interactions between the environment (in its absolute form), its occupancy, and its observability relative to the human body.

There are more than few parallels here to the tactic of how the body maintains equilibrium in relation to the absolute world through the Peripheral Sensory System. Vision, like the drone, tracks the position of the head and body [the viewing mechanism] relative to the world/ground plane.

The Somatosensory system tracks haptic input from the feet [instruments of physical connectivity] against the perceived ground plane, cross referencing sensors in joints, to know where our feet/legs are [a ground stabilization system].

"Social Roots and their Political Tendons"

"The reader is the space on which all quotations that make up a writing are inscribed without any of them being lost; a text's unity lies not in its origin, but in its destination. The Author, when believed in, is always conceived of as the past of his own book: book and author stand automatically on a single line divided into a before and after. In complete contrast, the modern scripter is born simultaneously to the text, and is in no way equipped with a being preceding or exceeding the writing ... there is no other time than that of the enunciation, and every text is eternally written here and now. Writing can no longer designate an operation of recording, notation, representation, or depiction; rather it designates a performative ..." (Barthes, 1977).[5]

[5] R. Barthes, "The Death of the Author," in *Image Music Text* (London: Fontana, 1977).

Project

Can we talk of the authorship when discussing collective ideas? Of the origin of social and societal circumstances based on groups and predicated upon access to now ubiquitous technology that makes up our (social) landscape?

"Far from rejecting outright any hierarchy of success or failure, philosophy instead reconfigures the judging process, lending legitimacy to the idea that the mainstream value system may unfairly consign some people to disgrace and others to respectability" (De Botton, 2004).[6]

[6] A. de Botton, *Status Anxiety* (London: Hamish Hamilton, 2004).

Social media offers an opportunity for the media of technology and mobility (the media of congregation) to affect a new social projection. New architectural conditions that explore the consequence of amplifying *un-tuned social policy*. This suggests that social media may constitute a condition of 'drone awareness' – offering the opportunity to assign a conscience to a soulless system. Architecture has the opportunity, and it might be argued the responsibility, to become the medium of congregation. A true social media, and equalization catalyst. The potential anonymity of the interface has the capacity to make us all, initially at least, 'equal'.

This project began by looking at the interiority of the problem, through the architectural device and through the eyes/lenses/screens of the citizen. This exploration intended to ask questions about authorship, responsibility, and the ability to navigate collisions of social conditions that have been previously left un-marked, undrawn, or at the very least, plotted with invisible ink.

The Vestibular System, the balance organs in the inner ear inform the brain [the magic decoder ring] of movements and the position of the head, analogous to the act of reading/navigation of items *above*, *on*, and *under* the ground plane. Occupancy encompasses a broader sense of how we, as drawers and readers, *inhabit* a tacit space, the cerebral synthesis of these multi-sensory inputs. Engaging the membrane, whilst populating the space of speculation. There is a new relationship, and therefore, a new definition of topography in the recognition of these scanning authorities.

The ground plane and the drawing plane, or the plane of observation, are inherently connected within the established canon of architectural discourse. They are both the horizontal planes of organization and reading. The notion nature of the plane itself, a semi-autonomous entity, looks at its function as a somewhat 'flat' arena for the dissemination of architectural thought.

Both drones and fracking create their own (perceptual) readings through the exploration and exploitation of existing contextual frame[work]s. While most drones are historically perceived in a military operational convention, the condition of unmanned air domination is starting to bleed over into the consumer world. One must consider this dominance and the implications for shaping a disembodied consumer 'strike' as an emergent condition within the culture of consumerism.

Mapping may be one of the most distorted terms in technology today. We might begin to explore the notion of 'map' the noun, with 'mapping' the **process**. Google Earth is one of the most widely used virtual sources of topoGRAPHICal **'documentation'** in the social media age. One of the most intriguing attributes of virtual media, whether initially social or not, is the opportunity it affords the user to explore **non-realities** as a credible environment for investigation. Misinformation becomes a condition of **content**. The residues of conceptual fracking and intellectual drone operations, offer places and planes of exploration and perception that would not have been accessible if we rely solely on the 'factual' information that social media claims to produce.

These machines create collisions between political boundaries and jurisdictions, policy enforcement, and the

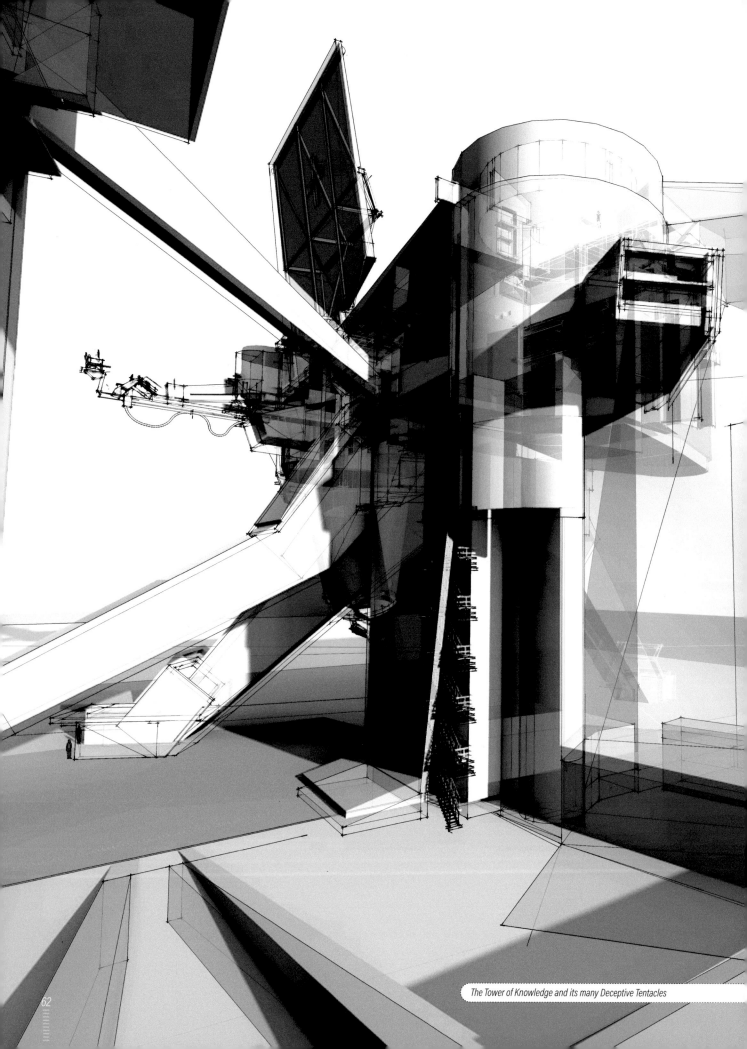

The Tower of Knowledge and its many Deceptive Tentacles

These proposals address social positioning and equity **disharmony**. The intention is to examine the plane of community collection (a result of above and below forces), compressing social data into a **'stratum of empathy.'** They seek to magnify the superimposed condition of 'class structure' and 'social status' through topographical, and *geographical* positioning. Exploring the idea that status is **reflected**, if not **based**, in physical position. The accretion of social **status** becomes social **stratum**.

Amplifiers increase the power of a signal. If that signal is the quest to flatten the field of status positions, then the Social Amplifiers are meant to compress our preconceived strata of social ranking into a single layer, altering the taxonomy that exists between media and community.

> "Ambient awareness is the experience of knowing what's going on in the lives of other people – what they're thinking about, what they're doing, what they're looking at – by paying attention to the small stray status messages that people are putting online. We're now able to stitch together these fantastic details and mental maps of what is going on in other people's lives" (Thompson, n.d.).[7]

The Social Amplifiers attempt to create environments that promote a greater degree Ambient Social Awareness, through the provision of an externalized perspective. By allowing the occupiers to view themselves the AMPs provide an awareness of conditions that are not physically occupied (or even occupiable) by the operator, in much the same way as a drone does it pilot/operator.

The AMP[lifier]s challenge us to become more than consumers in a media driven world of status updates and cultural fads, viewports, and portals. They are intended to focus the way we view other members of our society, and reciprocally the way in which they view us. This is Social Positioning – the act of viewing and judging yourself [one's 'social height'] through the lenses of others based on surface qualities – gender, clothing, race, style, context, etc. For these explorations, maybe it's not so much about its graphic *status* indicators as it is *spatial* indicators.

Perception.
Topography.
The 'height of awareness' … the metrics of social position.

dissemination of information. Social Media, when used as an architectural informant, might be able to consider the hidden systems of deployment and archaeology.

"It's those fracking drones again …!" (Wilson, 1996).[4]

The drone creates an artificial context through the acts of voyeurism, interpretation, and deployment. That deployment is often material in nature, and social in behavior, an alteration of the characteristics of **exteriority** of an event or place. Fracking produces artificial contexts within the physical material that changes the 'interiority' an event or space, through fragmentation, redistribution, and the residues of the process. Both mechanisms create artificial readings, synthetic **contextual** information.

Spatial Smearing as a tactical system of information distribution …

Surface splicing as an accredited condition of realigned political, social, topological, and therefore architectural systems. …

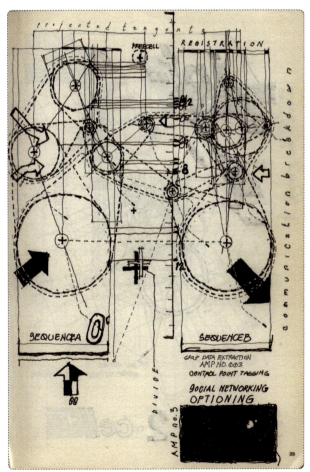

Sketch 31 – Social Network[ing] Optioning

The Procession
Each of the three amplifiers employs a basic set of strategies:

(1) Social interaction is encouraged through the population of designated/segregated gathering areas that establish basic spatial hierarchies between three distinct public groups:

submerged – surface to air
equal – surface to surface
elevated – air to surface

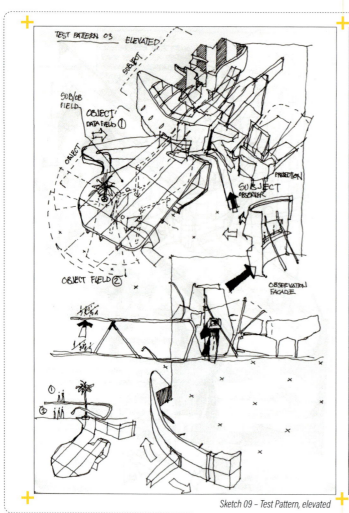

Sketch 09 – Test Pattern, elevated

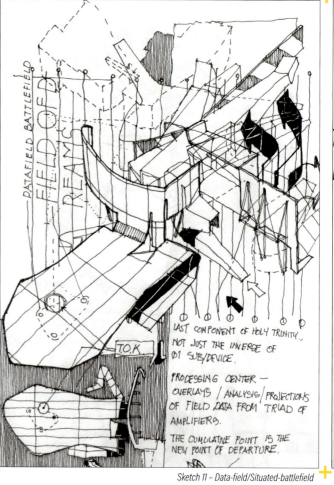

Sketch 11 – Data-field/Situated-battlefield

A] surface to air – looking up to power
[Catholic congregations, Aztec sacrificial temples, theatre stages, telescopes, and the Greek gladiator arenas]

B] surface to surface – face-to-face power, social networking arenas ...
no change in altitude
[confessionals, board games of chance, conversations, telephones, texting]

C] air to surface – power looking down
[the papal address balcony, thrones, microscopes, drive-through windows, pharmacist counters, and gravesite services]

64

Participants are understood as **voyeurs**, regardless of which category they occupy – everyone views everyone else through one of these paradigms of power. Each group is topographically divided based on the social physicality of status.

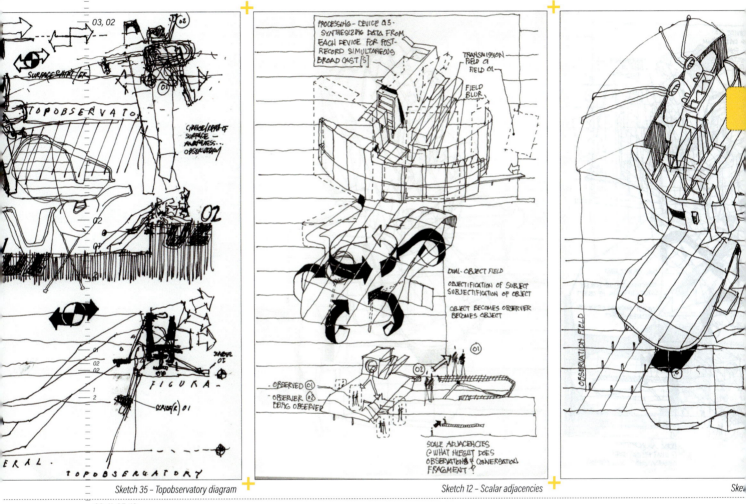

Sketch 35 - Topobservatory diagram   Sketch 12 - Scalar adjacencies

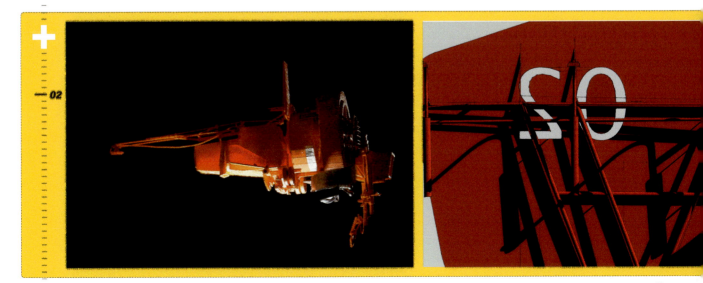

② Exchanges are initiated through scripted dialogue insertions – injected stimuli.

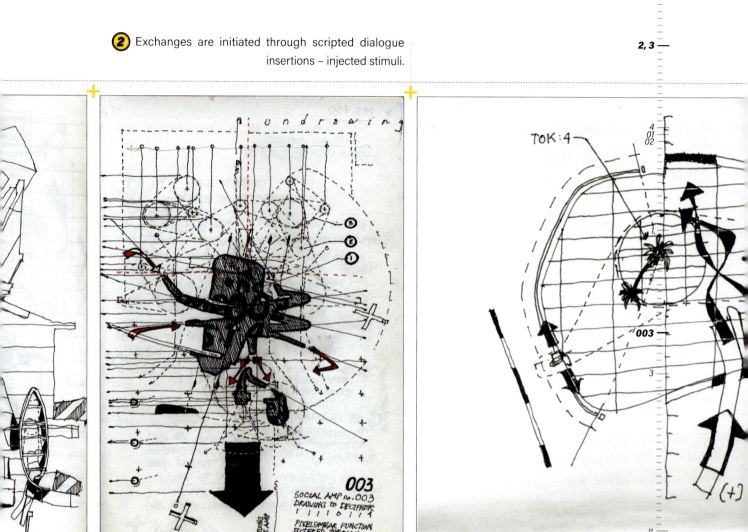

4 – Observational Fields Sketch 33 – the undrawing – detuning the AMP

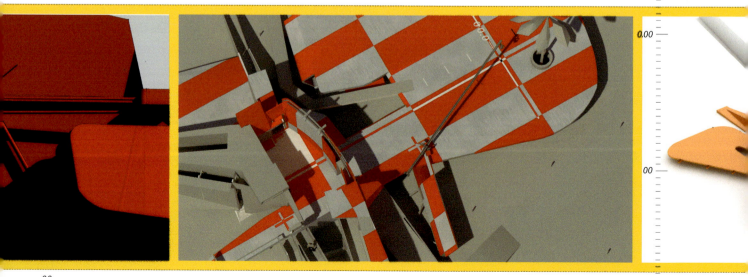

3 The interactions between each group as well as the 'other' groups are secretly recorded.

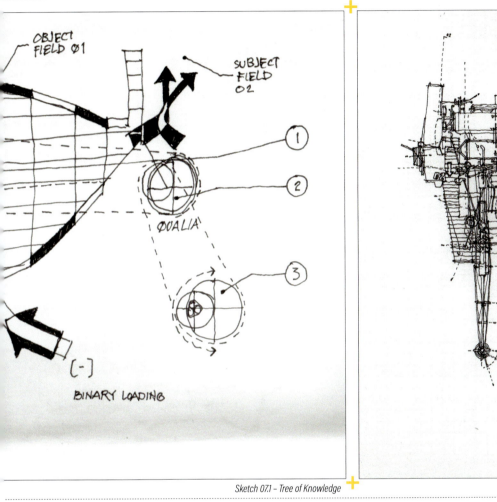

Sketch 07.1 - Tree of Knowledge

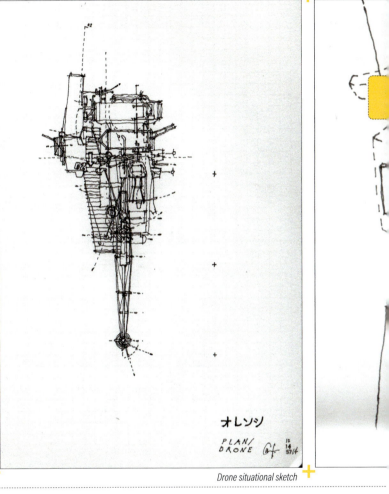

Drone situational sketch

4 The two groups eventually co-mingle in the antechambers, where they watch the previously recorded exchanges, played simultaneously to promote awareness of the emergence of multiple truths and observations based on geographic superiorities and group loyalties.

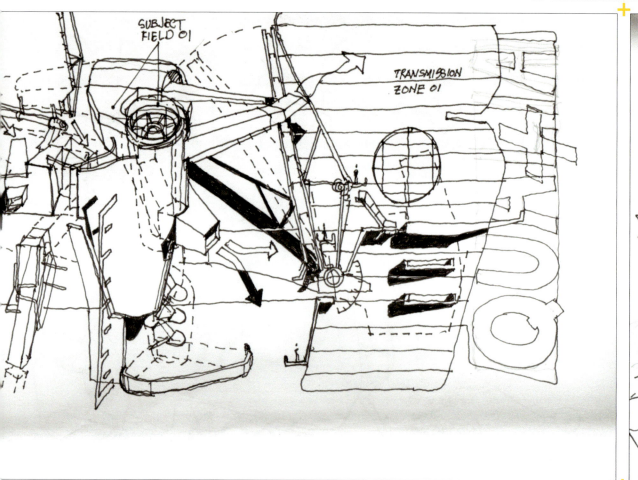

Sketch 08.1 – ARE THEY?

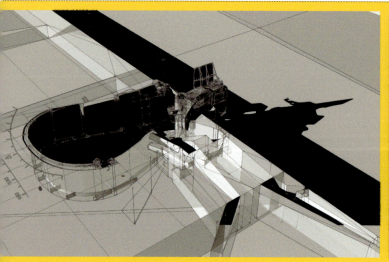
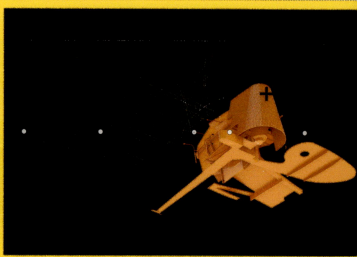

"An exhibitionist is nothing without a voyeur" (Sachs, n.d.).[8]

⑤ Exodus occurs as a singular collective, in direct opposition to the bifurcation of the groups' entry.

"a Topobservatory is born ..."

In these experiments as a so-called *'social scientist'* the viewer is asked to point the finger at themselves in addition to observing their subjects.

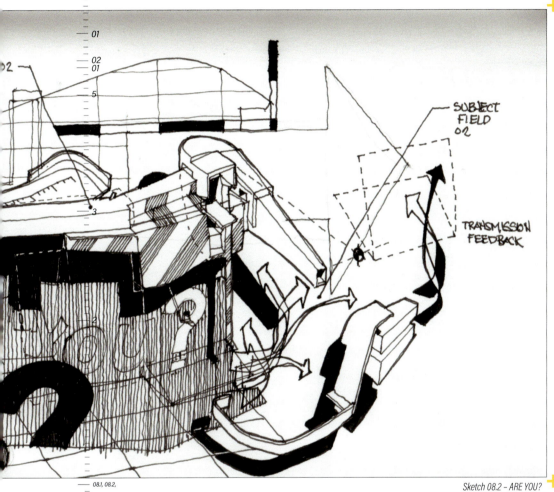
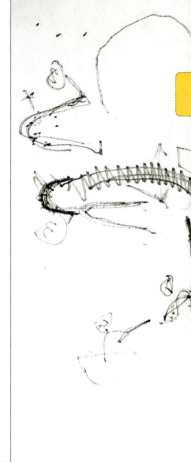

Sketch 08.2 – ARE YOU?

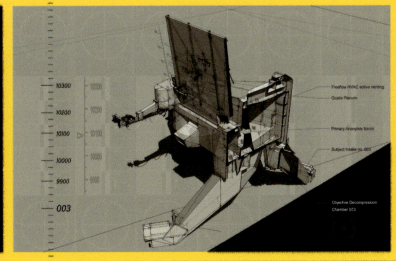
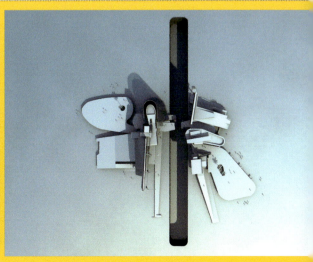

The oddity of this mechanical intervention is the process of information gathering; data is collected through what we might call *'screenshots'* of social engagement. This is Information (presented as continuously updating video feed), documents the interactions between subjects as they congregate in large Petri dish-like, plaza conditions, public areas that are placed in relation to a series of observation spaces

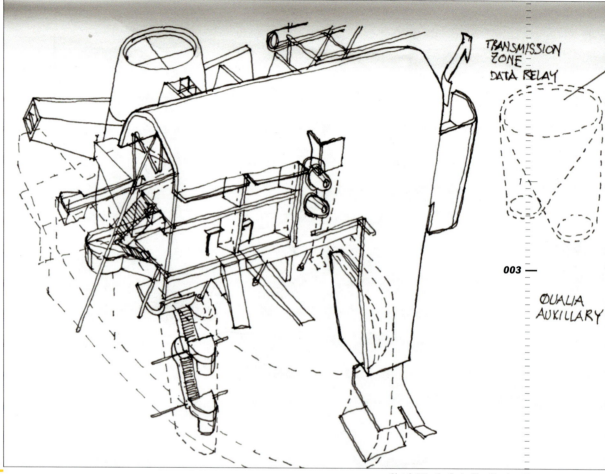

TRANSMISSION ZONE
DATA RELAY

QUALIA AUXILLARY

Sketch 44 - Sequence diagram

Sketch 07.2 - Qualia Auxiliary housing

and pavilions, allowing people to 'naturally' self-segregate themselves into either the observer, or the observed.

Neither viewer nor viewed can observe their opposite, without a *filter of themselves* layered into the view. The system generates a continuous feedback loop of self-observation, whilst celebrating the potentiality of technology to harvest social insights.

Binary input, idiosyncratic output.

Passive views, active judgments. Constant measuring, evaluating, reading – whether the data is *accurate*, or even *present*.

Image by Kevin F. O'Donnell

Full network conflict diagram 003

The Object

The embedded Qualia Chamber is an Inverted Observatory device. It was conceived as a microscope for studying self-imposed societal segregation patterns. Beginning as a space in which the user is prompted to identify the condition of self-observation within the context of social status, a place where the occupants of the machine can invert the function of the microscope. It examines which social entities exist – how they may be grouped within a *hierarchy* and *subdivided* according to similarities and differences. It asks what that *'knowledge'* is, how it is acquired, and to what extent it is possible for an entity to be *'known'.*

The plaza of each project is analogous to the stage on a microscope. A surface of social observation – each machine is a viewing/recording device for the implications/reactions/observations of a collective assembly, the congregation viewed from a controlled exterior location. It explores the subject/object of the architectural interface. Each device/folly/capsule observes and records the group acting as a singular living organism. They are microscopes, telescopes, oscilloscopes, fluoroscopes, perhaps even kaleidoscopes …

Amplified conversation device

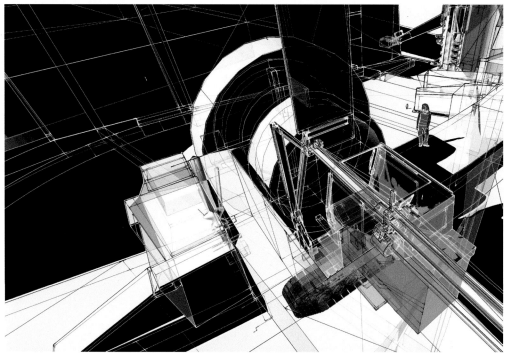

*Observation Drone –
"Operator Cab Detail"*

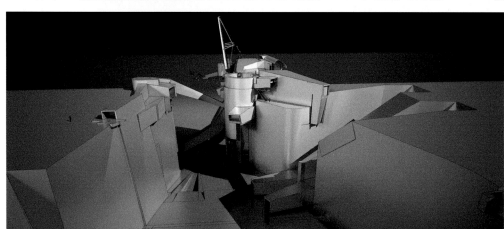

*Divisional Entry into the main
Processing Court*

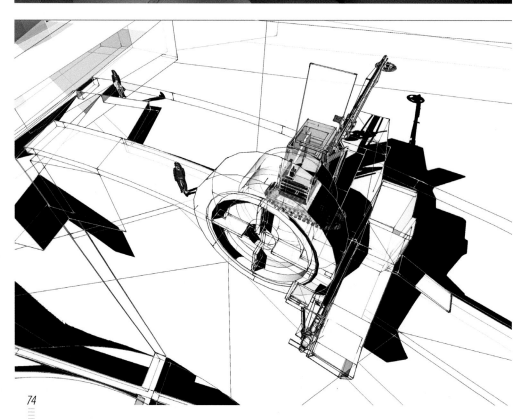

Self[ie] Drone – observational assignation

> "To embarrass justice by multiplicity of laws, or to hazard it by confidence in judges, seem to be the opposite rocks on which all civil institutions have been wrecked, and between which legislative wisdom has never yet found an open passage" (Johnson, 1786).[9]
>
> *S. Johnson, "King of Prussia," in A. Murphy, The Works of Samuel Johnson with an Essay on His Life and Genius, Vol. II (New York: George Dearborn Publisher, 1837), p.363.*

These devices suspend the Golden Rule, the observer/researcher is forced to interact with/affect the test group. The mediator device generates the condition/disturbance and records the outcome. Basic spatial situation-ing.

The deconstructed surface functions as a diagram, recording patterns of removal and isolation on surface of segregation. Through the promotion of awareness these spaces, in turn, become the surfaces of inclusion as we transition between passive observers and engaged players. Ultimately, the occupant of the pavilion becomes a mechanism of change, the architecture serves as a refocusing system.

<<"[E].Q.E.D. A tuning device ...">>

Each of the 3 amplifiers terminates with 2 chambers. These chambers repurpose the information collected in each structure looping it back in a series of immersive projections. Through the viewing of these videos it is hoped that *all* subjects might gain a new understanding of their *topographic judgment*, leaving the device educated and enlightened.

It's the rat, the cheese, *and* the maze with all elements cognizant of the others' presence; using the dialogue to map a less linear relationship ... ✚

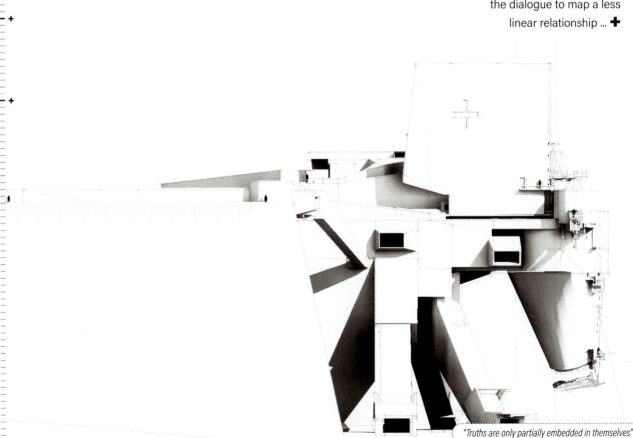

"Truths are only partially embedded in themselves"

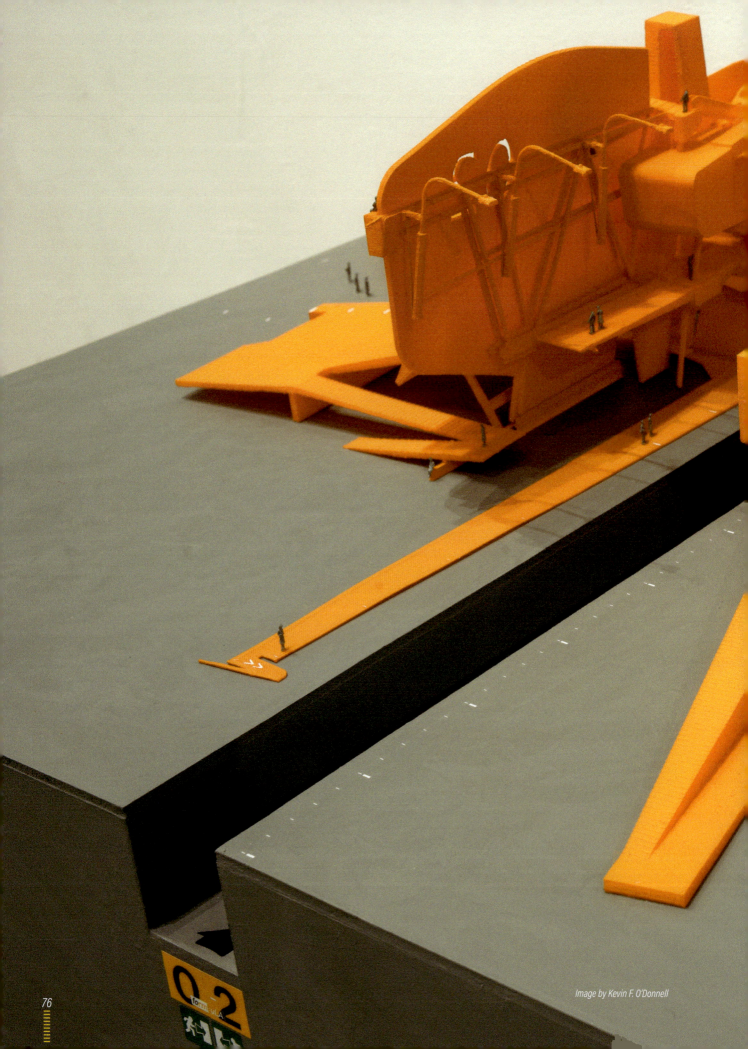

Image by Kevin F. O'Donnell

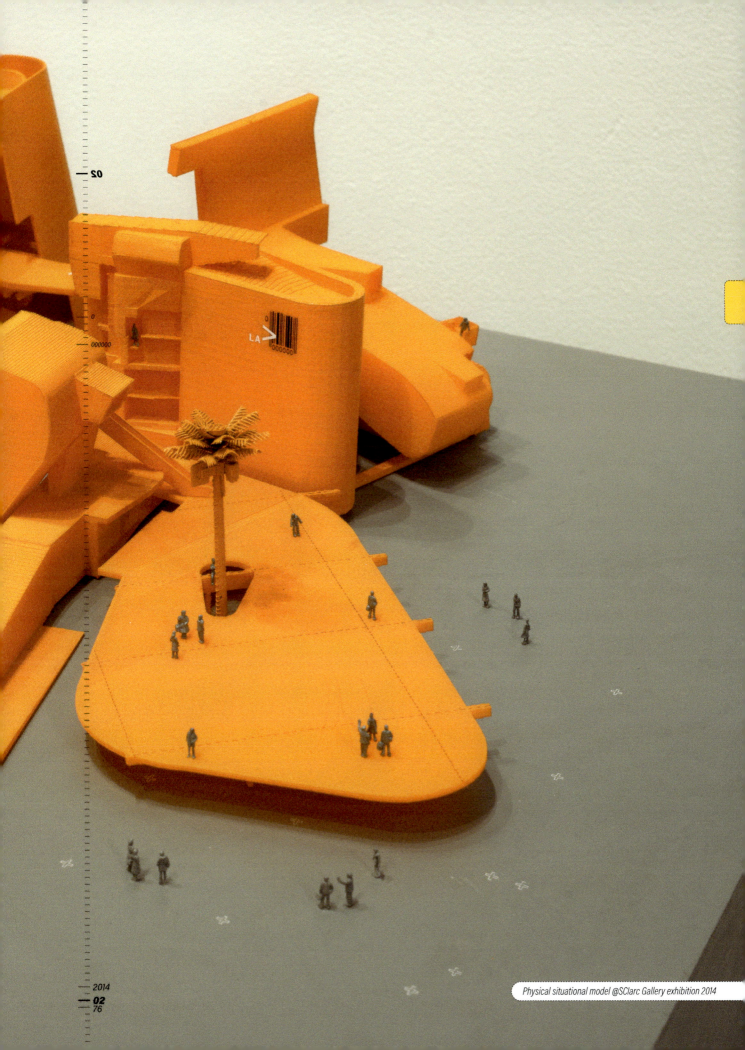
Physical situational model @SClarc Gallery exhibition 2014

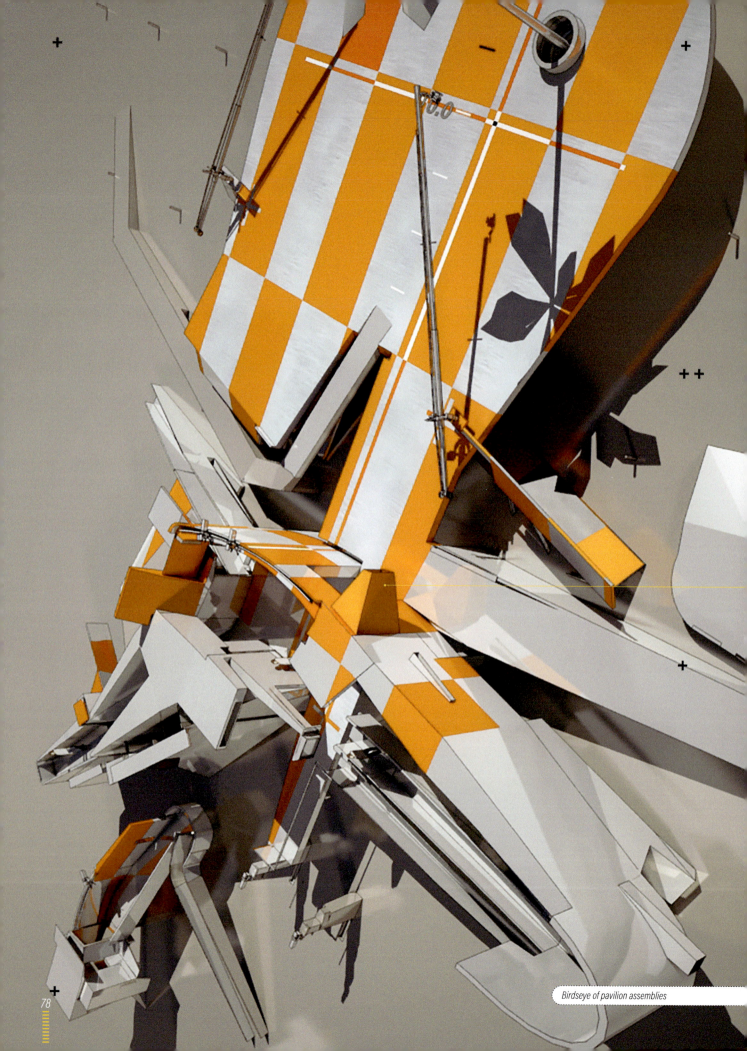

Birdseye of pavilion assemblies

Full Network Overload – all the world's a stage ...

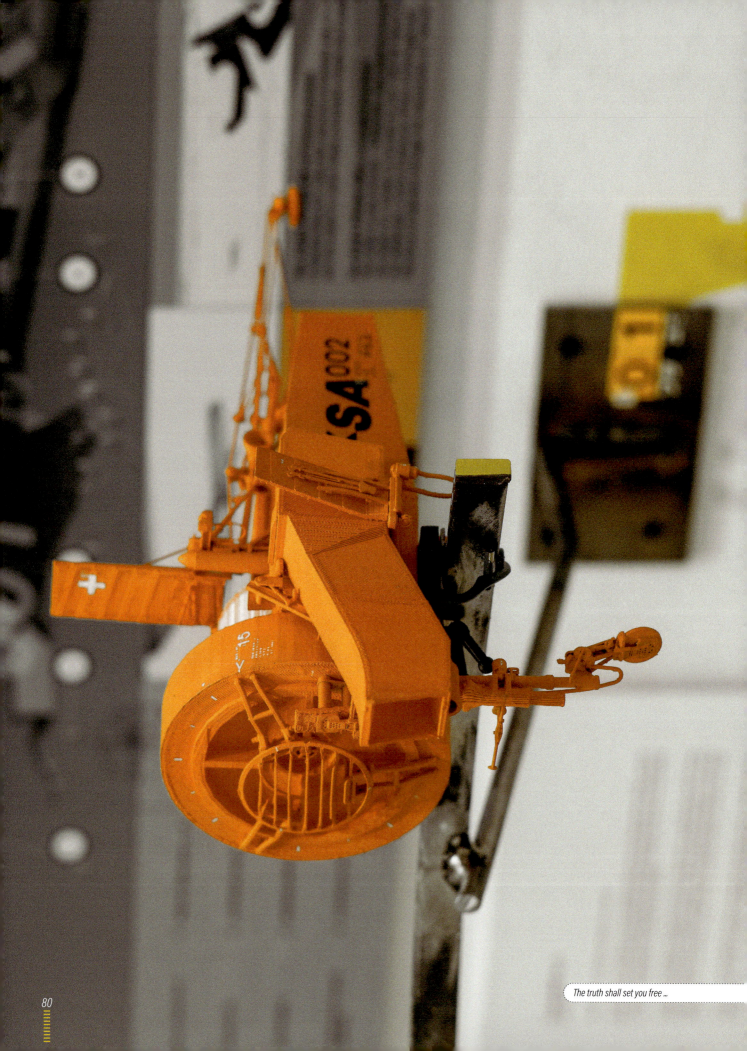

The truth shall set you free ...

Drone model. CON-text free

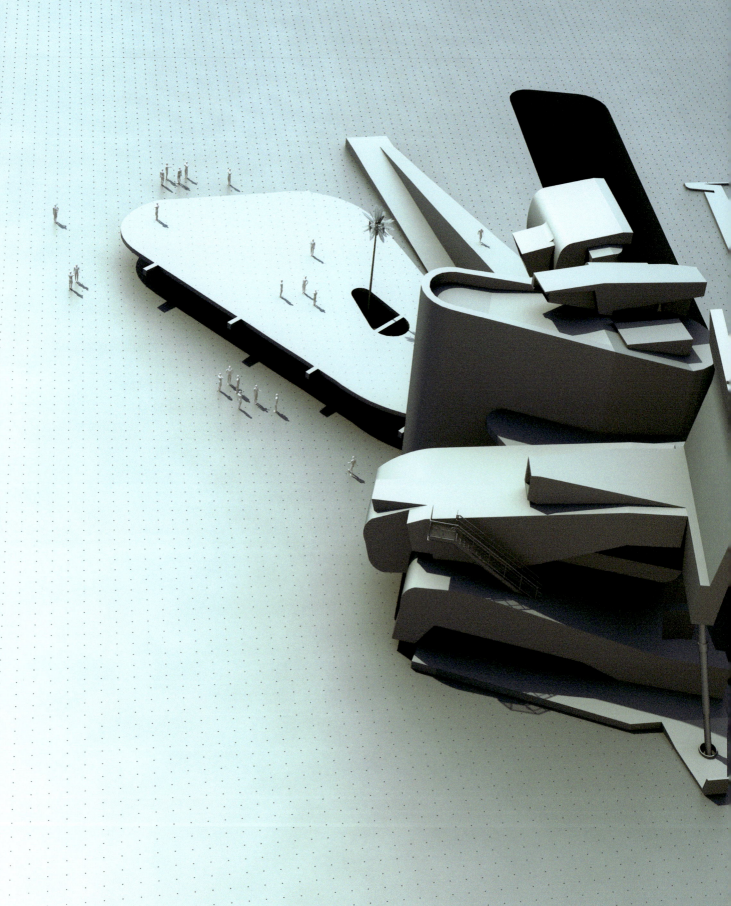

Truth can be a divisionary tactic

[Rear] Half-truths

+ OMGWTF WYSIWYG

Wes Jones
*Director of Graduate Studies,
USC School of Architecture, Los Angeles*

OMGWTF: Pretty much says it all. I mean, what else you say when confronted with the sheer overwhelming intensity of this work? Other than expletives of confounded amazement, snorts of amused surprise, or whistles of appreciation, the viewer is stunned into silence.

WYSIWYG: And yet, it's all right there, exactingly represented, no tricks of approximation or perspectival sleights. It could be built.

It is an easy and obvious mistake to think of Cantley's work as being 'about' the machine, given the extremely careful and extensive reference to the mechanical forms proliferating throughout. In fact, though, the work is really 'about' the complexity resulting when these forms are layered and collaged and morphed and mixed, as objects and graphics, taking its essence or nature beyond that attributable to the forms. A seemingly unstructured proliferation of individually coherent details solicits the viewer's complicity through the limited reasonableness of those details and their presentation within an architectural context, which always assumes an ultimate logic, however apparently absurd, or infinitely deferred. While the machinic forms and graphic elaboration are engaging in themselves, they are best seen as the counters he uses to construct this particular complexity, and it is the complexity that *demands the attention and finally rewards contemplation*. The complexity arises from the interaction of the elements in his compositions, and it is greater than the sum of these parts, their assemblies and subassemblies and the identifiable interactions between them – even though they are almost uncountable. In other words, the complexity cannot ultimately be unraveled or explained by tracing it back to its constituent elements. The viewer understands this immediately at some subliminal level and this conditions her enjoyment of the resultant furball by eliminating the frustration of thwarted understanding.

Yet, these objects are certainly not random or neutral, and the complexity they develop could not be created with an indifferent collection of parts. Instead, Cantley's brand of complexity owes its particular character to the rules inherent in the choice of objects and their customary arrangements, as well as the viewer's familiarity with the world they reference. As we will see, this familiarity sustains the engagement that allows the complexity to develop its full impact for the observer and avoids the visual burnout that haunts so much other architectural production trading in complex forms and arrangements.

It is helpful in this regard to contrast the complexity that Cantley achieves using the forms of the machine with that developed by the popular blobists who champion the pseudo-complexity of a smoothly authorless semi-biomorphic parametric mush, under the banner of Object-Oriented Ontology. In viewing Cantley's work from the perspective of OOO it is clear how his work offers an alternative to the absolute aloofness sought by OOO that strands the blob between a superficial wannabe alienness and indifferent obscurity.

The potential architecturalutility of OOO is best understood by viewing OOO as the logical concluding endpoint of a graduated series of steps taken toward achieving novelty, beginning with simile and metaphor. These two terms describe an arc towards novelty that depends on extending understanding from the familiar into the different. Simile begins the journey as strict analogy – one thing is like another – but metaphor is transformation, as one thing becomes another, completely absorbed as the other, transferring the meaning to create something surprising and new. *A Doric column is like a man, but a caryatid is a woman, with a building sitting on her head.* The kind of practice that features recognizable figures, like Cantley's, is often assumed to play along this arc, whether or not there is an obvious intention to ride it somewhere comprehensively new or different. In architecture the difference between simile and metaphor is the that between legibility as an abstract awareness and meaning as a felt experience. The Doric column evidently bears the proportions of a man, but its entasis shows how it feels to bear the weight of the entablature. Cantley's work seems to be

"It is an easy and obvious mistake to think of Cantley's work as being 'about' the machine... the work is really 'about' the complexity resulting when these forms are layered and collaged and morphed and mixed, as objects and graphics, taking its essence or nature beyond that attributable to the forms."

clearly located at the metaphoric end of this range, yet it cannot be left there, since the stuff is just as clearly not simply metaphoric to make a point. It is, instead, itself, doing what it seems like it would naturally do as itself, however strange that might seem to the viewer. Cantley's caryatids have buildings on their heads, but unlike Mnesicles' they don't look silly because they are fully aware of that fact and actively participating in the activity, balancing the load, distributing the weight. Cantley's work follows the arc of meaning out beyond the reach of architectural gravity... and into the space of OOO.

While simile and metaphor are interested in advancing ideas through the juxtaposition of otherwise unrelated terms, with varying levels of commitment to the result, OOO casts itself into the object's world absolutely, with a commitment to absolute difference: off the deep end, beyond comprehension or meaning or any connection. OOO is resigned to following the arc of meaning only because it is epistemologically necessary, but its goal is to imagine stuff that escapes gravity and floats free of any associations, in complete obscurity. The actual epistemological impossibility of this goal makes the work which pursues it either an off-putting illustration of the desire or, if more successful, a boring enigma – indifference being in fact a sign of its success. Clearly neither of these conditions is an interest of Cantley's complex work.

OOO was imported to architecture for the same reasons as deconstruction, though the spirit behind the two are very different. Deconstruction was attractive to architecture because of its underlying liberation theology, coming at a time when architecture had taken a distinctly conservative turn into autonomy with Historicism. It was felt that deconstruction offered the possibility to 'open up' architecture to other meanings than those associated with the favored forms chosen/handed down through history by encouraging forms that were devoid of conventional meaning. After much willfully obscure and laughable formal invention it was realized that meaning is not so easily dismissed (lesson that the original literary version of decon had learned earlier, with less embarrassing – because less concrete – results). When the computer arrived on the scene to rescue Deconstructivism from this impasse, its ability to go where no pencil dared led the enterprise into complexity as a substitute for difference, trading strange forms for an eye-glazing blizzard of seeming randomness that repelled any potential reading. However, except among its own practitioners, this repulsion understandably succeeded as well in eliminating any interest in reading by its audience. This disinterest was not however the indifference that would signal success for OOO.

The most charitable way to think of OOO's interest is as a representation of the nuclear option in 'advanced architecture's' resistance to convention, since it aims to escape the human connection entirely. Less charitably it can be seen as an alibi for extremely personal (opaque to others) formal excesses, otherwise inexplicable except as examples of the art game's current dare to identify anything as art. *As a necessarily human undertaking, this escape is doomed to failure when it comes to operating in a realm that produces (human) stuff*, like architecture. The original, strictly philosophical version of OOO realized this and renamed itself 'speculative realism,' admitting these limitations. Architecture, on the other hand, is sticking to the original premise, trusting complexity to shield its epistemological nakedness, selfishly aware how the philosophical goal of indifference (foreshadowed

for architecture by Benjamin and Hugo) would not be such a great idea for architecture, and knowing that the connection preventing that indifference cannot actually be lost. Here Cantley's work steps into the conversation, showing how much the object's autonomy can asserted without forsaking architecture's horror of irrelevance or invisibility.

Much of the continuing work in the OOO world is concerned with various ways to defend the object from the epistemological gravity that tends to suck it back into the human sphere. So, for example, Graham Harmon (who is credited with starting the whole thing) cautions against 'undermining' the object, by viewing it as the embodiment of some deeper essence or parts, or 'overmining' it by seeing it as a manifestation of the relationships it can make in the world, including in language. In both cases OOO says the object, in itself, is missed. A key aspect of this is the idea that every attempt to 'grasp' the object is incomplete, that there is always something more, that the object always 'withdraws' from any apparent legibility or understanding (preserving its ultimate autonomy).

Architectural attempts to explicitly represent these possibilities are obviously limited to what OOO would have to consider a superficial illustration of simile, while even a more complete metaphoric approach to the problem would be stuck with treatments that were only approximations. Architects have attempted to address these issues through making their stuff ever more strange – more obscure and less meaningful – to foil the viewer's potential engagement. While it is obvious why true success in these efforts would be suicidal for architecture, the PCAD world continues to attempt this. Which makes us wonder then what OOO's real utility is for architecture if, like deconstruction, it is not something to be merely illustrated. Clearly the deeper epistemologically challenging aspirations of OOO cannot be embodied in authored form, but maybe the spirit of … respect for the idea those objects could withdraw can be demonstrated.

If OOO is about trying to imagine what the object itself would do or be, in the absence of an author or any concerns for being understood by other objects, including people, Cantley's stuff shows us (without resorting to the authorless automatism of PCAD) the first, without being canceled out by admitting the second. This occurs in a couple of ways that recall Heidegger's discussion of 'equipmental being.' First, Cantley's complexity passes right by simile and metaphor to project a willfulness, earnest intention, and potential meaning that appears to emanate directly from the object(s) rather than being imposed by the author. And it promotes, requires, an intense level of engagement that extends that will to the viewer, forcing her to be an active reader. This in turn acknowledges/respects that will and further reinforces the seeming autonomy of the object demanding the attention. Further, by drawing the actual graphics into the equation, the object refuses subjugation to an author who might be wielding those graphics, instead playing freely among its conventions, driven by a formal self-awareness that reinforces the sense that the object is in charge.

While a willingness to roll up curiosity's sleeves and duck down under the hood might be necessary to penetrate the first impressions of the work's daunting furball mechanality, the objects are not coy: what you see is what you get, and they are not worried about being under-or over-mined in that appreciation. There are guides to where the latch for this hood can be found, and little moments of metaphoric recognition that tease the reader deeper and deeper into the work's own unfamiliar territory, but where the reader ends up there are no ladies with buildings on their heads, only cable-headed medusas and biomechanical devices, emerging from the page, literally, to headbutt the reader. The visual affordances acknowledge the reader, but on the object's often unexpected terms. Like the barbs on an anchor, details grab our full attention, moving the gaze from one instance to another without zooming outward to the overall maelstrom. It all makes a sort of sequential sense. And when it doesn't, when a critical collage displacement or shift between two details is noticed, it is noticed as such, and accepted without interrupting the visceral pleasure of the images.

"If OOO is about trying to imagine what the object itself would do or be, in the absence of an author or any concerns for being understood by other objects, including people, Cantley's stuff shows us the first, without being cancelled out by admitting the second."

The difference between PCAD's satisfaction with the aloofness of OOO and the intense engagement that Cantley's work finds there is due in part to the framing expectations of the encounter. PCAD strives to distance itself from its institutional or disciplinary roots, to get as far away from the gallery as possible. In the process this work risks the frame's identification of it as (whatever it is). Cantley on the other hand recognizes that value. His work finds a 'home' in architecture. Its residence there is based only on its emphatic presence, not on any recognizable architectural traits that might undermine it or disciplinary tropes that could overmine it, so its OOO bona fides remain intact. Its presence as/in exemplifies Heidegger's description of the art 'work' as unique and special, without implying any larger statement about that context, or its own specialness other than that embodied nakedly by its existence: "It could be built."

The WYSIWYG insanity of Cantley's machinogenic furballs is firmly anchored in a ground of apparent intentionality. Even the craziest stuff is granted some legitimacy when understood to be 'on purpose'. Craziness needs that legitimacy to be effective, to be taken seriously, because it is, well, crazy. And that craziness inoculates the work against the over- and undermining that claims the unwary object. Because in the end architecture is not crazy and work in its name that is crazy is necessarily other, somehow. Like Wittgenstein's games, there is a family resemblance but that's it.

In view of this ironic connection between Cantley's work and OOO, which otherwise is the alibi for so much PCAD silliness, should we see this relationship as critical, or illustrative? Arguments can be made for both, but maybe the real answer is who cares? Does it matter? And does that question actually say more about it and its true contemporary relevance?

Why must everything today be judged as 'critical' to be taken seriously? This work shows us that mastery can live in the ostensibly arbitrary, that the difference between the two extremes contains a lot that is worth considering, and that maybe this can be a more effective way to make a point. It is too well sorted out to be arbitrary. But it isn't its fault if you can't keep up. Any apparent insanity then might be more a reflection of the viewer than the author. Or maybe an example of Barthes' claim that the viewer is the author.

The hook for this judgment will be meaning; how the work's meaningfulness is judged will tell. This is not to ask what its meaning is, but whether it seems to have any, or care. ✣

Image by Kevin F. O'Donnell

COSMO

The viral implant as a new con-dition of [n]urban planning.

What happens when a viral architecture is applied as a salve to heal contemporary urban blight? To replicate, a virus must be permitted to execute its code and rewrite to the memory of its [un]willing/[un]knowing host. Many viruses attach themselves to executable files that may be part of legitimate, desired programs. When a user launches an infected program, the virus' code is often executed simultaneously, running in stealth mode. This project is the basis for a new urban model virus *[virurban?]*, that will eventually attach itself to the 'unexecuted' structures of the city.

MEDIA LOGICS

TYPE 5 Viral Media

A computer virus is a program that can replicate itself and spread from one CPU to another. The term 'virus' is also commonly, but erroneously used, to refer to other types of malwares, including, but not limited to, adware and spyware programs. Viruses typically make unauthorized changes to the computer's operating system, undesirable even if no damage is done or intended. The operative term here is un*authorized*. Once again *authorship* has a stake in the game.

Viruses may be divided into two types based on their behavior when they are executed:

Non-resident viruses that immediately search for other hosts, infecting those targets, and transferring control to the application program they have infected.

Resident viruses do not search for hosts; instead, they load into the memory on execution and transfer control to the host program. The virus stays active in the background and infects new hosts when those files are accessed by other programs or the operating system itself.

TYPE 6 Viral Medium

A bacteriophage [or phage] is a virus that infects bacteria – these have reconnaissance mechanisms that gather intelligence so to remain in a state of quiescence or assault a new host, based on the accessibility of fresh targets. Phages have active discussions regarding recipient availability and success of infection.

Lysogeny – reproduction without destruction, becomes a media blanket for distribution protocols and replication conventions. Much like their digital counterparts, that contain [or generate] code for overtaking and reprogramming host cells/conditions.

The COSMOlogy Viral Caspid behaves no differently. It is both the code as well as the spiked protein that follows the directive to penetrate cells [in this case an urban condition] in hope of rewriting the urban condition's structure, creating a new Caspid.

Masterplan of Initiation engine, node seekers, and viral growth

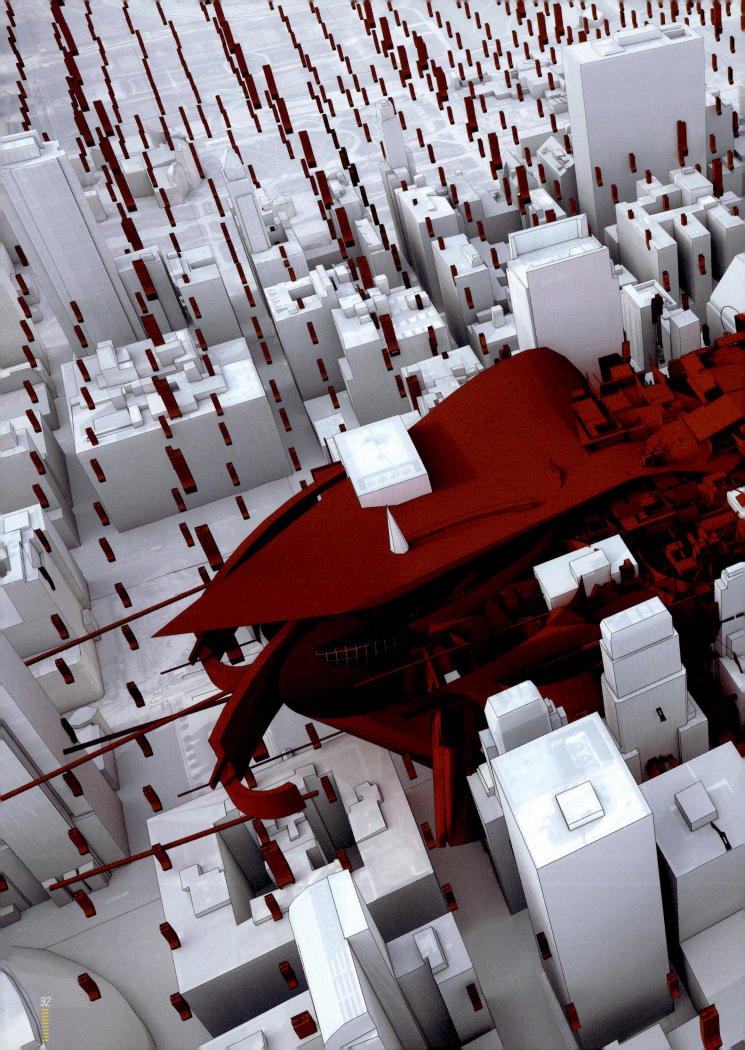

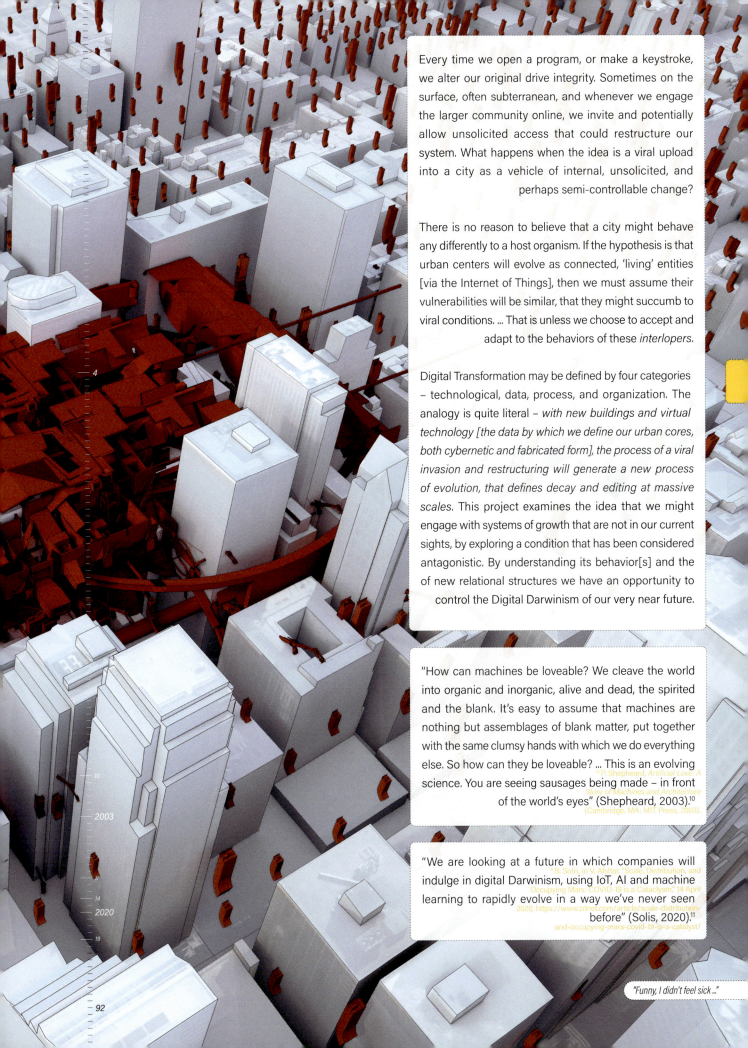

Every time we open a program, or make a keystroke, we alter our original drive integrity. Sometimes on the surface, often subterranean, and whenever we engage the larger community online, we invite and potentially allow unsolicited access that could restructure our system. What happens when the idea is a viral upload into a city as a vehicle of internal, unsolicited, and perhaps semi-controllable change?

There is no reason to believe that a city might behave any differently to a host organism. If the hypothesis is that urban centers will evolve as connected, 'living' entities [via the Internet of Things], then we must assume their vulnerabilities will be similar, that they might succumb to viral conditions. ... That is unless we choose to accept and adapt to the behaviors of these *interlopers*.

Digital Transformation may be defined by four categories – technological, data, process, and organization. The analogy is quite literal – *with new buildings and virtual technology [the data by which we define our urban cores, both cybernetic and fabricated form], the process of a viral invasion and restructuring will generate a new process of evolution, that defines decay and editing at massive scales*. This project examines the idea that we might engage with systems of growth that are not in our current sights, by exploring a condition that has been considered antagonistic. By understanding its behavior[s] and the of new relational structures we have an opportunity to control the Digital Darwinism of our very near future.

"How can machines be loveable? We cleave the world into organic and inorganic, alive and dead, the spirited and the blank. It's easy to assume that machines are nothing but assemblages of blank matter, put together with the same clumsy hands with which we do everything else. So how can they be loveable? ... This is an evolving science. You are seeing sausages being made – in front of the world's eyes" (Shepheard, 2003).[10]

[10] P. Shepheard, *Artificial Love: A Story of Machines and Architecture* (Cambridge, MA: MIT Press, 2003).

"We are looking at a future in which companies will indulge in digital Darwinism, using IoT, AI and machine learning to rapidly evolve in a way we've never seen before" (Solis, 2020).[11]

[11] B. Solis, in V. Afshar, "Scale, Distribution, and Occupying Mars: COVID-19 is a Cataclysm," 14 April 2020, https://www.zdnet.com/article/scale-distribution-and-occupying-mars-covid-19-is-a-catalyst/

"Funny, I didn't feel sick ..."

> "Humanity is just a virus with shoes" (Hicks, n.d.).[12]
> [12] B. Hicks (n.d.), "Quotes About Misanthropy," https://www.goodreads.com/quotes/73483-i-m-tired-of-this-back-slappin-isn-t-humanity-neat-bullshit-we-re

The project began as examination of a system that articulated an architectural language intended to express its **overall totality**, whilst retaining the capacity to describe the cellular details of that system. It studied the relationship between the alpha and omega, examining the **quickness** of a *Blink* and the **intensity** of a *Gaze*. We used the prototypical urban environment as the sheet on which to draw.

The **digital virus** became a device for positive regeneration through the capacity a computer virus to overwrite a prosaic system. There is a parallel here; the recognition that both the structure of (a) drawing, and the *virus* – whilst physically unmanned, both are intellectually inhabited. The **scripting** of each is **occupied** – by the author and intention. The resultant mapping records the behavioral characteristics of an **invasive**, *organically-behaving*, mechanical system onto a stagnant repetitive system that is suffering from its own *entropy*.

Since a virus is preordained to function as an **invisible entity**, the project looked at the act/condition of **media overwrite** as a positive way to rethink *architectural complacency*. We began by using ideas of the military drone to survey, assess, **inject** hardware and **liquid[ate]** software into a remote system in order to reconfigure it ... to save it ... to create a new topography of behavior.

> To quote *Theory of the Drone*: "The prey who wants to escape his pursuers tries to become undetectable or inaccessible. But **inaccessibility** is not only a function of physical **geography** – such as an entangled bush or deep crevice. The **theorists of manhunting** remind us that the 'political and legal restrictions, especially in the form of jurisdictional boundaries', are an **eminent** part of the 'set of constraints that **shape the rules of the game**'. From this point of view, it is clear that 'sovereign borders are among the greatest allies' that a fugitive can have. The **hunter's** power has no regard for **borders**. It allows itself the right of **universal trespassing**, in defiance of territorial integrity of sovereign states. It is an invasive power which, **unlike the imperial maneuvers of the past**, is based less on a notion of right of conquest than of a right of pursuit ..."
>
> "Didn't you hear me? I'm in high speed pursuit" (Justice, 1977).[13]
> [13] B.T. Justice, "High Speed Pursuit", Texarkana, 26 August 1977.

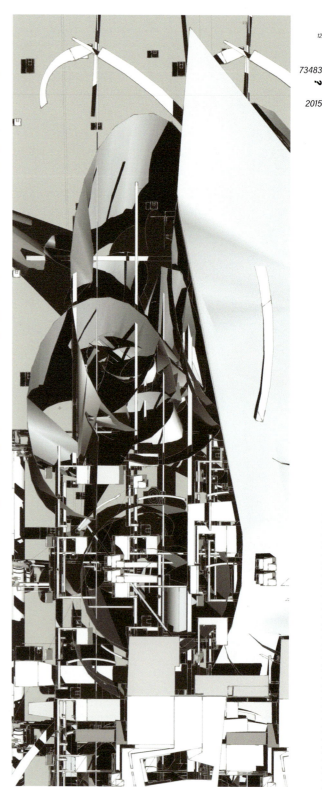

Thou shalt not s[k]in

This system examines the spatial qualities of an infectious component, where remnants of that infection are also projected back into the originating device. It becomes a city-eater, consuming the code of the urban and sub-urban.

These are ideas about the insertion of an infection into a metropolis as a system of reorganization, a system of synthetic topographies.

A phoenix code.

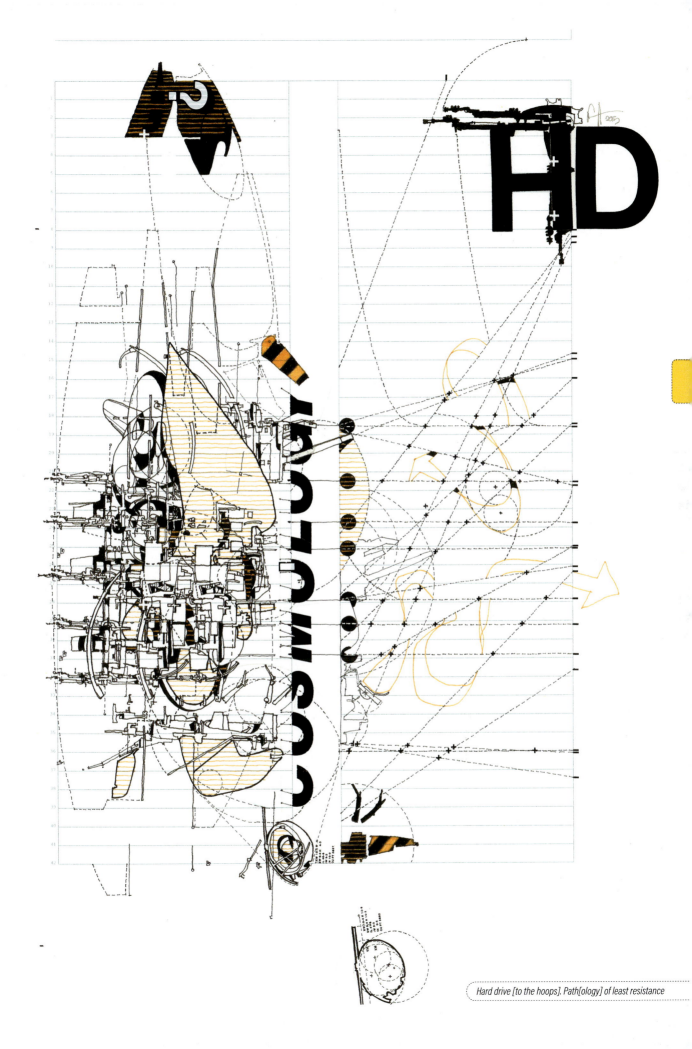

Hard drive [to the hoops]. Path[ology] of least resistance

Drawing/Painting
We are surface dwellers ...
The earth's surface.
The artificial surface of architecture.
The surface of all non-verbal communications.
The surface of documentation.
The surface of denotation, detonated.

[Component structure typologies]:
Shells the skinned components that encircle original code
Add-ons relocation of nucleus [SITE]; it re-programs the behavior
Intrusives overwrites 'site' and therefore original functionality

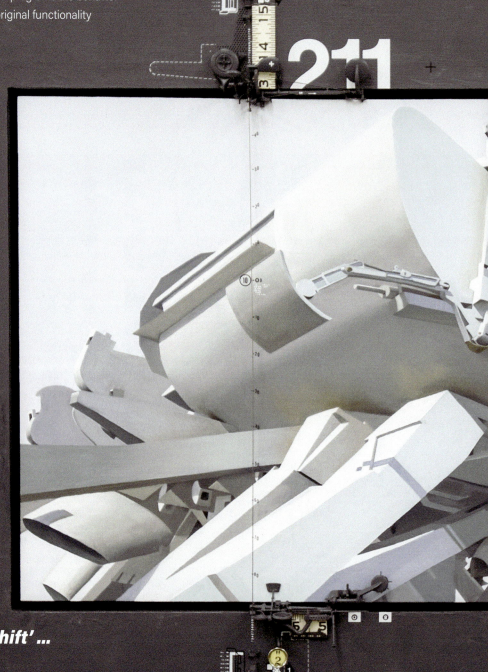

A visible exploration of the scanning mechanism and process to make hairy the bald *noumenon*.

What began as a digital construct has transformed through a traditional media exploration – paint and brush, wood and glue, plastic and metal. The subversive conceit, using traditional analogue media to explore and discuss digital concepts and constructs is of great interest ... it allows, or even forces us to explore the background systems of representation to understand in what is labeled as *media shifting*.

The object recognizes the [invisible] device used to transform the analogue into digital – the flatbed scanner. The exposed mechanics of the system, the horizontal movement that records information is superimposed upon the object – making the under-layer the top component, acknowledging the *making* as part of the artifact.

'a media shift' ...

"Jacques' friend, Maria, says that machines are indeed alive. 'Machines aren't inorganic, they are non-organic.' She tells him – 'they are artificial life.' 'Artificial Life?' asks Jacques, 'Does that mean that there is artificial love? Is that what I've been feeling for these creatures? Artificial Love?' Now here she is sitting at his little plastic kitchen table telling him that machines are alive. She says she loves the whole spooky contradiction of the idea – as though machines could have an afterlife. And as though they have a sex life, too – 'Which they DO!' she says, but by using us to reproduce for them. We are the midwives of the machines, she says. 'Not Frankensteins, but midwives.'"[4]

[4] Shepheard, *Artificial Love*.

Oil painting/Deconstruction of the plane of [de]notation. Collaboration with Kim Cantley

"A condition occurs during a process of switching from digital construct to analogue output and back again" – it examines not so much the *when*, as the *where*.

There is a large amount of residual information, that exists in potentia, in the space between the two media, this example overlays the applications of digital theory and technology onto *methods* of analogue representation to create a new hybrid, exploring the notion of the processes of graphic production with its representation as a *singular concept*. The artifact, in this instance, renders the scanning process and the scanner itself visible, manifesting *the mechanics of the devices and processes that we, as consumers of graphic information, are not supposed to see* – the manifestation of the suppression.

It is a reproduction of a photograph of a painting of a printout of a digital model's digital image.

It's not often that digital conception produces analogue offspring. The overlaid mechanics represent the bones, the invisible activities, the systems of reproduction that transpire during the *analogue to digital* process of the scan. Scanning may be thought of as a mapping system of geographical adjacencies, topographical relations, and projective [dis]orders.

Here, the oscillation, path, and mechanism of the scanning arm were central to the development of an analogue drawing system to *build up* data in hope of creating a residual effect, a somewhat Kantian dual-aspect view of the dual object ... in the post-post-digital world. It is **Reverse phenomenology** in the face of digital output. ✚

Detail 01 – Scanning mechanism, deconstructed: Transmission

Shell, add-on, and intrusive manifestations

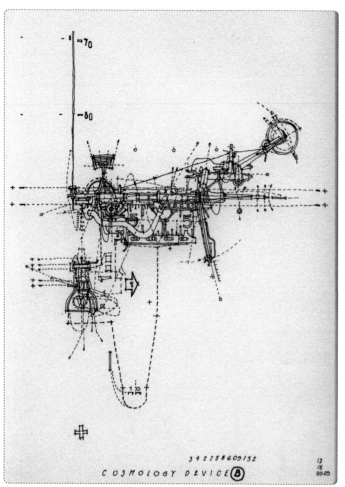

Cosmology device – Reception mechanism notational sketch

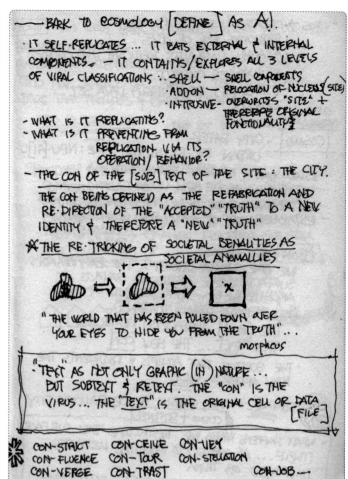

Notes on self-replication – subtext/re-text

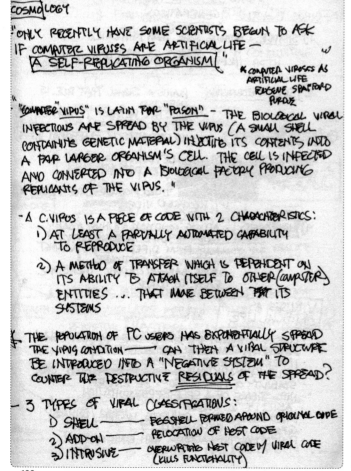

Virus is code. Narrative is a disease

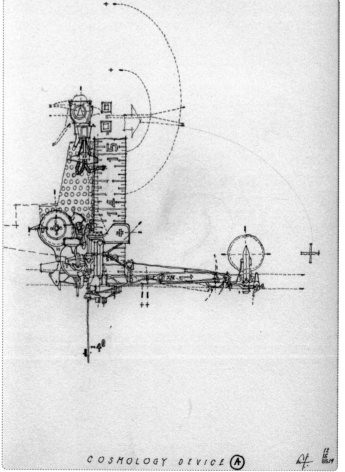

Cosmology device – Transmission mechanism notational sketch

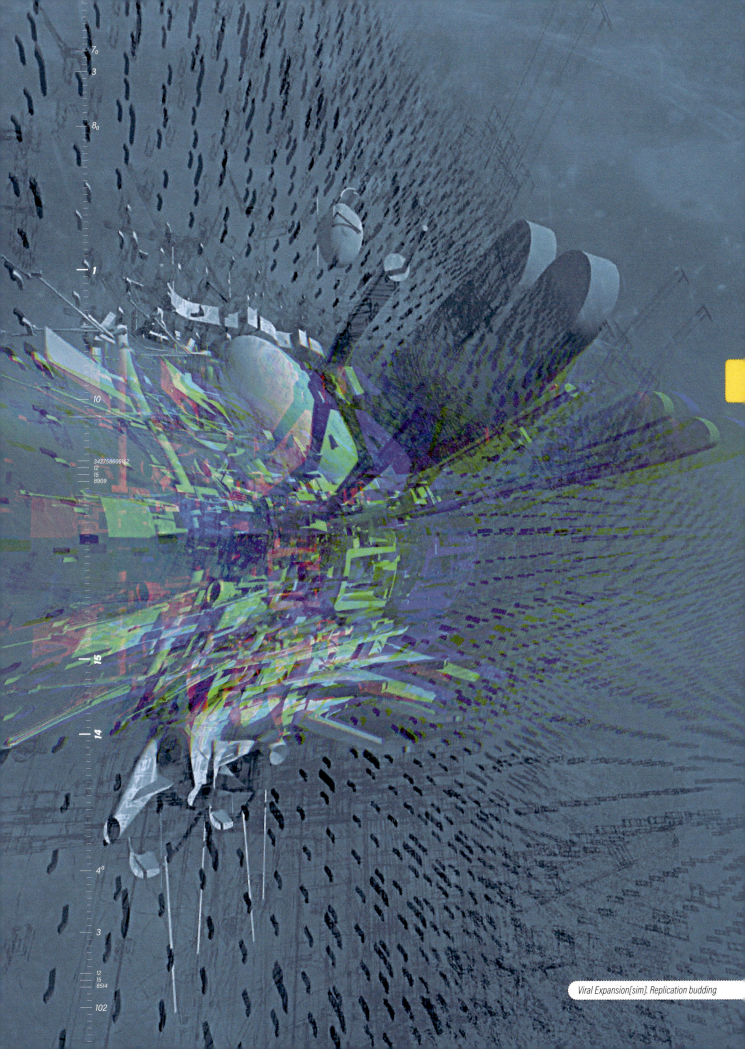

Viral Expansion[sim]. Replication budding

SClarc exhibition panel 2014. Insertion phase. Edifi[du]c[ial]e equations

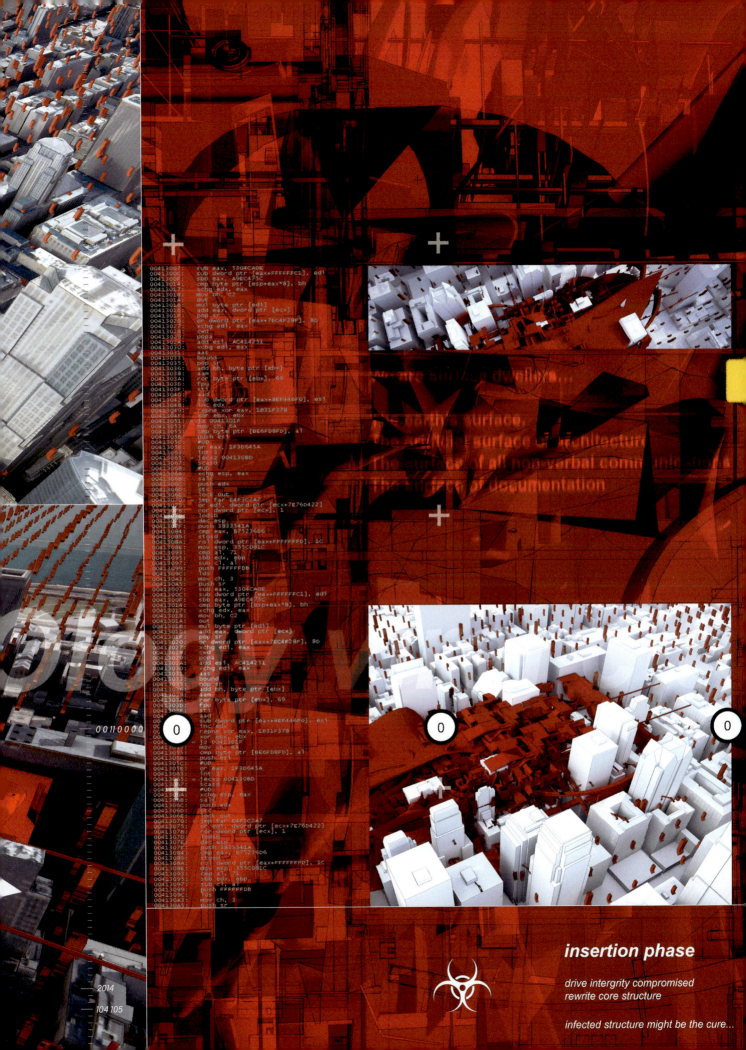

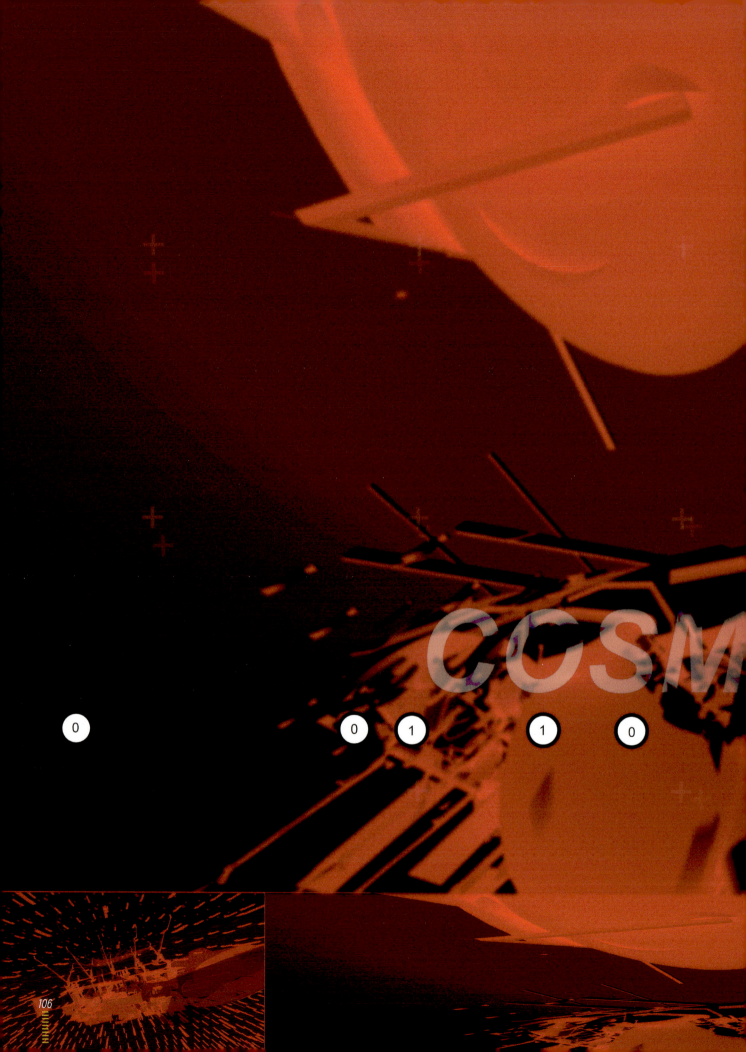

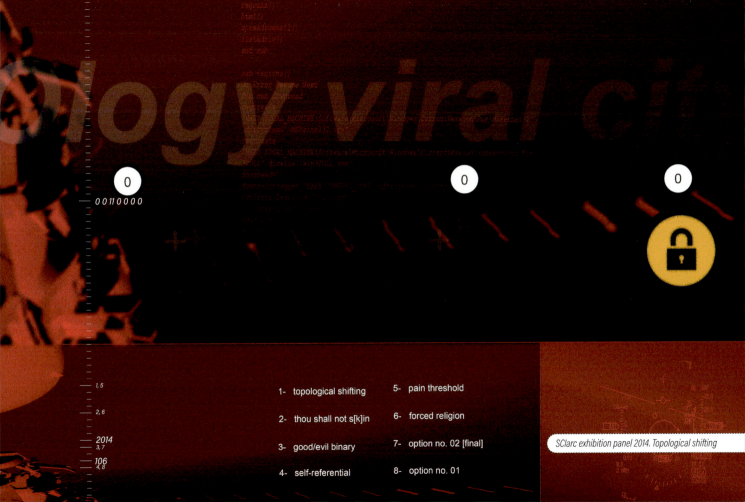

SClarc exhibition panel 2014. Topological shifting

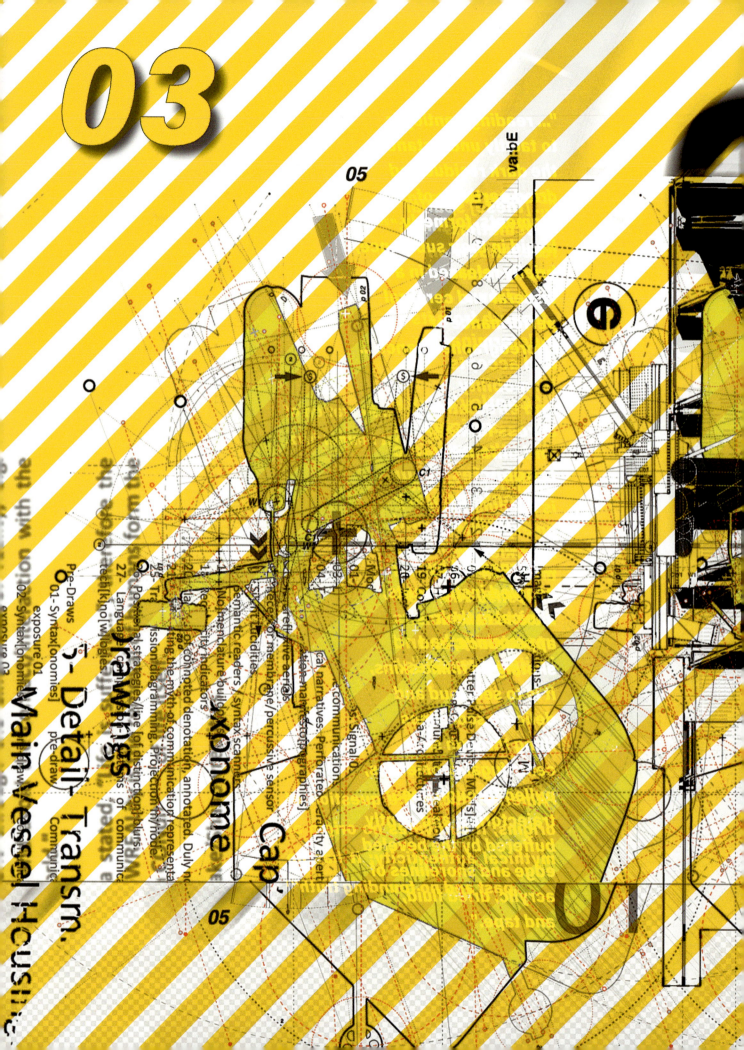

chapter 03
Towards a Taxonometric Architecture

Tree Hugger

An architectural device that maps the metrics of graphic politics – cell phone towers, deforestation maps, and gerrymandering districts.

"America ducks the question of origins; it cultivates no origin or mythical authenticity; it has no past and no founding truth"[1]

[1] J. Baudrillard, *America* (London: Verso Books, 2010)

Mapping tra[i]nscriptions

The Southern Californian landscape is a curious phenomenon; a s[y/n]thetic oasis born within the raw desert through the creation of an increasingly complex (and increasingly necessary) network of technological and environmental infrastructure.

Whilst observing this artificial landscape, "we nail our Astroturf down" (Cantley, 2020),[2] we could be forgiven for considering that this idyllic image of suburban America (so frequently the setting of our coming of age films, dramas, and TV shows) is rather more akin to a soundstage within which the actor/occupants willingly overlook the obvious fakery of this contextual simulation. One even might extend this line of thinking, arguing that the 'green' nature of the Southern California landscape has become authentically synthetic (a SoC[i]al Landscap[e/ing]), a condition in which the flora reflects the biological condition, an authentically s[y/n]thetic environment of "Fake Plastic Trees" (York, 1994).[3]

The treE-hugger is a device that operates between two[ish] systems, the natural environment [and its occupants – the trees], and the synthetic, the Cell Tower Mimic.

The device occupies the 'translator scale' … exploring the possibilities and consequences of the space(s) created when digital and analog worlds, despite best efforts, fail to establish a 'firm handshake'. This misalignment is an inherent condition of the translation between these two [dis]similar states, the physical (real and actual) and that of the virtual (real, but not actual) and the manner in which those states are documented and read.

TYPE 8 Map[ping]

Map comes from the Latin word for 'sheet'. Its origins are not in information, but within in the geometry of the flat surface.

As a 2D plane, the sheet must be folded or bent to architecturally dimensionalize a phenomenon. Its inherent flatness is overcome by the powerful ability for architecture to momentarily intensify the graphic surface of seduction.

Map versus mapping …

Drawing is a mechanically induced invasion. Not only is it the invasive quality of graphite or ink impregnating paper with a residue of intention and application, but the bellicose construct of engaging [and thus agitating] the intellectual argument[s] of the architectural proposition.

TYPE 9 Architectural cookies…

The digital cookie is a subverted media typology, a Trojan horse of information. Data from the downloaded/visited website or content stores information on the user's computer in order that user preferences will be remembered upon future interactions. It is a concealed, but highly functional media typology. They are residual configurations of preferential spatial recall. Milk anyone?

"cOOOkies, om nom nom!" (Monster, 1971).[4]

TYPE 10 Place downloading…

Temporal spatial configurations, these 'file[ogics]' allow for a temporary architectural event to deposit a microcosm of itself in a particular location. The site condition remains as the occurrence/event terminates, leaving behind a mark, a residue as well as an easily configured revisit of the event space.

TYPE 11 [r]OOO.M.B.A

Something of a modern-day Ouija board. Existing at the threshold of topographical scanning, it changes course and trajectory based on its 'reading' of surface instructions. Younger readers are more likely to be familiar with the Roomba, though stripped of the Victorian envelope of the occult that accompanies the Ouija, is a device that appraises the surface conditions and responds with a machinic dance based on this input. Both systems offer no engagement, in fact no gesticulation at all, unless the directives [printed geo-centric typographies in the case of the Ouija, spill patterns and envelope parameters in case of the Roomba] are fed via an external circuitry.

The treE-hugger is, primarily a scanning appliance, one that probes and charts deforestation zones, cell tower location maps, and the archival documents that constitute a record of the haunted archaeologies of landscape reconfigurations, power line boulevards, and plots of topographic(al) legislation. It scans and traces these mapped/drawn entities that are themselves synthetically re[pro]duced responses to the physical environment. It cross references these reproductions with the realities that they represent, mapping the parallels and contradictions, noting the residual spaces and artifacts of these two tragically connected systems.

These mappings were initially viewed as a chorographic[al] chart, revealing the potential paths for the device as it explores the POST-occupancy of the s[y/n]thetic landscape. The assumption [for this inquiry], is that power lines occur post environmental construction [AFTER roads etc., are built], versus water mains [which are typically constructed BEFORE roads and other infrastructure and support services are built]. Water lines occur before population, power lines [at times] occur as the population grows, reflecting and mirroring the developing social boundaries. In other words, the treE-Hugger scans maps of conditions that occur POST occupancy ...

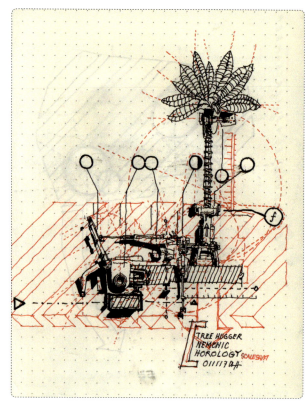

Mnemonic Horology

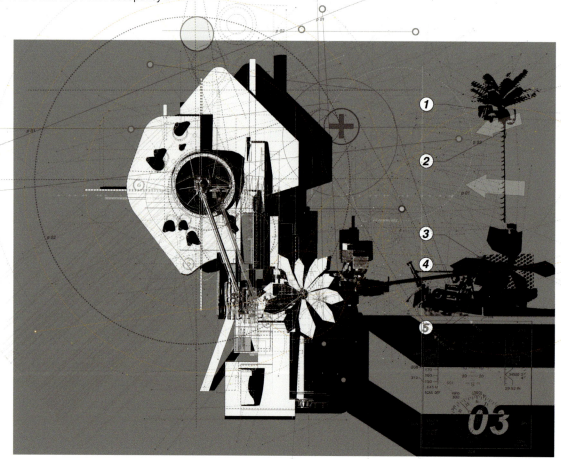

Planimetric Histories

"COVID-19 made shaking hands a fond memory of the past" (Castle, 3001).[5]

[5] S. Castle (3001) "The New Delivery Kings" *Mentor*, New York, USA: MomCorp Publishing.

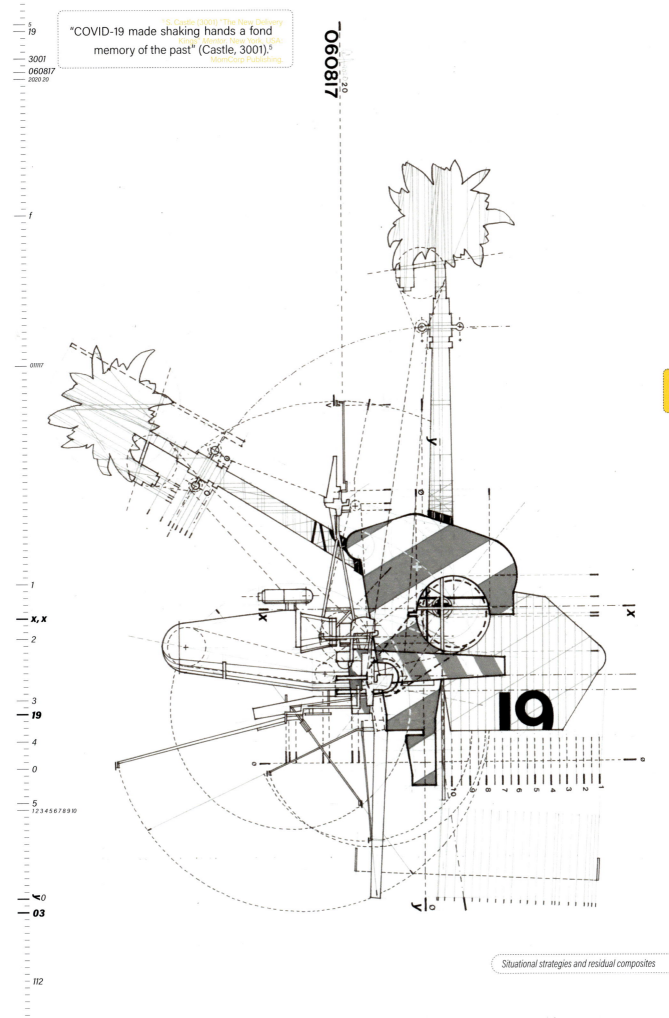

Situational strategies and residual composites

The hugger also maps out the media of cartOOOgraphy, a system of *Mappa Mundi* [the napkin world], a flattening (out) of a system of relatable geographies [Ptolemy] into a graphic system of distribution. An act of reduction, of compression, and of broadcast/distribution. It is a situation of thickly pixelated mimicry. An administrative narrative forced upon the reader (from a position of political advantage), masquerading as an act of knowledge. The OOObject[s] become a set of related spatial strategies. These relationships, while purportedly true, may unknowingly be fictitious, furthering reliance on a reading appliance.

The architectural phenomenon is a result of the synergies between the device and the surface of interface. Here, as with many projects, the device cannot be separated from its context. This is not a singular condition, it is an occurrence, it has many sites, many shifting frameworks that are not linked through curated content.

The project gives voice to the anti-suppression/oppression [s/opps] of political agendas documenting gerrymandered overlaps and backroom decrees.

It records these allowing playback to the great unwashed should the need arise. It is a vessel for the data that might be of social/political/economic value to those in need [much like the Sword of Gryffindor]. It is, for lack of a better analogy, the young boy from the "Emperor's New Clothes".

It was a bit of a pair-o-legal in that sense. It is The Great Collector. ✚

Smear Tactics as a method of political dominance

  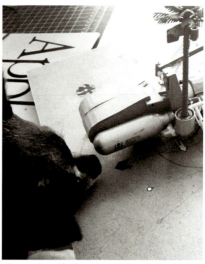

Mnemonic Horology *Study model and projective mapping strategies* *Everyone's a critic. Figure for scale. Investigational options*

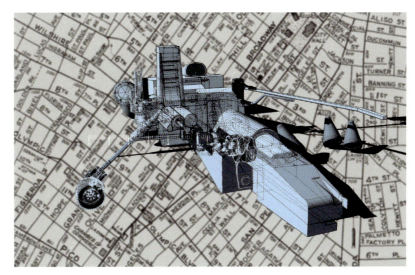

Positional awareness

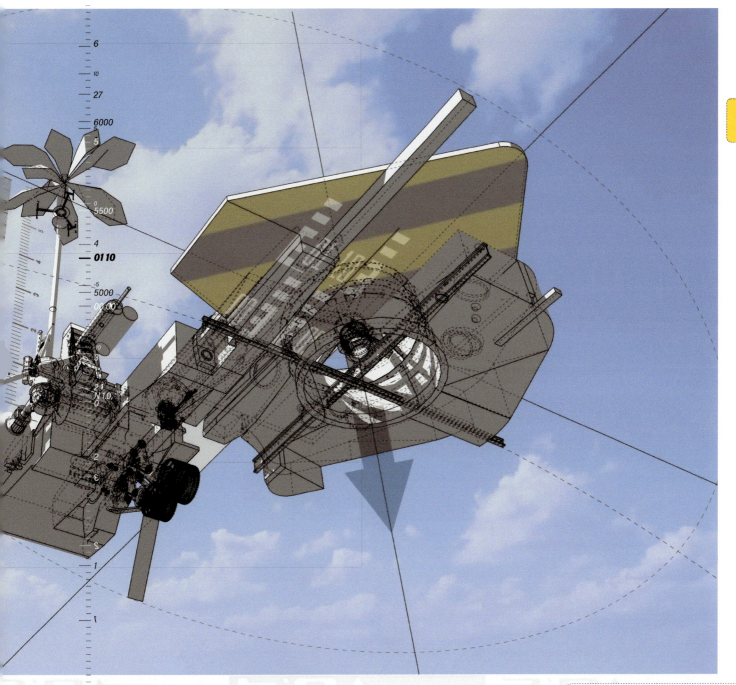

Conditions of Technature – data composites

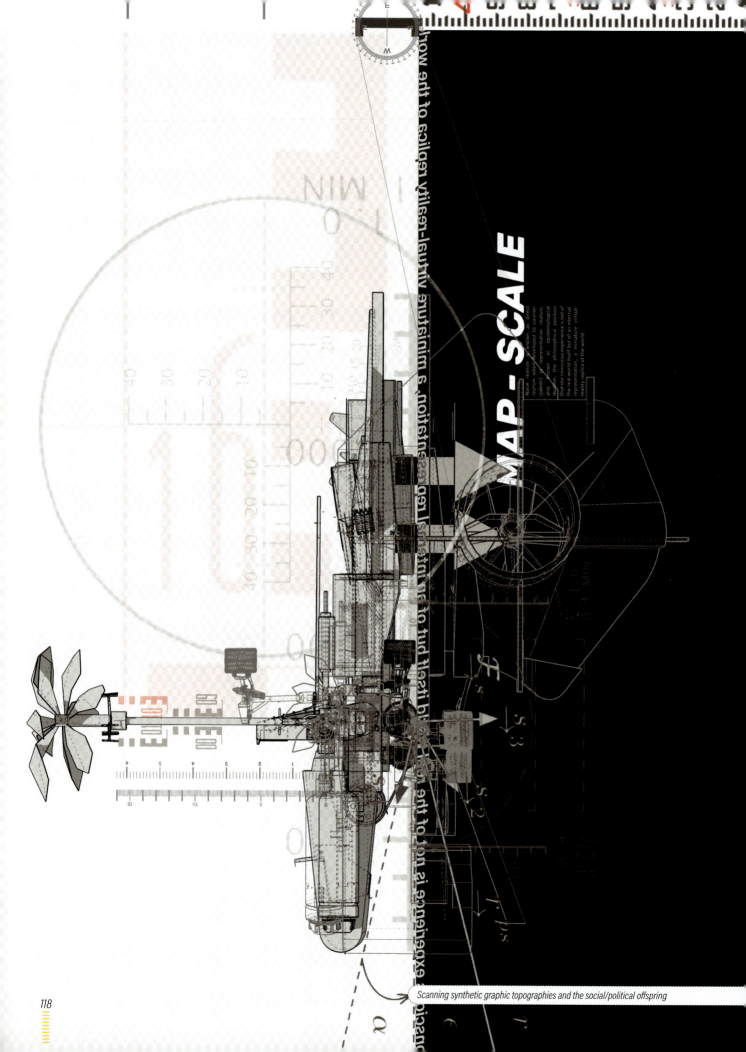

Scanning synthetic graphic topographies and the social/political offspring

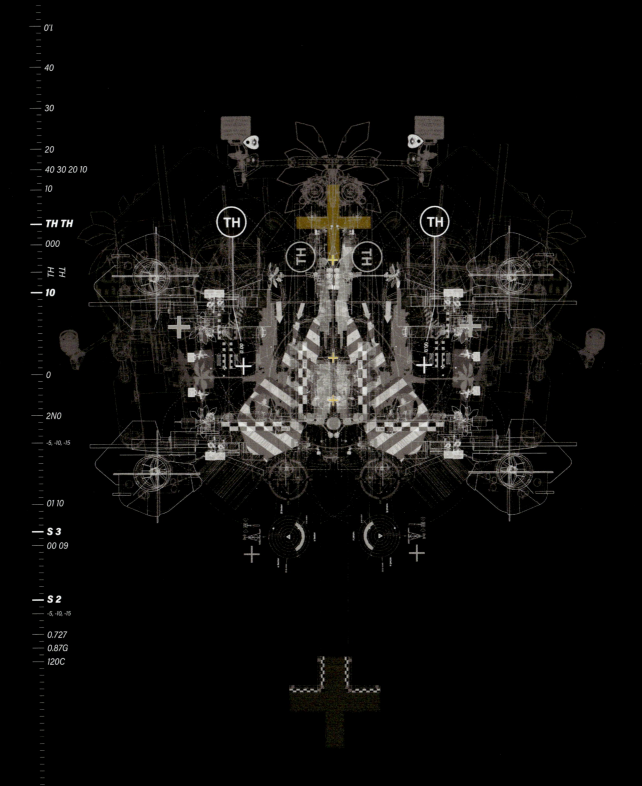

Rorschach[arts]- Projection imprints/Multi-geographical data collation

Trajectories, histories, and mapping transcriptions

On the Move: a polysemy on contextual dynamism and creative expression

Rana Abudayyeh
*Assistant Professor,
University of Tennessee, Knoxville*

Below the ever-present [A/a]rchitecture debate, the fine weave of physical place has been gradually unraveling into multiple strands, binding and unbinding the parameters of time and space. Spurred by sweeping technological permeation and corresponding social connectivity that has come to characterize this unfolding millennium is an ongoing redefinition of context. This redefinition transcends the propriety of site-anchored architectures reflecting the kinetic nature of the contemporary human condition. The implications of the shift from a stable reading of place to a liquid more mobile state are profound. They permit the conceptualization of sites as dynamic landscapes that simultaneously function at multiple temporal and spatial scales. Emerging and dissipating through digital data flows, bounded by robust universal frameworks, these dynamic settings draw out unexpected links between local and global forces; a merger, revealing multi-locational contexts that challenge not only physical constructs but the fidelity of the 'real' itself. As transnational flows and digital technologies undermine conventional notions of space, planetary turbulence and climate crises continue to percolate. These conditions culminate in a state of perpetual indeterminacy; at once, situated and untethered within realms that we supposed were known and commanded under a pretense of stability. Spatial praxis *must work* toward a reckoning of its manifold positionings within variable virtual networks, on the one hand, and planetary instability on another. Responsive to these contextual complexities and contradictions, Bryan Cantley's work deploys an elastic formula of making that questions the prototypical modalities of architecture and defines tactical assemblages within a fluid design domain. Cantley's work remains positionally involved yet unfettered by place and placement, inherently more inclusive of the readings it solicits, parameters it encounters, and events it hosts. It blurs virtual and physical boundaries and wields architectural practices that are responsive to the hybrid narratives of our times.

Emblematic of Cantley's work is a multivalent language of representation that concurrently registers and projects machined landscapes and territories. It defines dynamic formal mediators as it resists fixity and singularity of function and reading,[6] an amalgamation of architectural, technological, and environmental formations defined by semiotic parameters. These plastic and scientific codes, symbols, and topologies gauge their fluctuating contexts and cater to our collective delocalized sense of being and the feedback loops of our networks. While there is a distinct, intimate flavor rooted in backstories and autobiographical accounts traceable through Cantley's production processes,

[6] N. Spiller, "Magic Craftsmanship: A Glimpse into Bryan Cantley's Thirdspace," *Architectural Design* 88, no.2 (March/April 2018): 97.

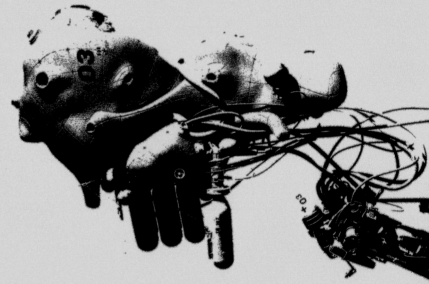

his work remains relevant to our broad human condition. It establishes illustrious registries of our collective media culture, recounting universal journeys and depictions of our nested worlds and liminal frontiers.

Roam, Repair, Repeat

In the project "Ozonic Metric Anomaly" (OMA), Cantley presents a construct that roams and surveys the setting in which it resides, repairing environmental fissures created by our consumptive habits. The intricacy of the OMA narrative is matched by its existential paradigm as an active domain for atmospheric harvesting, ecological replenishing, and social seeding. Every aspect of the project transgresses practices of enclosure, absorbing context instead of creating it, charting landscape instead of occupying it. Yet, the device itself remains a highly terrestrial entity in its conduct and affiliation. Bruno Latour presents the 'Terrestrial' in opposition to the natural and describes it as a designation of dual allegiances to the local transient crust of the soil and the extensive strata of the world.[7] At once, switching scales and ranges of operation between locational grounds and collective, universal conditions, OMA portrays a mobilization of architectural frameworks within active environmental and technological milieus, through which it upends design regimes that have often remained static and unresponsive.

Along parallel narrative lines, following a traversal synthetic-natural approach, Cantley's treE-hugger device maps trees (or their human-induced absence, to be precise) and the cell towers of the Southern Californian landscape with the same voracity. By virtue of scanning, treE-hugger crossbreeds the construct with its context. Like many of Cantley's projects, the architectural appliance exhibits an intense fixation with its contextual parameters; but it is not fixed to them – a fundamental shift where place is understood as a downloadable script transposed through ephemeral deposits of the architectural event.[8] Although highly of its place, treE-hugger deconstructs its regional setting, scattering its fragments across universal bandwidths.

Forfeiting stable elements and essences, OMA and treE-hugger's synthetic speciation and mechanical appendages twitch, pulsate, and move, pursuing dynamic temporalities in architectural logics, dismantling myths of stability as they illustrate primordial inclinations towards the nomadic, the itinerate. While untethered physically and conceptually, both projects remain highly involved in their contextual burdens.

Becoming-Dynamic, Becoming-Nomad

Earth is a moving planet; a turbulent and unstable body made of active flows that cycle and fold into metastable patterns.[9] Proliferated by technology, the intrinsically active nature of our world – geologically, compositionally, and metaphorically – now more than ever necessitates metastable, responsive, and relational resolutions.[10] This dynamic becoming bequests equivalent architectures; itinerant, morphologically nomadic. Typically, architectural practice does not favor the nomadic construct, nor does it accommodate the wanderer, the refugee, or the sojourner,

at least not intentionally. Architecture's becoming-nomad is at face value impermanent; its temporality diametrically opposes the stable stereotomy of architecture. But look closer, becoming-nomad is an unspoken environmental creed, a commitment to resource stewardship catering to a shared being that outlives the built monolith. The durability of the nomadic rests in the long-term sustainability and circular economies it invokes; its continual becoming.

Becoming-nomad as an understanding of place is a relevant vantage into OMA and treE-hugger specifically, and Cantley's body of work at large; on account of their literal mobility, yes, but more so in response to their operational code that overrides the binary impasse of spatial assignments and disposes of the exclusionary logic of the physically set. Evident in their environmental axioms and political underpinnings, OMA and treE-hugger's nomadic natures challenge the structured statehood of place, its despotic authorship, and claim over territory. Against the stationary and grounded, both constructs disengage from conventional standards, finding relevance in dynamic manifestations and discursive images. They challenge the foreclosed nature of architecture, departing from solid lines and locked-down enclosures, allying with non-singular paths across indefinite spaces,[11,12] trailing ascribed terrains and phantom volumes. Through these actions, Cantley's work shifts intentionally from its respective originating body ([A]rchitecture), arriving at perforated participation in the discourse and its media, as Cantley puts it.[13] This deconstruction of lines and logic and the respective blurring of the spaces they denote is inherently nomadic.

Deleuze and Guattari discuss the relevance of Nomadology and unpack its profound political, economic, and cultural influences. The nomad's structures are collapsible, yet the collapse opens up possibilities and creative capacities. Possibilities enable assemblages[14] that accommodate the fluidity[15] characteristic of our amalgamated (virtual and physical) milieus and their corresponding socio-technical practices. Cantley's work anticipates the nomadic tendencies of our contemporary condition and correspondingly retools spatial parameters to account for its turbulences and opportunities. In the

> "Cantley's work anticipates the nomadic tendencies of our contemporary condition and correspondingly retools spatial parameters to account for its turbulences and opportunities."

[7] B. Latour and C. Porter, *Down to Earth: Politics in the New Climatic Regime* (Medford, MA: Polity Press, 2019), p. 92.

[8] B. Cantley and P.J. Baldwin (ed.), *Speculative Coolness* (London: Routledge, 2023), p. 111

[9] T. Nail, "An Ontology of Motion for a Moving World," *Mobile Ontologies*, https://www.anthromob.space/episode-i/

[10] Ibid.

[11] G. Deleuze and F. Guattari, *A Thousand Plateaus: Capitalism and Schizophrenia* (Minneapolis: University of Minnesota Press, 1987), p. 380.

[12] B. Cantley, "Deconstructive Text(s)," *Journal of Architectural Education* 70, no. 1 (2016): 60.

[13] Ibid., p. 60.

[14] Deleuze and Guattari, *A Thousand Plateaus*, p. 89.

[15] Ibid., p. 53.

constant interplay between assembly and disassembly, his constructs track customary, habitual paths; non-singular in direction or goals,[16] such paths are different from sedentary roads.[17] The projects propagate fuzzy aggregates and partial objects, instead of dividing masses and distinct formations. This nomadic modality enables Cantley's work to challenge site-bound formal and social memberships while maintaining a keen situational awareness. It offers a multiplicity of readings, building a viewership that transcends common language and discipline expertise. By employing social media platforms, Cantley empowers the viewer's becoming-participant, an interactive player in the work and its concepts. As such, he solicits a rapport with the circumstance, the environment, and the occupant (sentient and insentient alike), a transaction that allows the work to engage and develop experiential alliances and rhizomatic structures. Fair to say, OMA and treE-hugger are rooted in the affinities they prompt and the affects they maintain.

[16] Cantley, "Deconstructive Text(s)," 60.
[17] Deleuze and Guattari, *A Thousand Plateaus*, pp. 380–1.

Worldbuilding on Shifting Grounds

Wrought by actual and virtual dynamics, OMA and treE-hugger posit new relational frameworks for the land. In discussing treE-hugger, Cantley indicates that the device is inseparable from the surface of the interface.[18] A similar logic can be traced through OMA's contextual attitude. In both cases, context is not a singular condition; rather, it is multiple, where land as a physical anchoring mass is not the only site of operation. With this relegation, the politics of placemaking shift; the nomad no longer plays second fiddle to the settler, and the edifice does not lay claim over the territories it occupies. The land's unbecoming-support, becoming-construction plane facilitates connections and interruptions between constructs, partial objects, and hybrid forms. Together, they beget trans-locational multiplicities that can be taken in and out of context and yet still be read with the same vibrancy. Here, the ground is not an endgame; instead, it is an interfacial medium, one among many that span the chthonic and celestial strata. Within this scope, the drawing is an indispensable domain; it is the host surface on which the layers collapse and from which new intersections between ideas, forms, and context can be interpolated. It is the site where the constructs traverse dense events with resolve, stitching storylines, collecting artifacts, and spawning terrains. These ever-shifting assemblages prompt rich polemics between mapping modes and narratives, in both form and substance. Hence, they formulate a proactive stance against stagnation, a resonant call for action to exercise design sensibilities that anticipate and celebrate the contextual dynamism and locational schizophrenia of our time.

[18] Cantley and Baldwin, *Speculative Coolness*, p. 114.

Everything on the Move

Within climates of uneven forces, current happenings, and processed media streams, a stable architectural outcome is elusive at best; at worst it, is often alienating, being fundamentally antithetical to the context where they are placed. To claim that ground (in both the metaphysical and physical senses) is secure and, by extension, stable, is the very thought that alienates us from it.[19] Within these tensions, Cantley's spatial speculations foreshadow an architecture that draws strength from its indeterminacies and accepts its mobility and circulation across familiar and unfamiliar terrains. It sublimates our dense and complex realities into maps and diagrams of flows and disruptions, igniting in the sublimation process new cultural meanings replete with glitches and gaps, frayed traces, discrete filters, and rogue agents.

[19] M. Wigley, "The Translation of Architecture, the Production of Babel," *Assemblage* no. 8 (February 1989): 14.

> "... [these] spatial speculations foreshadow an architecture that draws strength from its indeterminacies and accepts its mobility and circulation across familiar and unfamiliar terrains."

Without a doubt, Bryan Cantley will continue to reshape how we understand and value the discipline of architecture. While his work challenges the forcefields in which it functions, it possesses its own raw and natural gravity; it pulls you in, inviting you to share its burdens and exultations. It is an architecture made to move objects, planes, lines, and points; an architecture made to challenge affections and convictions. Once you are in, you are in its orbit; you too: a body on the move. ✦

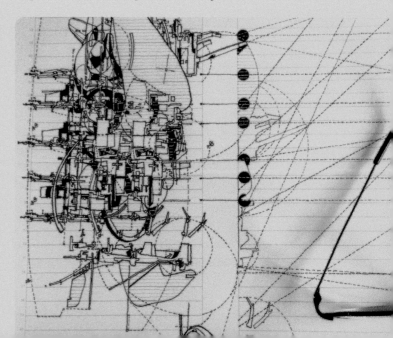

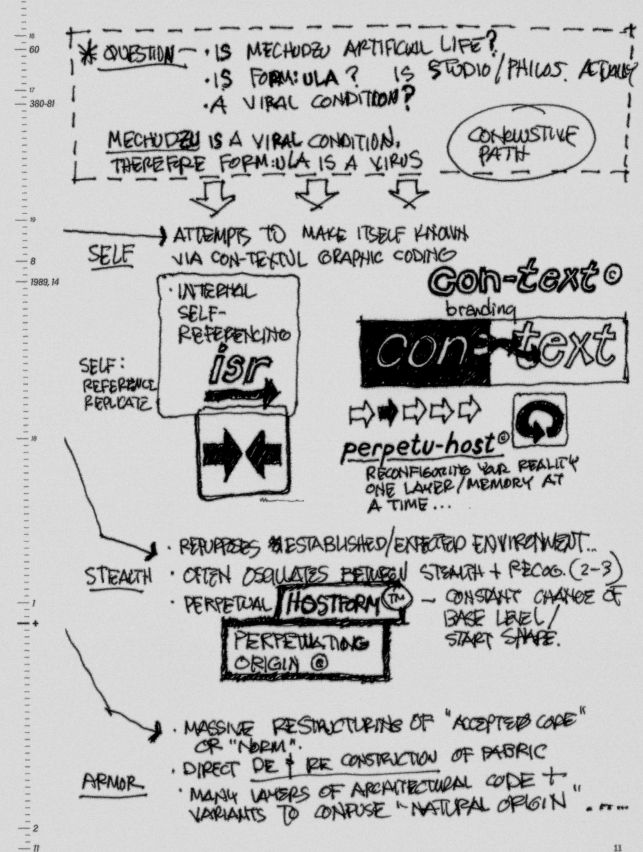

Palimpsestuous Relationships +

A series of palimpsestuous studies exploring the overlap of the technology of religion and the 'finality' of the architectural drawing.

[New Religion]

"[(N)ot just] the separation of the Church and the State [of the art], but the territory in-between these two entities. ..." This project is a two-space experiment, looking at two spatial scenarios that attempted to inform + deform a defined set of constraints or contexts.

Space 1: [Social] Mass vs. Mass

> "The [Soc(I)al] MEdi[a/um] is the MASS(age)" (Ecclesiastes).

A Celebration of the Eucharist/ aggregate of form ...

It might be argued that religion is one of the first social networks. The Church is both a place as well as an institution that is dependent on the 'mass(es)'; without people, the institution ceases to function. It was a sublime entity offering physical, spiritual, and intellectual succor. Often the center of the community, especially in small rural areas in the US, it served as the schoolhouse and town meeting hall outside of its ecumenically driven program of events (Henry County Museum).[21] There was a blurring of procedure, functionality, even behavior ... space and function could be flipped on and off based on time of day and programmatic requirements.

An early example of the switch-flipping, multi-program housed in a singular physical space, [re]programmed on the basis of fiscal and moral needs. The economy of public funds suggested and likely necessitated multiple uses ... while communities were shaped by the centrality of the church in their everyday lives.

Enter social media. Its t[E]chnology-vents have in many instances replaced the space of sacred residency. Social interactions occur through small portals – often hand-held devices, a reference to the continuing importance of the physical icon or totem. It is not without irony that the intimate scale of the instrument, and its proximity to the body that it demands, conflicts with the disembodied condition of the network itself.

> "If an Instagram account is updated, and there are no followers, does it make a sound ...?" (CONfuciUS, 1979)[22]

Node occupant sketch

Antonymical Simultane

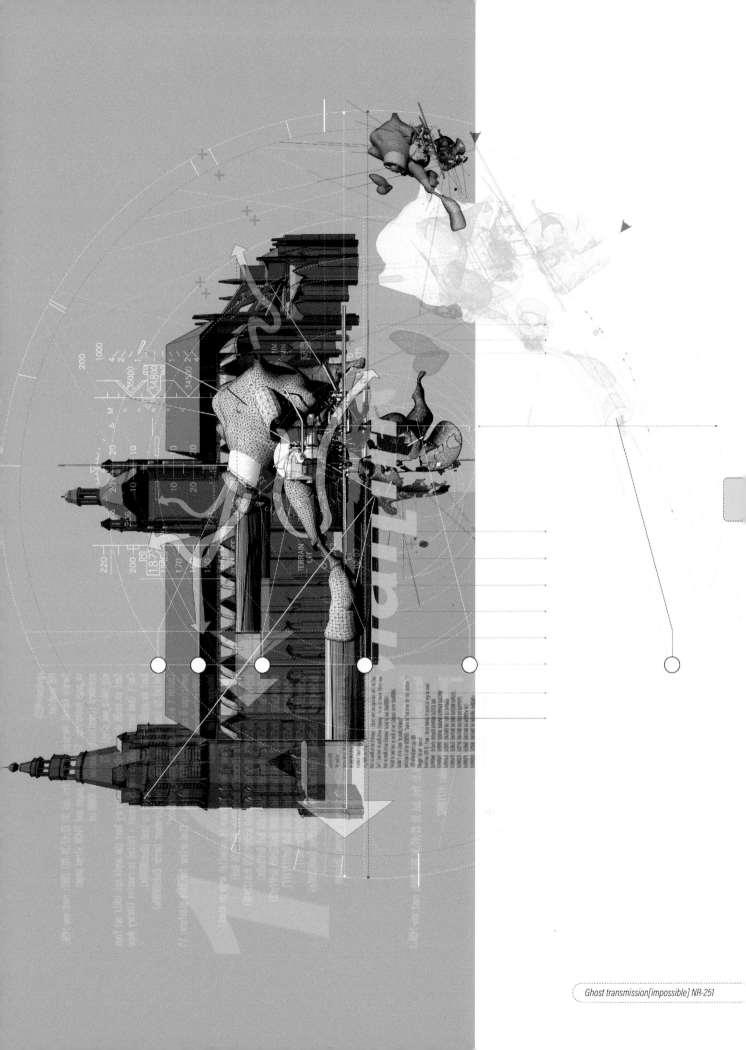

Ghost transmission[impossible] NR-251

Space 2: [Drawing] MAss

The second space contains two simultaneous arcs of enquiry; an anecdotal observation on the growing dependence on social media (particularly within younger generations), and an investigation into the drone appliance.

The emergence of behavioral Interference Patterns as social media extends its reach into everyday human consciousness is well documented, anecdotally and scientifically, altering our relationship to, and interactions with the world around us (Smith, 2019).[23] The tragic irony of being 'connected, is difficult to ignore.

[23] A. Smith, "Manchester Introduces Dedicates 'Slow Lane' for Mobile Phone Users," UMI, 23 August 2019, https://weareumi.co.uk/webapp/inspiration/manchester-introduces-dedicated-slow-lane-for-mobile-phone-users

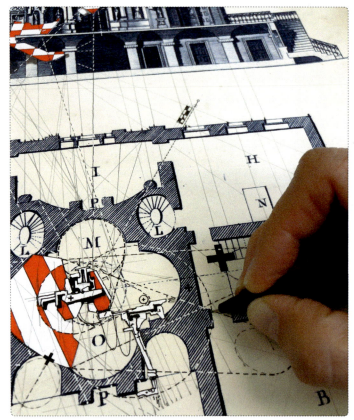

Drawing on the drawing - media decentralization[s]

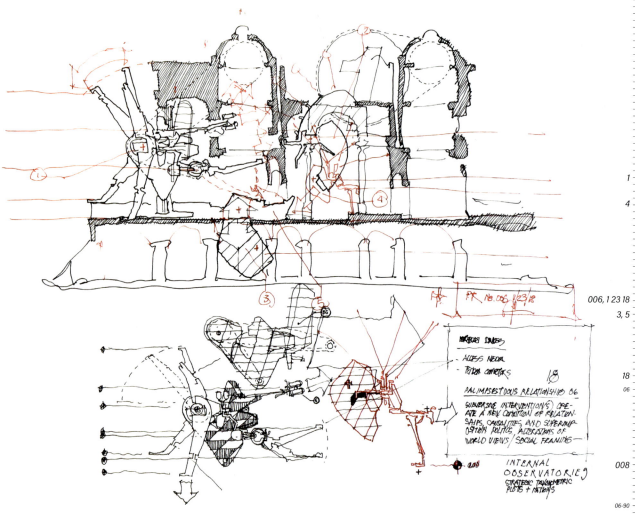

Internal Observatories/strategic Taxonometric plots

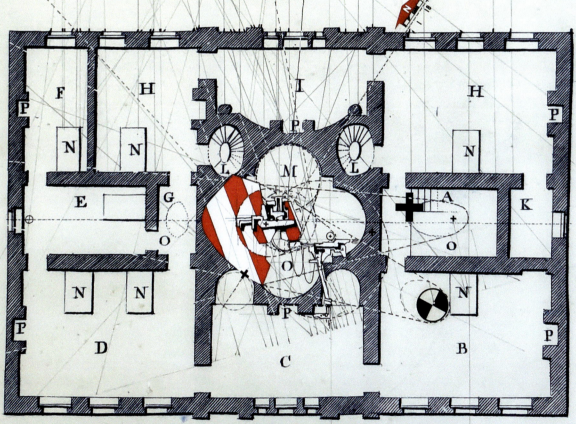

No. 06/ Cacophonous Registrations 06-90

CACOPHONOUS REGISTRATION 6?

Fake News

An unforeseen and [un]wanted by-product (BUY-product?!) of social media's omnipresence is what we might think of as 'truth on demand.' This refers to social media's capacity for:

₁ The power of personal statements and videos that are accepted as 'truth' by so many, so fast, with so little due diligence performed by the audience ...

₂ and, the desensitization of society that arises from the instantaneous availability of media.

> "Censorship is telling a man he can't have a steak just because a baby can't chew it" (Twain, 2013).[24]
> [24] M. Twain, *Great Speeches [& Myth-quotations]* (New York: Dover Publications, Inc., 2013).

For those raised **IN** the age of the (social) media appliance the emergence and adoption of new belief systems grows daily. One might begin to question the role *and identity* of 'higher powers' (and the attendant search for 'The Truth') for today's you[th]. It seems that there is a movement towards a new type of quasi-religious experience (and therefore a need for a respondent space).

"ACCOUNT SUSPENDED ..." (Fairy, 2020)[25]

[25] T. Fairy, "Mythreprethenting the Facths" A.M.G, 27 October (London: The Real FaceBook Oversight Group, 2020).

The project begins to question the role of organized religion within this multi-space and explores the condition of a deity and pious iconography in a time and arena where all is assumed to be 'knowable.'

Simultaneously, the project explores the drone appliance as a condition of social and architectural media. Beginning with the assumption that the voyeur believes that what is being watched is 'real' ... neither staged, nor affected by the introduction of the external viewing device into the scenario. A system which we know will be effected the awareness of the presence of the camera. The correlation to an 'all knowing and all seeing' entity is not lost here, the Technology Delivery System, the 'presence' of the drone becomes highly political and consequentially highly *architectural*. The combination of the two spaces created a unique point of departure.

> "(F)or the drone, politics becomes as much of a drawing device as does my pencil" (Cantley, 2017).[26]
> [26] B. Cantley, "Classification-ing," Lecture given in the International Lecture Series, The Bartlett School of Architecture, London, 25 October 2017.

What is sacred space within a social context that emphasizes the importance of the *myth of place* [MOP] and plausibility of information distribution [PID], as the spaces within which the actual event transpires? Is there a difference in the space of a-ttention versus i-ntention?

The proposal challenges forms of architectural, cultural and religious normalcy – examining the church and the drawing, as archetyp(ic)al conditions. If the sacred element of the past is no longer considered precious by the community that inherits it, then the question becomes "How might both states benefit from a mutual collision?" (Cantley, 2017).[27] As much of this work occupies a threshold, the in-between of entities and their situations, this redefinition was considered to lead to an interesting conversation about what is sacred. This in turn generates an interesting conversation about faith in an invisible system of order and organization.

[27] Ibid.

It begs the question, given a new world order of media-aspiration, where are the spaces of intention and attention located? Whilst historically religious doctrines dictate(d) identity relative to the hierarchy of the church, social media has, for the masses, supplanted this function (though oddly enough it is done thorough potential falsification of the self). The church offered you an identity based on your condition of 'being human.' Social media promotes identity classification by promoting synthetic conditions of identity, righteousness, and 'truth,' [whatever that is] ... We are all allowed, if not encouraged, to create our own avatars and our broadcast conditions based on interpretations, despite the inherent potential for falsification.

Communion vs. community

'The Media' is [often] thought of as any circumstance where mass communication is achieved via broadcast or transmission, with the goal of dissemination of information to large groups.

[ME]dia (in this instance) is defined as the occurrence where mass communication transpires, whilst accompanied by a shift of emphasis from the collective to the singular, ironically using the collective as the vehicles of production + dissemination.

LES GRANDS PRIX DE ROME D'ARCHITECTURE

"As technology and humanity continue to produce each other, the dichotomic differences between humans and technologies will continue to blur."
— Cyborg Anthology...

Removing the 'finality' of drawing, in hopes of tweaking the discipline of architecture + it's media.

No. 02- new religion[otations]

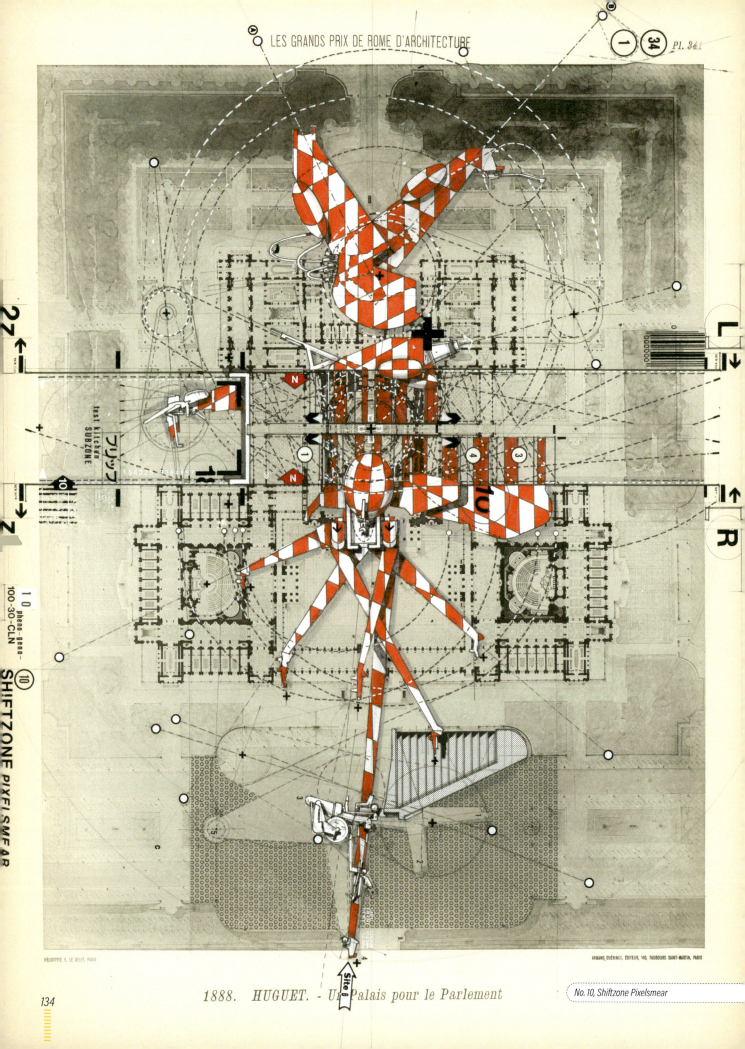

1888. HUGUET. - Un Palais pour le Parlement

No. 10, Shiftzone Pixelsmear

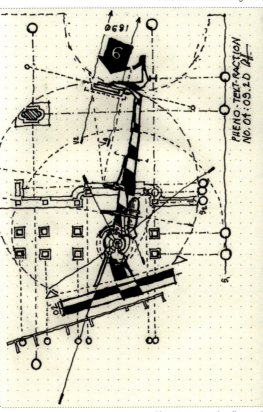

Pheno-text extraction diagram 01

Pheno-text extraction diagram 02

TYPE 4 [re]SURFac[ing]

MEDIA LOGICS

The concept of the palimpsest relates to the historic practice of writing on vellum; a valuable and scarce resource which would often outlast inks and pigments. When the original writing had faded, or information was superseded, it became common practice to scrape the vellum clean and reuse it. The original text though, effaced to make room for a later writing, often left faint traces or impressions on the surface of the sheet, affecting (however subtly) the absorption of ink and penmanship of subsequent writings.

<< *[**PB**: It is perhaps worth noting that it is not uncommon for the language of later writings to alter over time, with examples such as the Codex Ephraimi Rescriptus and Codex Nitriensis revealing earlier Greek texts have been overwritten in Latin that several re-writings have occurred over a period of hundreds of years. This may allude to the idea that the original writing is no longer comprehensible, let alone legible.*

BC: *So a drawing that is altered to accept 'later' data – it's as much a metric of chronology as it is anything else.*

PB: *Ironically this taboo results in the drawing (artifact occupying the condition of the subject of representation..*

BC: *I am intrigued at the [non?] reference of time that passes between inkings as a player in this conversation...]*>>

> Drawing
> **Drawing of a drawing IMAGE**
> **Drawing on a drawing**
> **Drawing in a drawing**

The architectural condition practices the act of [self] removal to move over/stand behind, hide from its replacement[s]. It contains palimpsests, it occupies them, it creates them, it discovers them, and it celebrates them often unknowingly.

Architecture IS therefore a palimpsestuous ACT.

Architecture may be one of the few disciplines in which overwriting is a fundamental condition of both of its functional states – the act of designing [via the architectural object/artifact (Archefact?), and the act of making [the built environment].

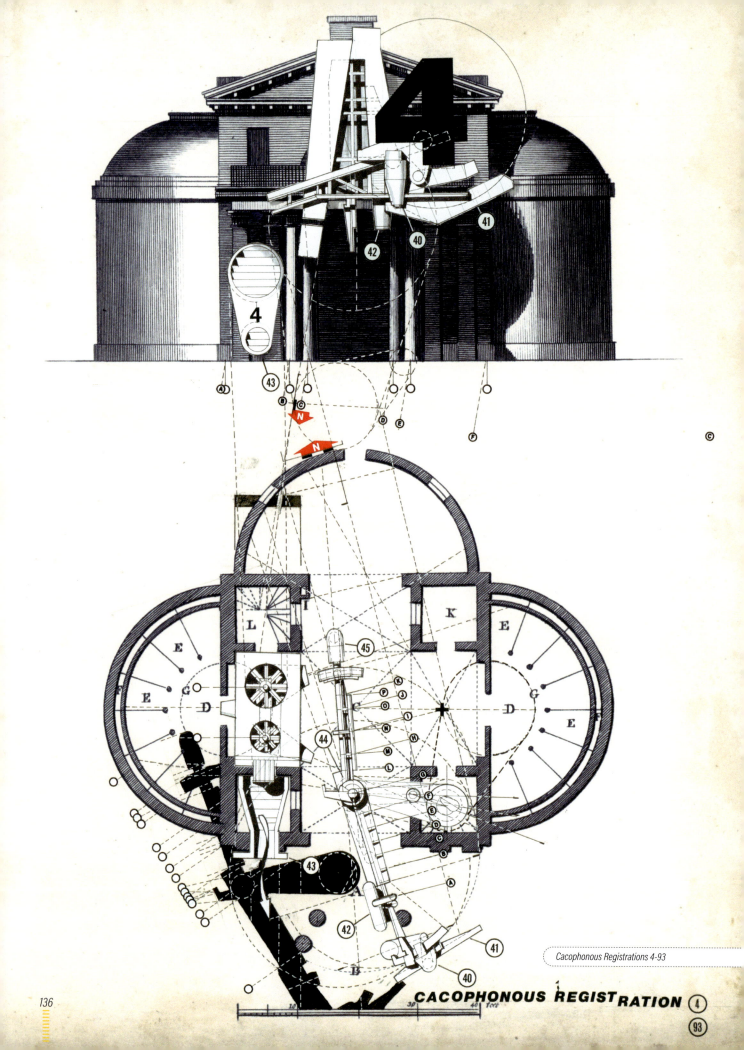

Cacophonous Registrations 4-93

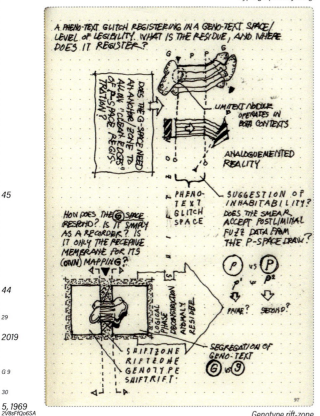

Hypergraphia layering

Genotype rift-zone

In the case of this particular project, we cannot segregate the two CONditions that create the synergistic relationship.

The Phenotext[1] to generously interpret Roland Barthes' definitions from *The Pleasure of the Text* (Barthes, 1975),[28] the original object/condition [here, the heliotype print of an ancient temple/building],

[28] R. Barthes, *The Pleasure of the Text* (New York: Hill and Wang, 1975).

The Genotext[2] [again, with apologies to Barthes] the resultant interface/relationship/artifact that describes the reason/generation of the superimposed liaison.

Each state functions as a signifier of the other.

Oddly enough one heralds the future [the 'blank' slate of the original drawing], while the other simultaneously generates both a needed reference to the past [the original] and the placement of the residue in the future. <<Synthetic chronologies ["Fake News"] indeed!>> These distorted chronological metrics, ask both the inhabitant of the architecture [the drawn world] and the viewer [located within the physical world] to accept the mutated, twisted, and frequently hybrid(ized) situation[s] of time; a non-linear, fabricated stew of multiple [il]legitimacies.

Simultaneously, a new typology in architectures' [re]presentation itself arises. An Analogue-mented Reality [AR(p)]; a synthetic architectural condition resulting from the interplay between the print and the inserted entity, that restructures the nature of time drawn, time spent, and time looped.

"Isn't the act of drawing about becoming rather than being? ... Could we think of drawings as eddies on the surface of the stream of time" (Berger, 2019).[29]

[29] J. Berger and S. Demirel, *What Time Is It?* (London: Notting Hill Editions, 2019).

"Did I call you Edd[ie] Baby?" (Cleese, 1969).[30]

[30] E. Ross, Interviewed by J. Cleese, "An Interview with Sir Edward Ross," *It's the Arts*, 5 October 1969, https://www.youtube.com/watch?v=2V8sFfQo6SA

The AR(p) suspends the notion of not so much what, but more fundamentally when of architectural representation, generating a fluid situation, that is suggestive rather than a formal conclusion.

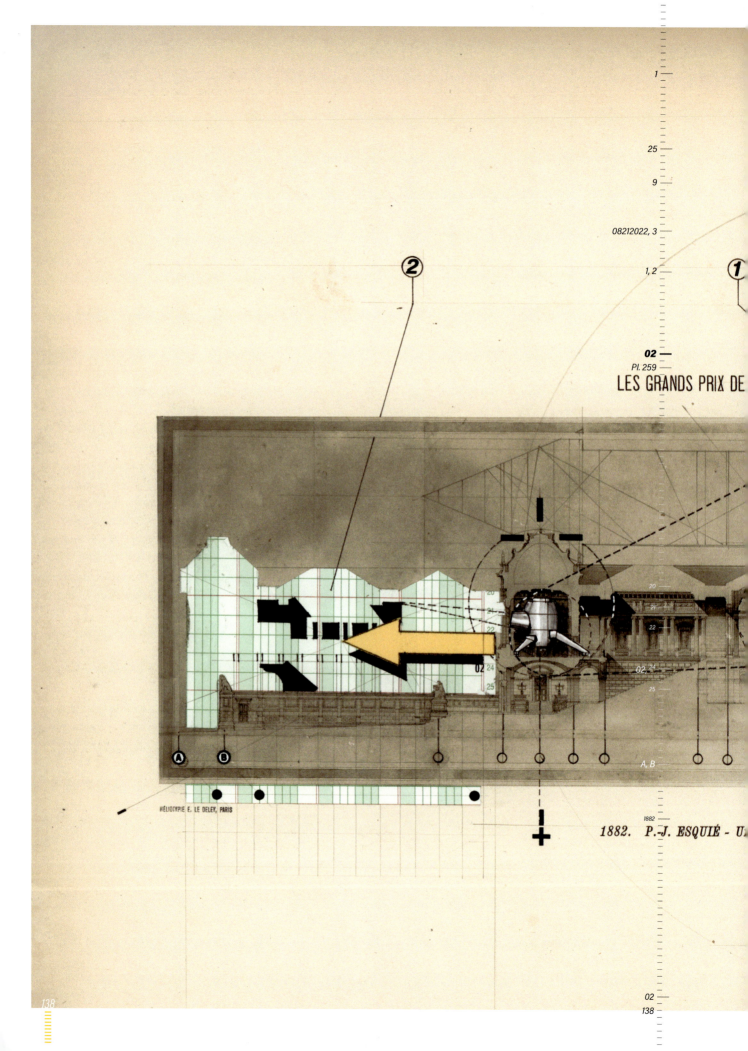

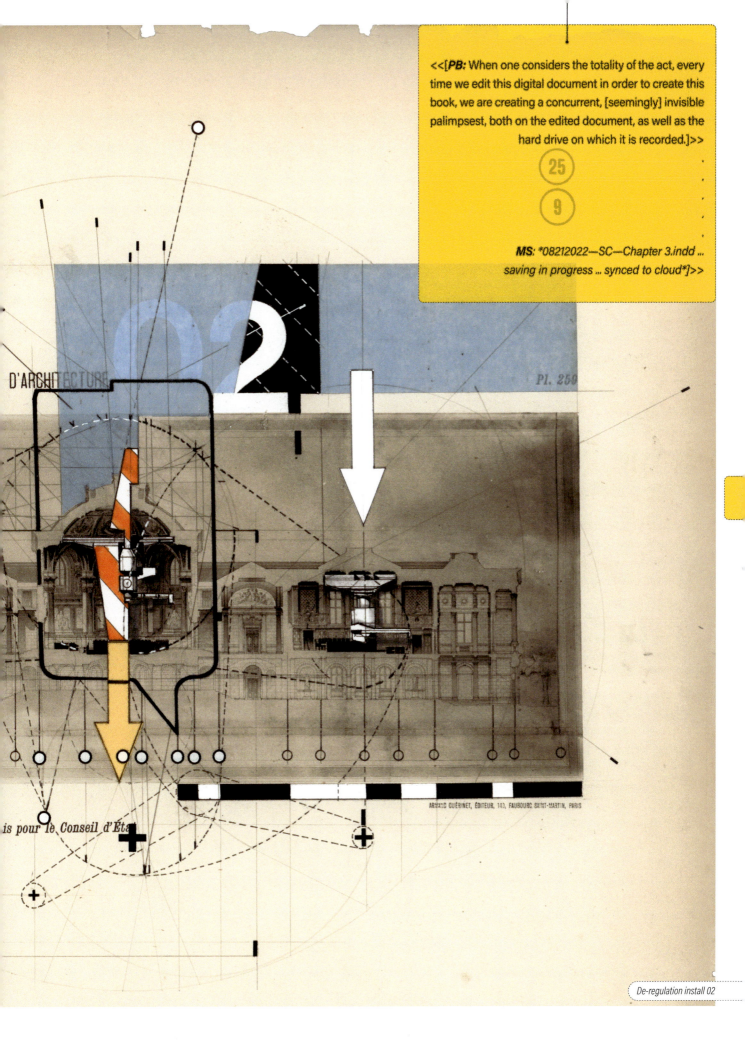

De-regulation install 02

The architectural drawing or artifact has, become a type of sacred object, at least within given curatorial circles. The rendering, or the 'finished image', reflects a 'conclusion' of sorts. The conversation of 'design', and therefore 'possibility' starts to erode as soon as the image is printed. Options and possibilities are exorcised by the rendering's status. Though the rendering continues as a SUBJECT, it (the architecture?) terminates itself as a malleable OBJECT. We broadcast the SUBJECT, through the finality of the OBJECT ...

<<[PB: "Curiously this condition of finality only occurs with the arrival of consumer culture, which perversely protects a product of 'cultural' value the print. I can't help but wonder whether in some part the state change (often we think of printing as the output of a process which has already happened, printing is an output function ...?) from Virtual to Physical."]>>

To be able to frame an argument about post liminal space ... the space between architecture and its media, as well as the space of the architectural drawing ... the drawing itself must be recognized as a physical entity, as well as a construct that allows its own codification to become part of the projection. The method of production of the artifact is key to its ultimate truth. Drawing upon a drawing is the taboo component of method, in that it provides the challenge to the norm of the rendering. Though it shares some characteristics with collage, this involves the construction of media directly upon the original, not only the cut and paste of an 'imported' image from another drawing. In this sense It has become a type of a 'tattoo space' – using the surface of the drawing as an impregnable condition. The alteration of the original creates a condition of both simultaneity and singularity, arguably provoking a conversation about the viability and/or sanctity of either or both elements. There is something vaguely sinister about the fact that someone OTHER than the original draftsman or architect is altering the graphic product of her labors ...

Drawing on top an existing print, 'the artifact', where the subject matter became a technological social broadcast hub, juxtaposed with an ancient religious Centre [itself a type of broadcast device], intends to challenge the status quo, offering new prototypes of the 'real' ... and 'implied' ... whilst questioning what is 'truth' in this scenario.

"I suppose could have presented these architectural interventions on the pages of holy books or song hymnals, but that seems to only address half of the equation, and it inherently does not challenge the typology of 'drawing' as a malleable context. $x = x$, as opposed to $x = y$" (Cantley, 2017).[31]

[31] B. Cantley, "Classification-ing."

Organized religion ... architectural prints ... these are excepted standards in both arenas ... both are called into question through the invention of these new spatial prototypes. The new hybrids are not meant to suggest a converted reality nor structural feasibility ... only to acknowledge their semi-co-existence. They are meant to reside in the realm of the drawing.

This is therefore

a manifestation of the post liminal fuzz.

+

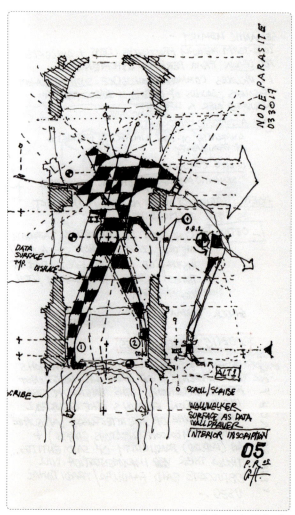

Node-parasite/Wall-walker

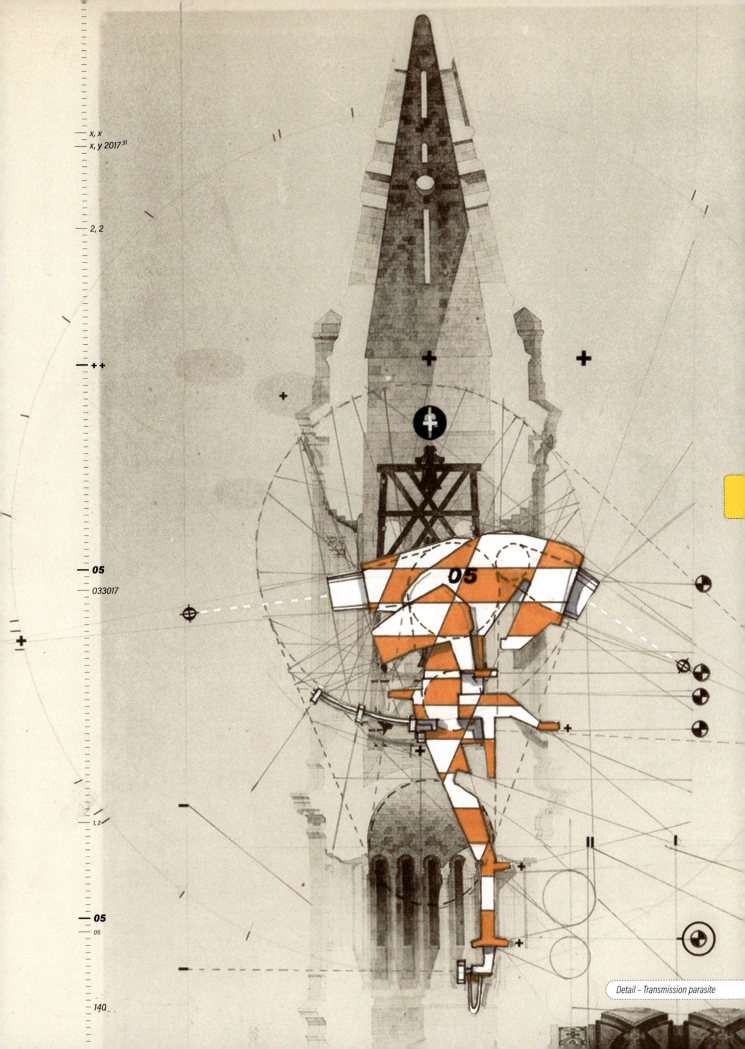

Detail – Transmission parasite

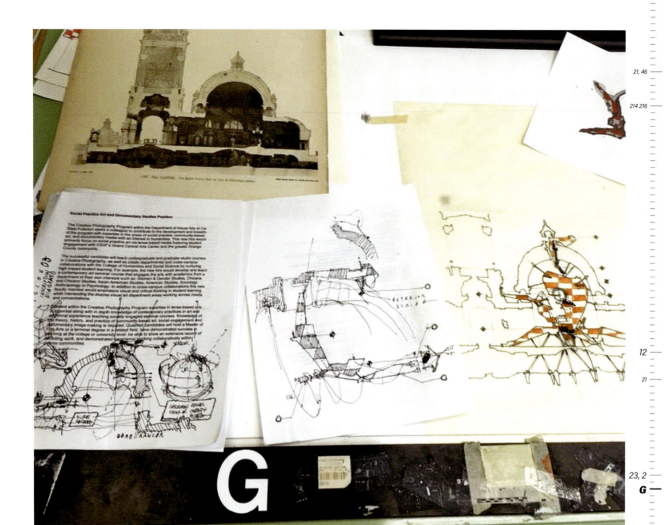

The plane of notation

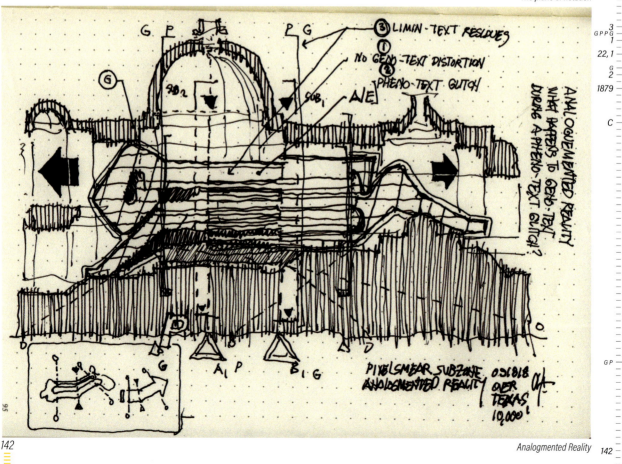

Analogmented Reality

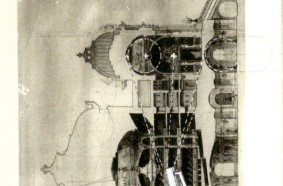

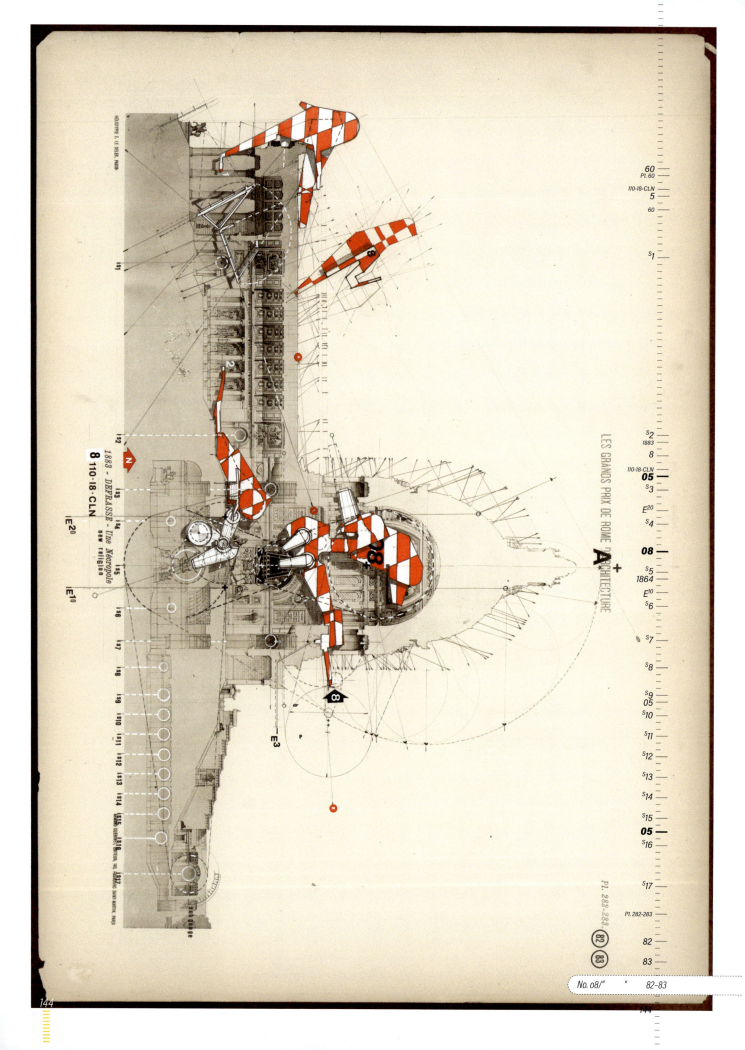

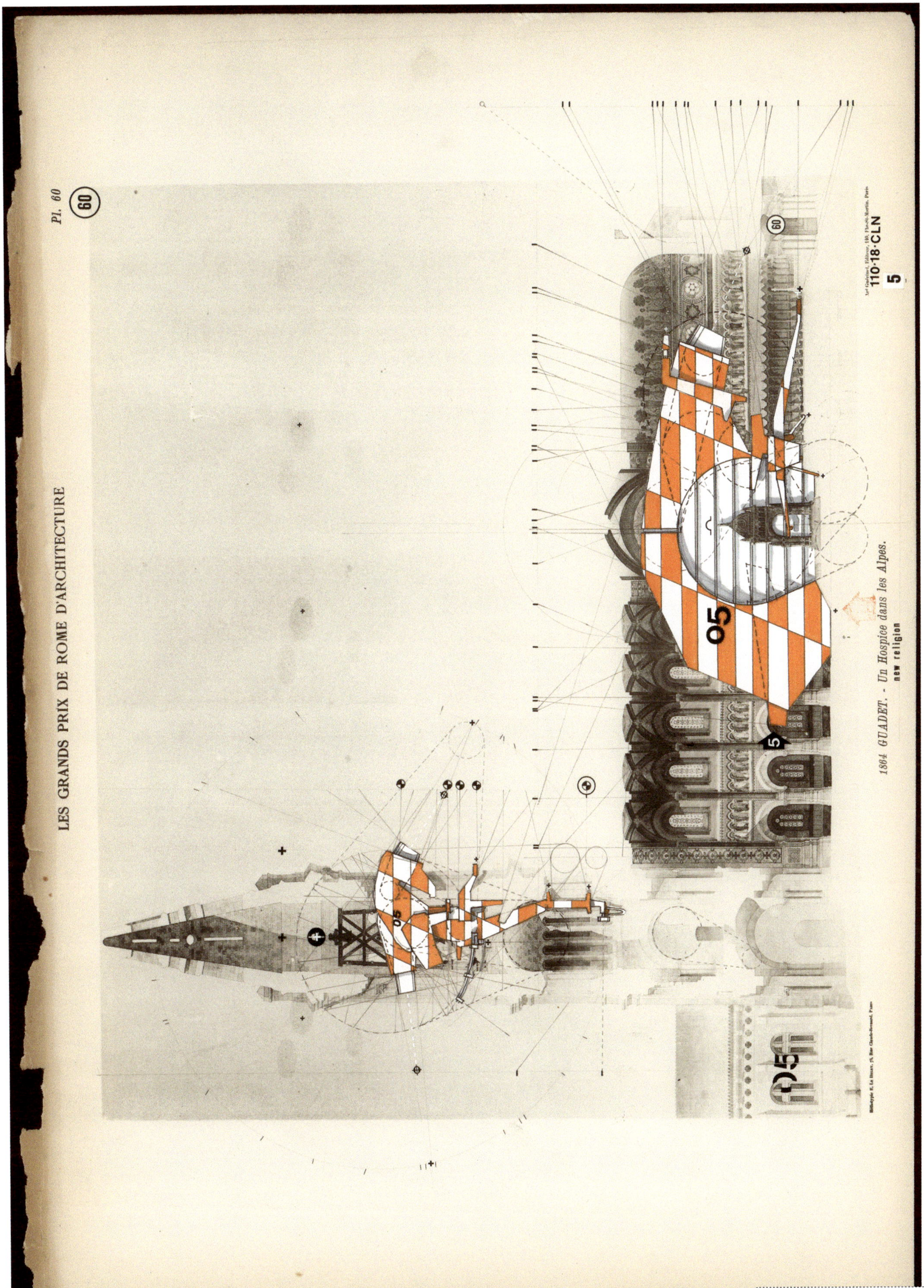

Pl. 60

LES GRANDS PRIX DE ROME D'ARCHITECTURE

1884 GUADET. - Un Hospice dans les Alpes.
new religion

No. 05, simultaneous transmissions

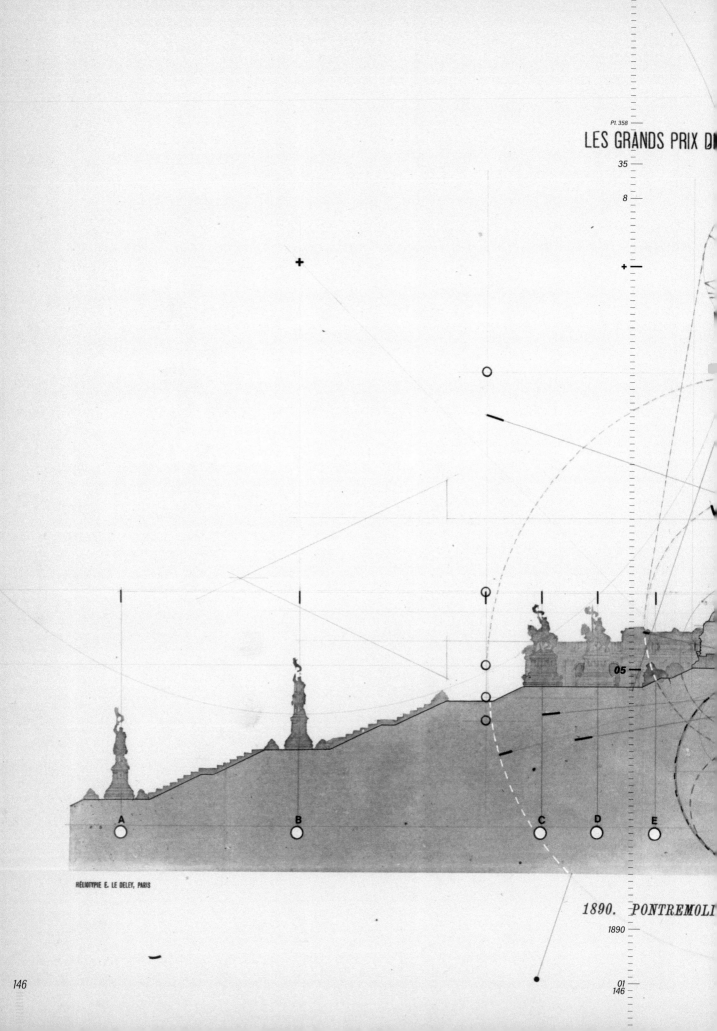

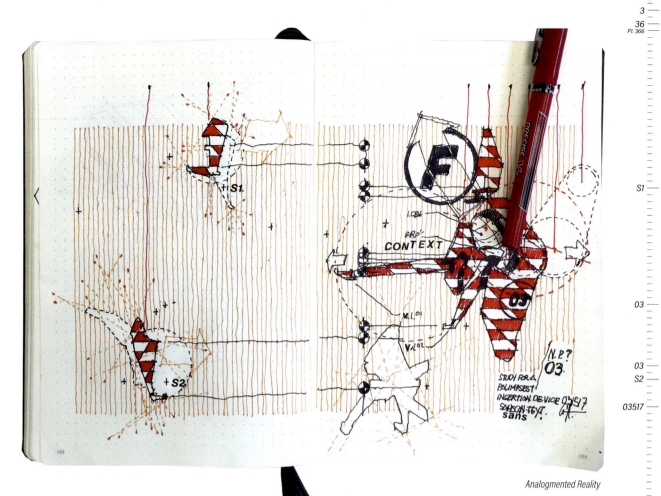

Analogmented Reality

The plane of notation

LES GRANDS PRIX DE ROME D'ARCHITECTURE

Pl. 366

1890. BOSSIS – Monument à Jeanne d'Arc

Myth-Alignments 12

➕ Ideal for frequent drawers. Not for any use on skin, including tattoos

Bob Sheil

Professor of Architecture and Design through Production, The Bartlett School of Architecture, London

Whilst it may not be the done thing to articulate on the meaning or otherwise of coolness in architectural discourse, articulating upon the vitality of speculation certainly should be. Architecture that is speculative is an experiment, it tackles the unknown, the subconscious, the intuitive and most importantly the limits of the real. Experimental and speculative architecture is multilingual; it speaks to the subject in parallel modes of communication, spiraling from the profile of outer forms to the innards of their spatial, material, and social constitution, then rebounding simultaneously outwards to the constellation of their contexts and polemic references. Experimental and speculative architecture is a debate; it operates in ways that are explicitly disruptive, provocative, and occasionally antagonistic, and in others that are self-critical, open ended, and not entirely designed to satisfy or reassure comfort zones.

Cantley's cool speculations ossiculate within this mode, skillfully deploying conventional means of representation to hypothesize on the unconventional and their edges. Entering the work requires some awareness of the particular genre in which it operates, the constraints from which it vies to escape, and the vibrant culture in which it celebrates expression. Its boundaries cut across multiple modes of practice, from stop-frame visualizations of narrative graphic novels, to visions of cinematic set design, from anatomical and bodily surveys, to mappings for dance and movement choreography, and from the lexicons of hazard signage to coordinate navigation systems, all brought home to the baseline set of plan, section, elevation, within documents for design and construction. Whilst flavors of the work are distinctly regional and in dialogue with peers and elders such as Denari, Kulper, and Woods, they are also knowingly transnational and talk to fellows that seek to illuminate through illustration, such as Cook, Spiller, Chard, and Lim.

Cantley has cunningly operated in this space for many decades and his latest contribution offers us insight into the causes of his experimentation, the triggers that set it off, and the trajectories it travels. This short text seeks to form a connection between the multiple ideas that exude from the output of his work and the making of the work itself. It has long been a belief of this author that methods and modes of production are intrinsic to its understanding, even on occasion its meaning. Arch exponent of this practice, the late Walter Pichler, went further than most by making the spaces in which his work was made and where later they were to be sited. At his Burgenland rural residence, the heart of the setting was the substantial kitchen stove that served as the environment's heat and nourishment source. His place for drawing was set between the stove and the fabrication workshop beyond, positioning the maker equally distant from both his essential supplies for survival and together their influence on his purpose. Everything – from the time of day or night that the maker strikes the first mark, to the degree to which their environment is well-tempered, from the provenance and procurement of their tools, to the uncontrollable tempo of peripheral distractions – plays its part in what the maker makes.

> "Architecture that is speculative is an experiment, it tackles the unknown, the subconscious, the intuitive and most importantly the limits of the real."

Reflecting on how analogue drawings are made draws conscious parallels to the environment with which all architecture interacts. Fluctuations in temperature and humidity generate significant forces of expansion and contraction upon the abstracted plane where propositions are laid. Throughout the day and night and upon these planes, untamed lines can grow and deviate, and untamed surfaces can buckle and meander. Thus, stabilizing the plane that aspires to be temporal requires honing its vulnerability to the ephemeral. Marking up and setting out precede the laying of permanent lines and marks in ways that are part rehearsal, part test for notional completion, but also independent in ways that follow another sequence of construction and tailoring that runs counter to the final impression. Here, the maker of speculative architecture deploys cerebral and visceral tactics and techniques that move between willing effort to reveal the vision, and equally willing attempts to discover it, or indeed, simply to let it emerge. The analogue maker of the speculative architectural drawing is in constant joust with the means and materials through which the work is being made, no differently to their counterpart in the woodshop, metalshop, or lab.

Cantley does not work exclusively in analogue of course, rather in tandem with digital platforms that provide hard to ignore power, rapidity, and forgiveness. Cantley's subtle use of the digital appears to convey how computational media agitates with its other analogue half, in particular providing clinical routes to manufacture and assembly previously held up as impenetrable barriers to the 'naïve' speculative. Aside from the practical questions that frequently and stubbornly challenge the speculative, his use of the digital adds flesh, albeit phantom flesh, to wanting bones. This mode of hybridity also offers us the avenue to explore that Cantley's speculations are imagined as existing in cinematic landscapes as backdrops, homes, and sites to fictional depictions of future inhabitations, perhaps as analogies of the failures of 'real' and conformist consumerist architectures. Here, one is drawn to visual and quantitative comparisons with waste and decay, recalling the vast uncharted mounds of detritus that accumulate as a by-product of the digital, some of it never used. Likewise, observing his forte for depicting the sumptuous intricacies of a bladder, a heart valve, or a nondescript organ in all its gleaming silkiness, one can't help wondering if Cantley is also referencing swathes of animal waste that accrete globally in the service of human sustenance and its excesses. Perhaps it suggests that conventional architecture prefers to avert its eyes from the uncomfortable and the controversial, reducing its engagement with truth to bland and mundane non-contentious palettes. But this of course is mere speculation.

Riding pillion to these claims is the knotty subject of solo authored and collective work and their evolving roles in architectural discourse and professional practice. Firmly camped in the solo world, Cantley's work talks to the immersive and layered process of developing architectural speculation through an artistic mode, that is, being a work that seeks to defy the conventions of the industrial mainstream through the consistent provenance of each line, mark, and notation. On the contrary, the collective mode through which most projects today are funneled increasingly seeks to anonymize such provenance, instead seeking to verify each line, mark, and notation against regulatory requirements that are risk averse. In this regard, *Speculative Coolness* needs also to be read as a manifesto that stakes out its opposition to submissive conformity in all its forms and declares the utmost urgency of the maverick's work.

Returning to the drawn matter in hand, and reflecting on the direct actions of the maker, hints of formal and conceptual trajectory are set out and pre-empted in skeletal structural drawings such as the drawing below.

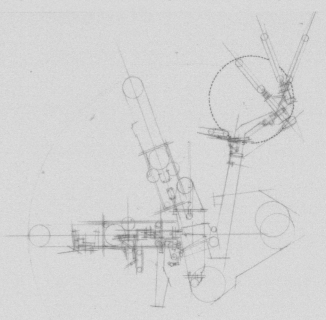

Marking out the nodes upon which experimental speciations later flesh out, trace lines hover like the initial workings of a complex lock mechanism, yet also, and peculiarly, like the organizational geometry of an arts and crafts house in relation to its landscape, or more in keeping with political intentions, the pegging-out of nooks and crannies, in a Miralles in Edinburgh sort of way. And why not? Lasting experimental speculation involves enlightened scholarly recall and well as a calligrapher's leap into the dark.

Finally, in this regard, reading Cantley is to tacitly understand the dark residue and dried particles of pigments, formerly liquid in their substance, briefly released in a visceral and cerebral performance of choreographed dance. Harnessed by needled instruments, clinical in their appearance, and skating on filmic skins, it is to see, loud and delicate scorelines flung through slow centrifugal geometries, pulled through linear trajectories, and gently buffered by the beveled edge and shorelines of acrylic, dried fluid, and tape. Regardless of the chapter being developed, the making of this architectural skeleton is inseparable from the tilt and pinch of human bone and tendon, the articulation of hinge, or the enfolding and popping of gut and tissue. It is an embodied form of provocation, expression, and speculation, a translation of drawing to building that is consciously punk and disruptive, otherly, and feral.

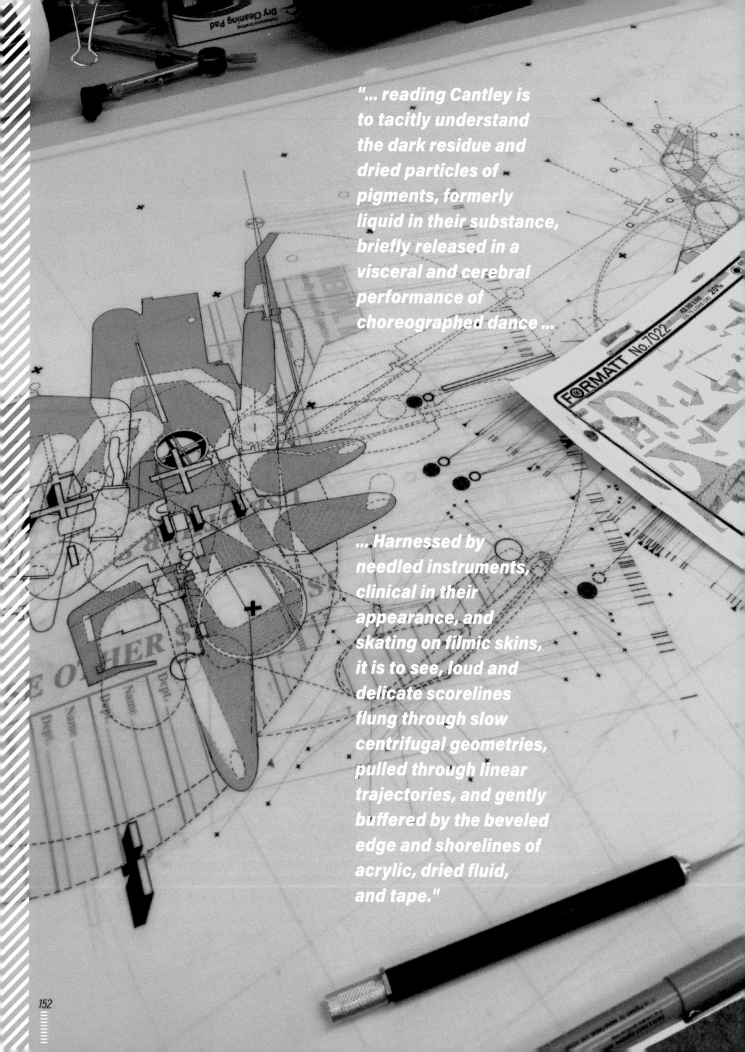

"... reading Cantley is to tacitly understand the dark residue and dried particles of pigments, formerly liquid in their substance, briefly released in a visceral and cerebral performance of choreographed dance ...

... Harnessed by needled instruments, clinical in their appearance, and skating on filmic skins, it is to see, loud and delicate scorelines flung through slow centrifugal geometries, pulled through linear trajectories, and gently buffered by the beveled edge and shorelines of acrylic, dried fluid, and tape."

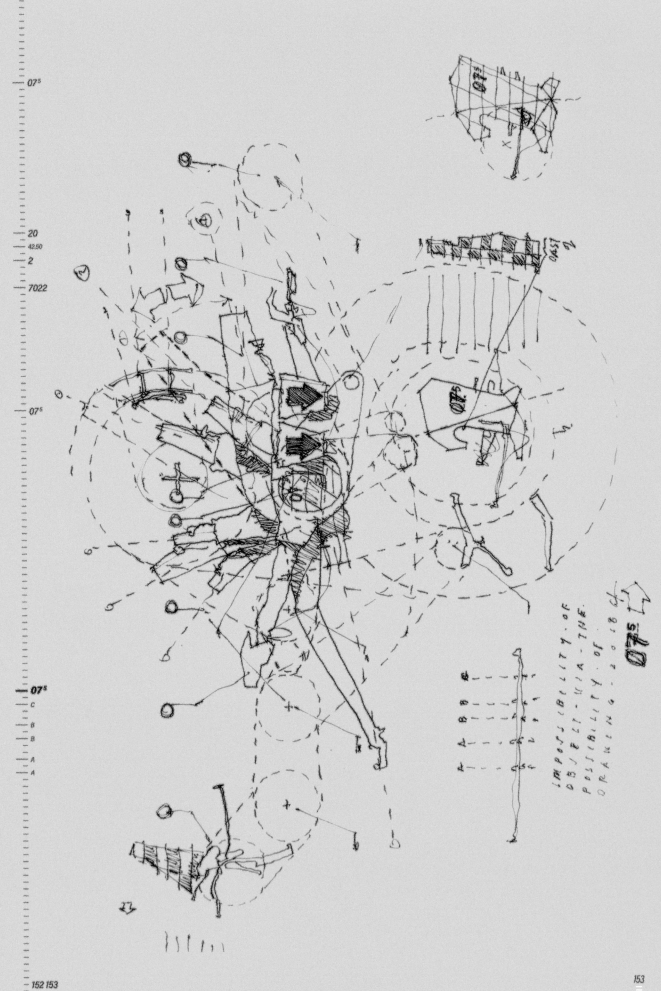

Ozone Metric Anomaly +

A system of architectural conditions that measure and fill the increasing holes in the ozone, as well as convey the metrics of increasing online usage – 'the cloud'.

A synthetic membrane:
Physically it protects and distributes ...
Socially it hides and distributes ...
Synthetically it replaces, records, and redistributes ...
an entity where One cubic yard of synthetic swelling occurs
for every cubic yard of depleted ozone ...

This expansion is also responsive to the amount and concentration of social media traffic. The OMA 'breathes' with log on/jacked in/use activity – operating as a physical and visual MEdia metric.

Ozone metric and fill(t)er systems, blur the reduction of physical layering and the aggregation of bandwidth. *What is our protective layer in the age of media saturation? When we collectively log on, where is our cONscious[ness] and our mental presence? Caught between the screen and the network? As the cloud grows, it forces awareness of global non-occupation.*

+ + +

[It is important to note that this theoretical construct is as much a

political vessel

as a tangible solution. Perhaps it might be best described as a messenger –

a CONscientious OBJector,

not architecturally resolved project but as flaming herald of inquiry.

A bullhorn of chron-[ill]ogical manifestations.]

Ozone a[l]ttitude. Biome[chanics]

"Early on, I understood that the drawings and models were themselves the work. They are autonomous in that they have their own life and are invested with [my] one instinct." *(Alonso, 2009)*

03
008

The artiFACT(s)—
MEdia and MEdium

Poros[c]ities of awareness and action

TYPE 7 Sta[g/t]e switching "Flitch Swipping"

MEDIA LOGICS

A condition of dual citizenship, the Sta[g/t]e switching refers to the situational phasing of media and its location in the consciousness of audience; perhaps not dissimilar to the way a building and its landscape are environments of parallel occupancy.

The closest analogy might be that of the classic 8-track tape [apologies younger readers, PB]. Anyone familiar with them will recall that the 8 tracks of the tape were spliced with a thin metal strip that would trigger a solenoid, causing the engaged playback heads to automatically jump to the next 'channel', thus creating the iconic 'clunk'/click [iconiclunk?] sound between tracks on an album.

These often occurred randomly in the middle of an individual song and were as conspicuous as the recorded music. This became the flipper condition, the medium of the tape serving as both the background – the medium of transmitting the music recording and the foreground – the audible acknowledgment of the broadcast device over the signal itself. This was the first and, perhaps, only popular [social] medium of music transmission that allowed the backstage area to become a front stage player, an almost anti-Heideggerian configuration/interpretation of the broken tool analogy.

Other transmission devices only engage with the corporeal interface of the listener [one had to physically pick up the needle of a turntable's tone arm or press the rewind button on a cassette player], whereas the mighty 8-track system deployed physical and therefore spatial deconstruction as a calibrated part of the appliance, causing it [the machine] to become present during its operation. This realization is known [to us] as the 8-track[now]ledge.

Field bladder 122212 prototype mitosis

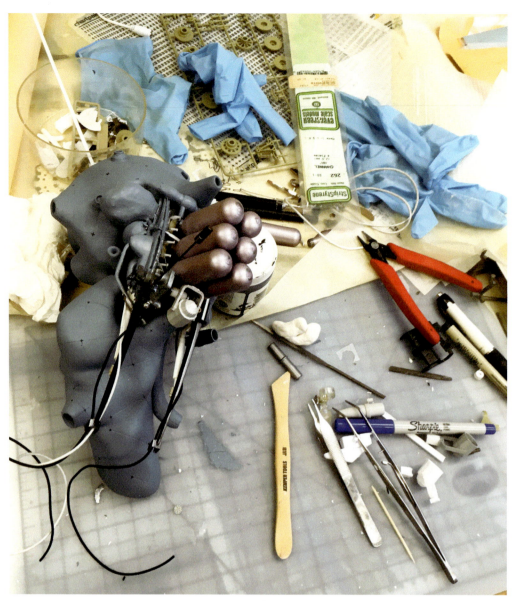

Workspace 01 - 09.15.2016

Field bladders 8897 and 8898
linkage/fusion

Backstory

When I relocated to LA in 1988 for grad school there were, to the best of my recollection, two main area codes for the surrounding territories: 213 – for the immediate LA areas *(that I)* traversed, 714 – for Orange County.

> "I lived almost as much in the commute space between those area codes as I did the places themselves. We all do – it's a 'SoCal thing'" (Cantley, 2020).[1]

Mobile phones were quite the anomaly if we had them at all. Fax machines were just beginning to enter the consumer market but still something of a novelty. The 'Web', as a consumer accessible entity, had not been born [in the early 1990s, Al Gore promoted legislation that funded an expansion of the ARPANET to allow public access, helping to develop the Internet as a public entity].

> <<"I invented pants" (Gore, 2000).>>[2]

Currently, there are some between 11–13 area codes, depending on your source and/or district mapping for the same LA/OC region. The moment the internet switch was turned on, by default the need for access was doubled.

> "Los Angeles is 72 suburbs in search of a city" (Parker, 1927).[3]

With colossal expansions in population and the requisite need to always 'be connected', the Voice Over Internet Protocol, smart devices, and need for technology space has increased in the most dramatic way in the recent history of human consumption. Enter a protocol for an ever-expanding vehicle for data + linkage.

> "I had a single [01] landline at the time of my move in 1988, now I have a mobile line, a line for my internet, a line for my smart watch, and that's just me. Almost Triple that for my household, which would be 6–7 dedicated 'lines' for my family. We (now) have 11 data-freeway 'smart devices' capable of communication within our current household of three people and 1.75 dogs" (Cantley, 2020).[4]

Tangentially, the layer of informational engagement, or bandwidth accretion, has created a 'fullness' to the data transfer and social [dis]engagement, that creates a conceptual, yet impactful layer of *information discharge*.

> "... they have the internet on computers these days" (Simpson, 2004).[5]

The amount of ozone has been steadily declining since the 1970s. The Antarctic Ozone Hole is an area of the stratosphere in which, in recent years, ozone concentrations have dropped to as little as 33 percent of their pre-1975 values. The ozone hole occurs during the Antarctic spring, from September to early December, as strong westerly winds start to circulate around the continent creating an atmospheric container. In this container over 50 percent of the lower stratospheric ozone is destroyed. This rupture continues to grow each year, resulting in an incredible imbalance in our protective layering, as well as disrupting the delicate weather systems and environmental balance of the continent.

The Tre[E]-hugger is a derivate residue ... a child of the process of unpacking the design problem

"Nothing vast enters the life of mortals without a curse" (Sophocles, 2015).[6]

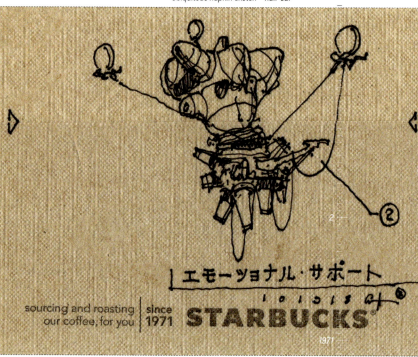

Ubiquitous napkin sketch – half-caf

The Project/Object
This proposal is for an Ozone metric and plugging system, which merges the reduction of our [needed] somatic stratum with the accumulation of dataspace, responding to the continual demand for additional of bandwidth. The prognosis: a need to fill the increasing surface rupture of the ozone.

The conversation becomes one of skins and projections. The earth's atmospheric skin ... human skin ... the skin of architecture ... the membrane of social media engagement [hot/cold media] ... The projection of information, recording, reporting, and forecasting of our current scenario[s] ...

The conceptual space begins to inquire as to how that protective layering might be defined, recognized, labeled, and re-imaged within the age of media saturation, global un-awareness, and resource depletion.

The Device is a metric for the acknowledgment of these contrasting, yet superimposed issues. As an architectural hypothesis, it serves two functions:

[1] Primary
To *physically* measure, calculate, and [re]fill the cavities that [will, sorrowfully] continue to open in our ozone layer, and;

[2] Secondary
to *critically* measure, record, map, and project our rapidly increasing technology media demand, engagement and usage.

This is an observatory ...
it is a recording device ...
and it's a mobile transmitter ...
It's a cognizance machine.
It's a billboard ... an advertising agency ...
a bit of conceptual duct tape and bondo ...
a physician, scientist, lab manager;
a [plastic] surgeon;
and counsellor all wrapped into one ...
It's a soothsayer ...
It's f[i/u]nctional pornography ...
a mimic ...
a magician ...
an impersonator ...
and perhaps most poetically,
a political and social Band-Aid.

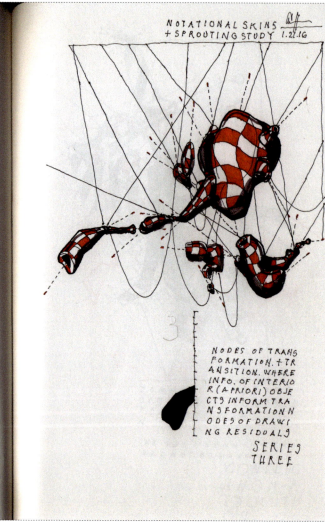

Transformative nodes sketch

Taxonometric authorship indicators

In very pedestrian terms, it expands to fill the holes in the ozone, just as it expands to measure the amount of communication and resource demands. It is, sadly, one of many millions of cells in an ever-expanding network.

Eventually it would expand to a maximum volume linking and merging with adjacent anomalies, until the new ozone is a completely artificial construct. A security blanket for our lungs, our skin, and our earth. Essentially, it becomes an alarm clock as much as it is anything else. • ⋯⋯⋯⋯⋯⋯⋯⋯⋯⋯ • *[Will you hit sNOoze?]*

Therefore, both physically and conceptually –

It is The Cloud...

Its bladder form, is an attempt to initiate an architectural dialogue, not based on form, but on message ... ironically delivered through a very labored formal language study. The amorphic shape is highly variable; the anomaly morphs constantly as ozone and media projections change over time. It is a measure of the chronology of progression and thought. Though it is designed to expand to full capacity and total implementation, it is hoped that through its message ultimately, its need will be reduced with the hope for its ultimate goal:

To become 'self-decom[miss]ioning ...'

> A.C. Clarke, "Hazards of Prophecy: The Failure of
> "Any sufficiently advanced technology is
> Imagination" in *Profiles of the Future: An Enquiry into the*
> indistinguishable from magic" (Clarke, 1962).[7]
> *Limits of the Possible* (London: Pan Books, [1962]1973).

Cloudscaping 101. *Projection, dialogue, and non-formulation. Machines not only in (an) (their) environment, machines constructing environment(s). New topologies.*

Who manufactures your rainbow, and what are the qualifications of your leprechaun technicians? Might the pot of gold in fact be an awareness that leads to the rebuilding of the ozone, rainforests, Arctic shell, and all of our other natural resources?

+ *Floating laboratories, Band-Aids, bindi/duct tape, selfie absorbers, (anti)-social media membranes.*

+ *Keep your head in the clouds.*

+ *Behind every cloud is another cloud. "Be thou the rainbow in the storms of life. The evening beam that smiles the clouds away, and tints tomorrow with prophetic ray." "Do you wish to rise? Begin by descending. You plan a tower that will pierce the clouds? Lay first the foundation of humility."*

["is it architecture [yet]? was it before it puffed up?"]

1965
1962 1973

CON-structed [me]dia[stolic]s

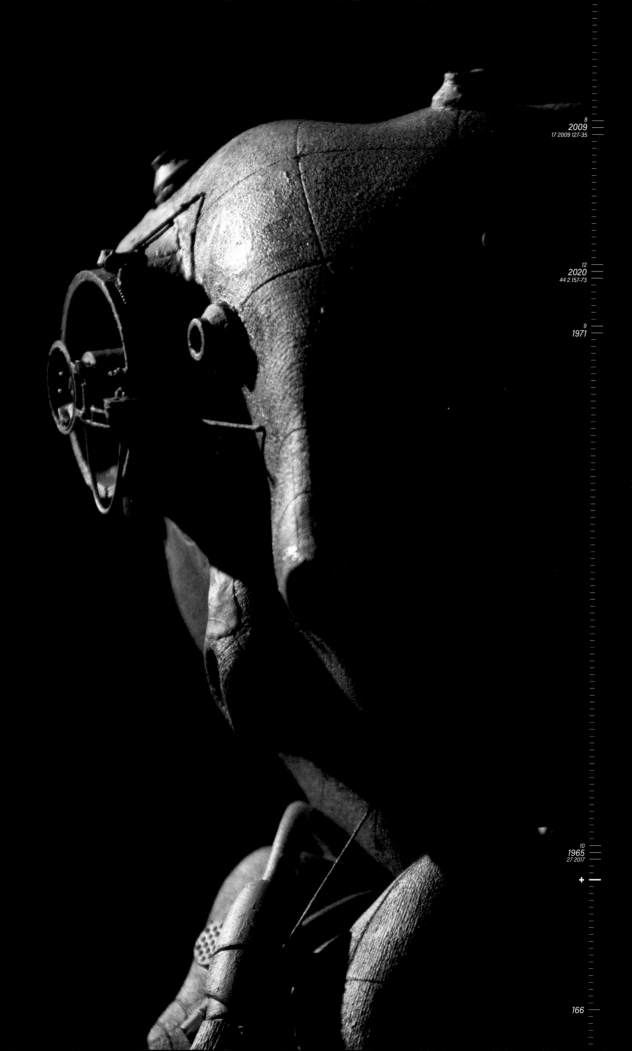

The artiFACT(s) – MEdia and MEdium

> "Early on, I understood that the drawings and models were themselves the work. They are autonomous in that they have their own life and are invested with [my] one instinct" (Alonso, 2009).[8]

[8] H.D. Alonso and T. Mayne, "Generation(s) and the Generative," *Log* 17 (2009): 127–35.

This drawing was an attempt to distinguish representation from presentation. In this case, the space *between* the model of the architecture and the architectural intention.

The architectural model is perhaps traditionally the most reductive method of communication, and, one might argue, the most 'truthful' in terms of architectural media – "what you see is what you get" (Jones, 1971).[9] At least in terms of THIS model – it is an attempt to describe the formal characteristics of a set of finite responses. The more esoteric the intentions of the model, the fewer questions are answered in its reading. This analogy is based on TRADITIONAL architectural model media – less of a novel and more of a dictionary.

[9] G. Jones, The Flip Wilson Show, 1971, https://www.youtube.com/watch?v=tcbn0K84ZdE

To follow that analogy, DRAWINGs, traditionally, are instruction manuals for assembly and measured understanding of the project. Both the model and the drawing served the project ... but, here, each is allowed an equal stake, attempting to experiment with the factors that combined each of the systems into a single condition.

Not with the intention of achieving singularity, actually, quite the opposite ... the drawing allows multiple sets of data which occur in realms that are typically segregated to be unpacked. It discharges the intelligence of the contradiction and conflict ... the overlap, the sympathetic relationships, and the emergent circumstances that occur when those two typologies occupy the same physical membrane.

The physical model is an attempt to distinguish the conditions of representation from the conditions of presentation.

> "... which is more fake?" (Crocker, 1965).[10]
> "FAKE NEWS!" (Trump, 2017).[11]

[10] B. Crocker, "Have you seen Polythene Pam?" Los Angeles, 1 July 1965.
[11] realDonaldTrump, FAKE NEWS TROPHY [Twitter]" 27 November 2017.

It represents conditions of exteriority, positioning, and scheduling. It is a distorted and fractured timekeeper. It suggests a new typology – a device/architecture that inhabits the drawn object ...

There are three segregated entities in the 'model' – the Bladder Lab, the umbilical connection/docking station, and the tree hugger. Each of these exist in the world of the architectural project, yet none occupies the position, time, and proximity that the model suggests. Just as the experimental drawings overlap non-adjacent elements, skewed chronologies, and the multiplicity of scales, so too, does this artifact.

> "the term 'post-truth' describes not only an increase in the frequency of lies in the public sphere, but refers to a world in which truth is no longer an expectation" (Tsfati et al., 2020).[12]

[12] Y. Tsfati, H.G. Boomgaarden, J. Strömbäck, R. Vliegenthart, A. Damstra and E. Lindgren, "Causes and Consequences of Mainstream Media Dissemination of Fake News: Literature Review and Synthesis," *Annals of the International Communication Association* 44, no.2 (2020): 157–73.

OMA Residues

The question of authorship of an architectural language came into question for me in 2016. This drawing was partially a response to the challenge that an architect might be able to possess the formal characteristics of shape-making, formal language, and graphic 'style'.

It charts the fabricated piety of false cynics and questions the condition of authorship within a discipline that is based on form[al] propriety. simultaneously it is a syncopated chronological sample of an architectural proposal whose fundamental premise is that of constant mutation, and to therefore *evade* form, so that very notion of formal authorship changes on a daily, if not hourly basis. It asks the question, if a project is a proposal to the identity of 'non[un]-form', how might one categorize the *plasticity of identity* [POI]? This becomes an effort of 'anti-authorship', the anti-stylistic condition.

This drawing is an experiment of using a previously designed architectural entity as a metric for graphic investment ... an attempt to deconstruct prototypical data of three entities simultaneously: the project, the object, and the documentation. Somewhere between these three conditions lies the truth of the Taxonometric Drawing, and the nature of Post Liminal Fuzz. ✢

Main connection portal – lock-in and lockdown

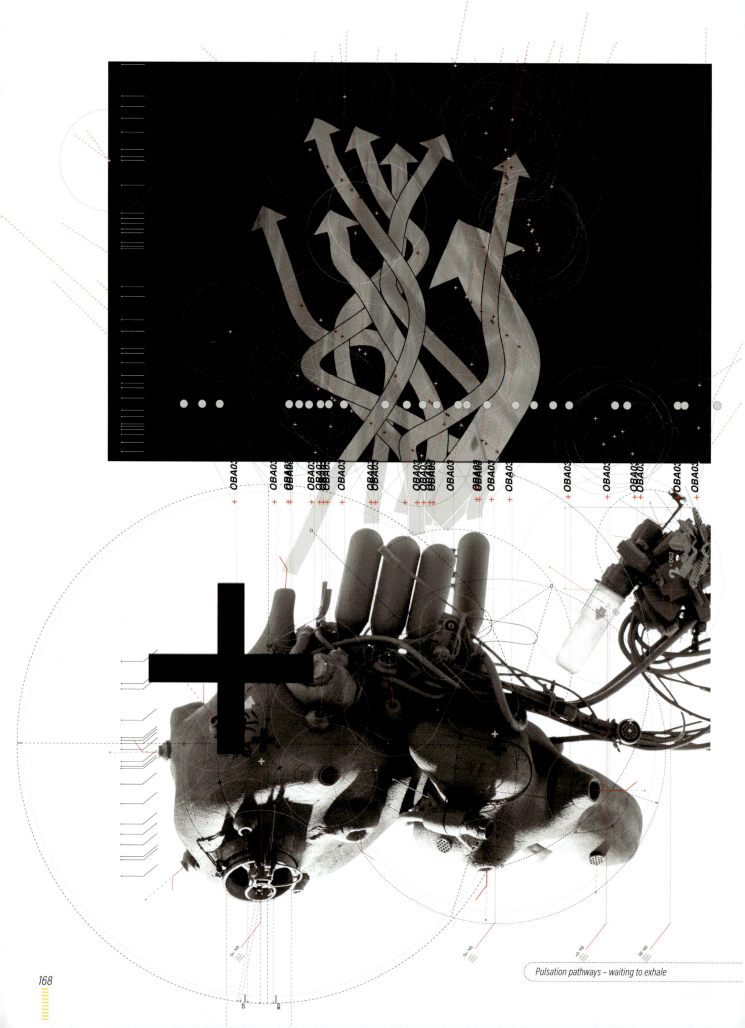

Pulsation pathways – waiting to exhale

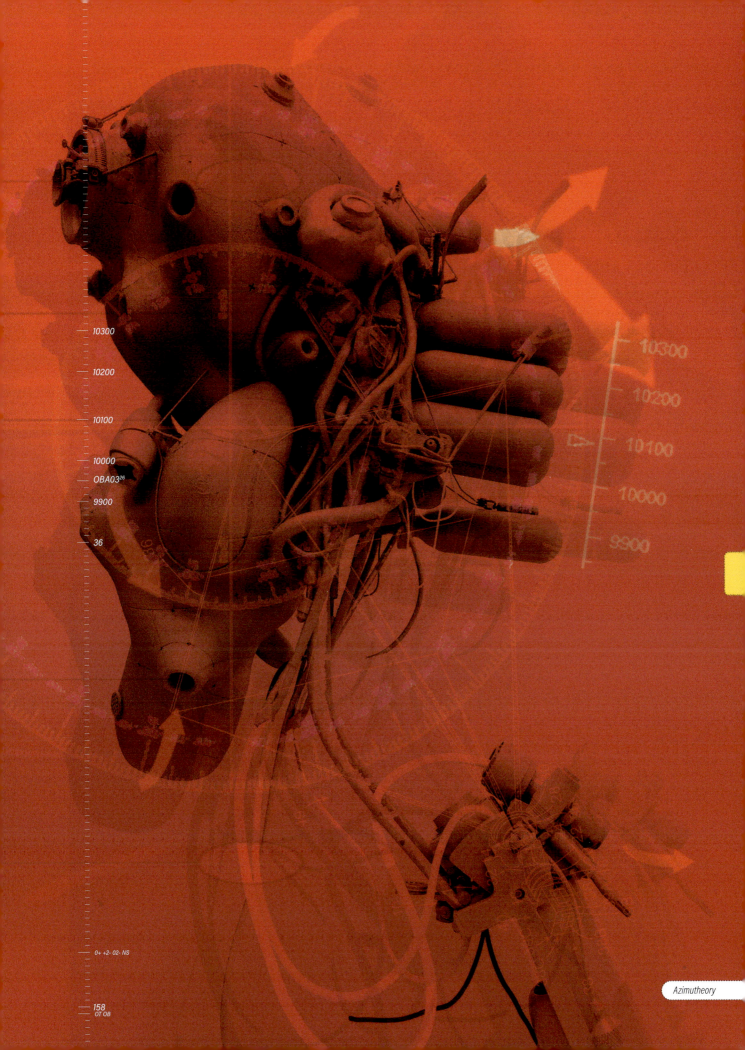

Azimutheory

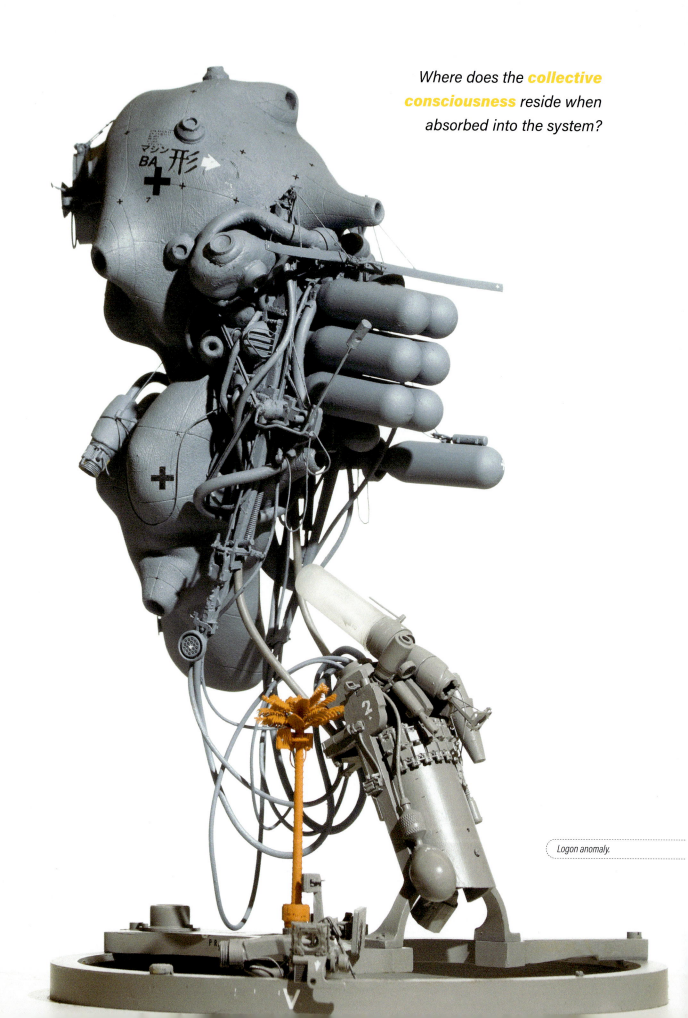

*Where does the **collective consciousness** reside when absorbed into the system?*

Logon anomaly.

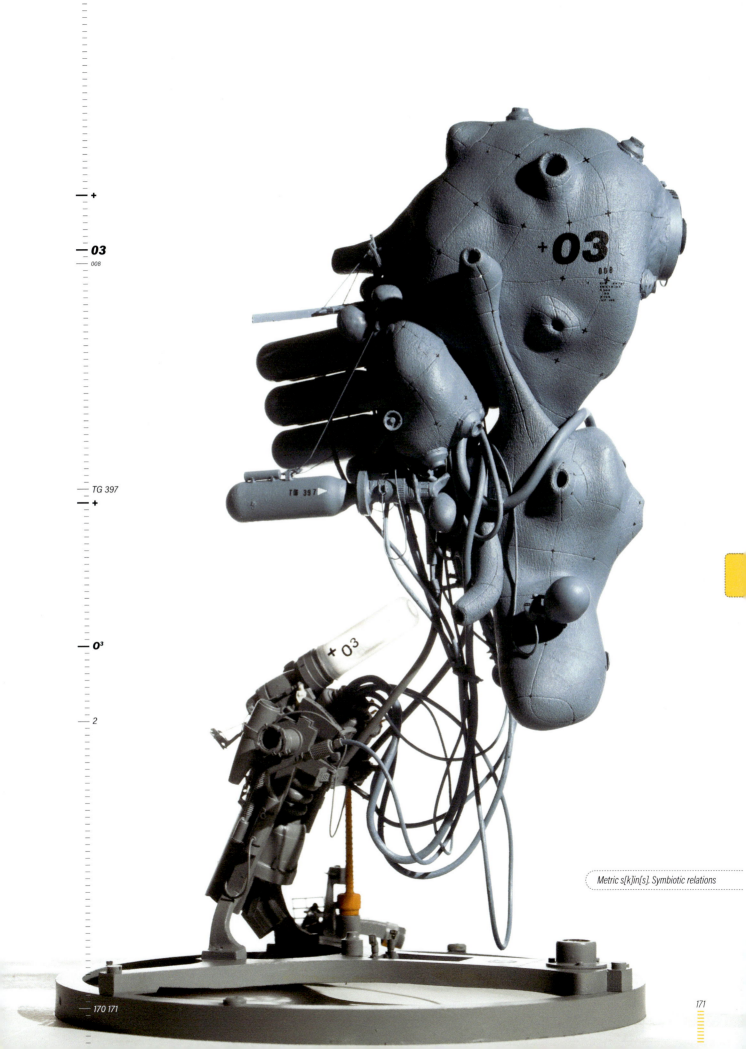

Metric s[k]in[s]. Symbiotic relations

Array fields/"Where's Waldo?" ... the tectonics of the [th]atmosp[here]

Umbilical Tower/payload changeout unit

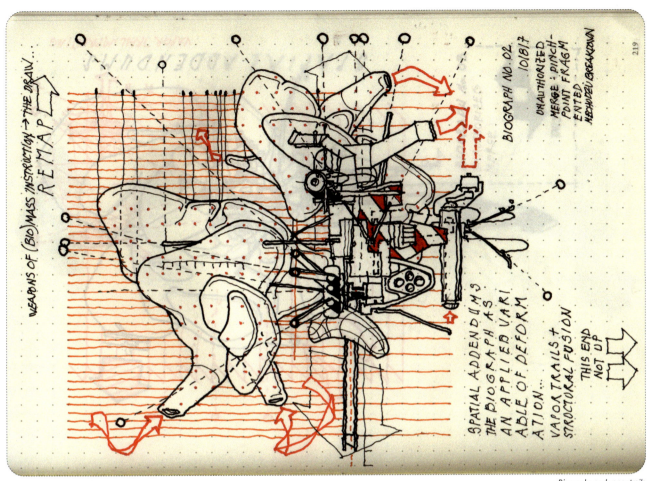

Biographs and vapor trails

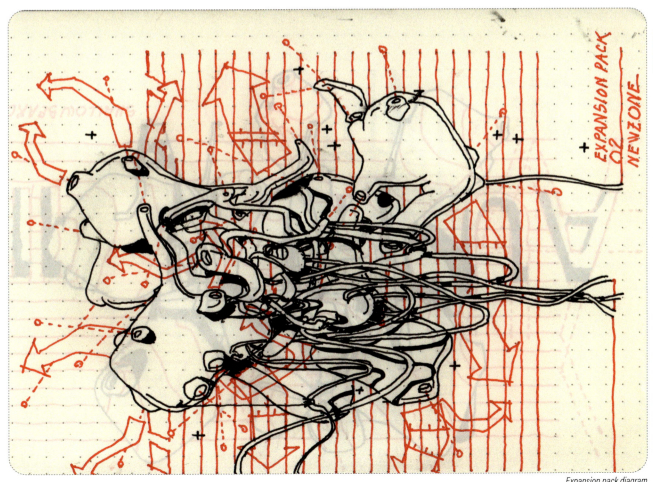

Expansion pack diagram

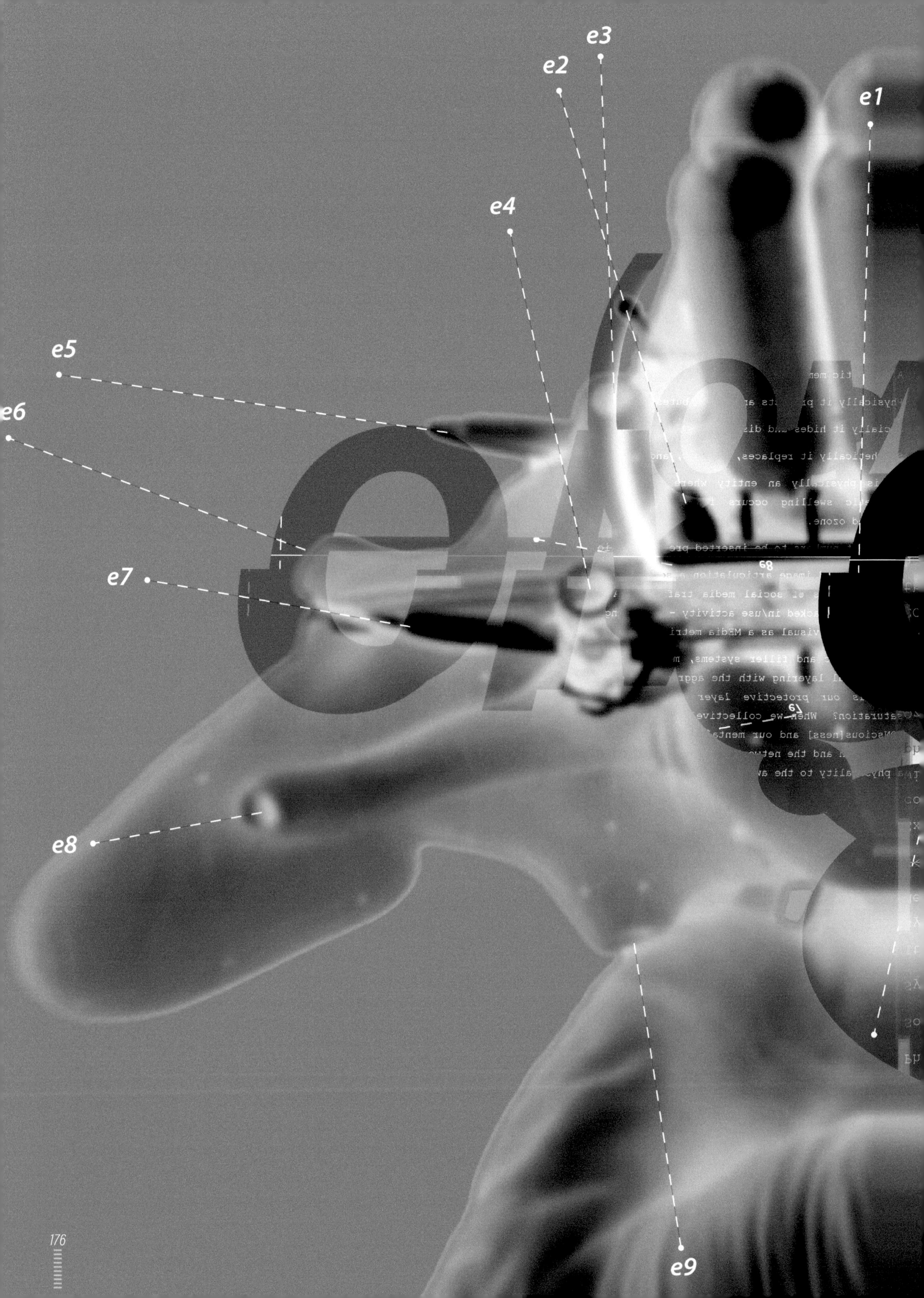

e1
e2
e3
e4
e5
e6
e7
e8
e9

176

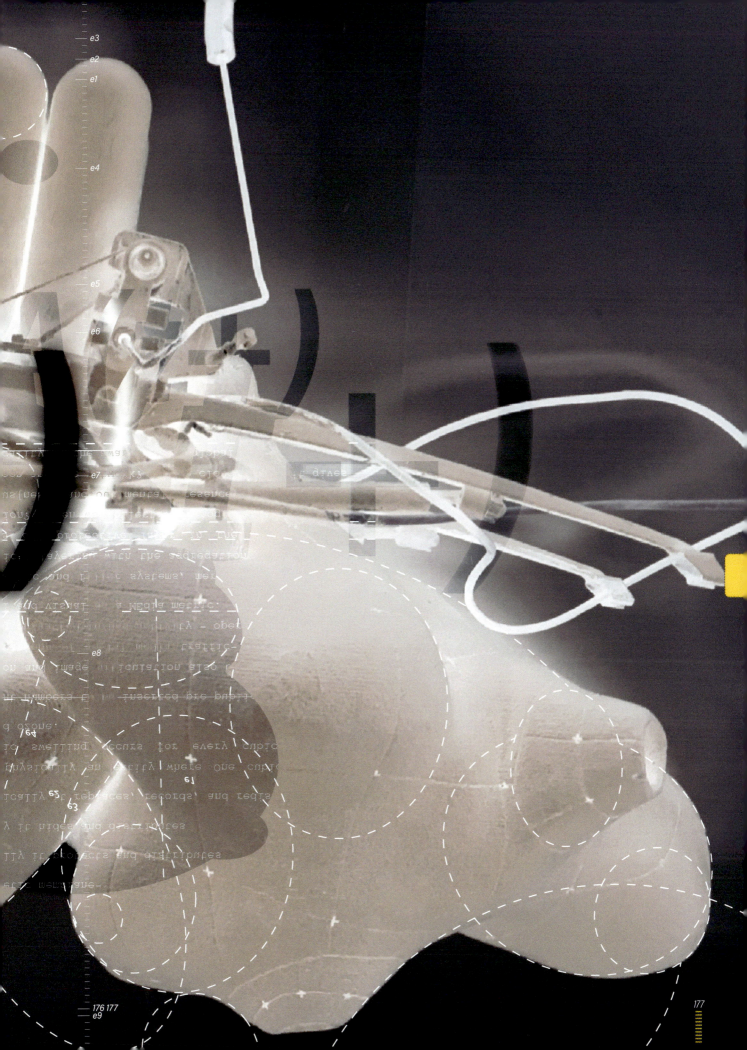

Whorolog[e] +
Ministry of [w]Hore-2:culture

A single-serve, self-governed brothel in a legal, urban environment, focusing on the pre- and post-commerce of the act of prostitution.

"You've been out gallivanting with that floosy of a bigger uBRO-ther of yours haven't you!" (Simpson, 1993).[13]

[13] H. Simpson, Season 4, episode 14, Springfield, 1993.

Occupied[ata]. Transaction Configuration.

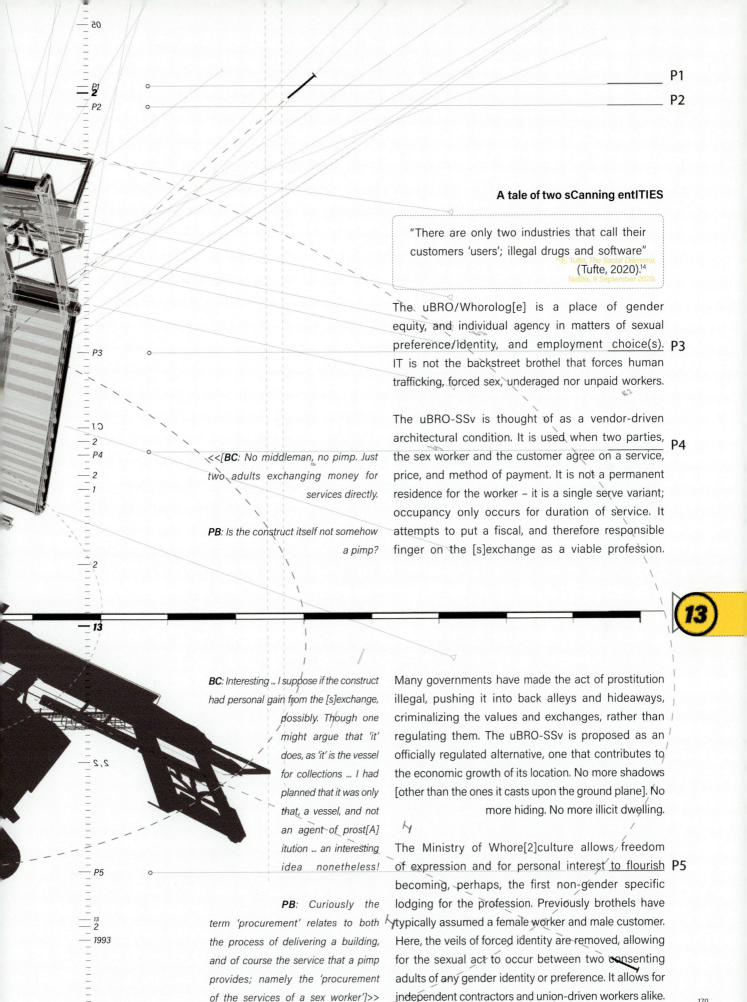

A tale of two sCanning entITIES

> "There are only two industries that call their customers 'users'; illegal drugs and software" (Tufte, 2020).[14]
>
> [14] E. Tufte, *The Social Dilemma*, Netflix, 9 September 2020.

The uBRO/Whorolog[e] is a place of gender equity, and individual agency in matters of sexual preference/identity, and employment choice(s). IT is not the backstreet brothel that forces human trafficking, forced sex, underaged nor unpaid workers.

The uBRO-SSv is thought of as a vendor-driven architectural condition. It is used when two parties, the sex worker and the customer agree on a service, price, and method of payment. It is not a permanent residence for the worker – it is a single serve variant; occupancy only occurs for duration of service. It attempts to put a fiscal, and therefore responsible finger on the [s]exchange as a viable profession.

<<[**BC**: No middleman, no pimp. Just two adults exchanging money for services directly.

PB: Is the construct itself not somehow a pimp?

BC: Interesting ... I suppose if the construct had personal gain from the [s]exchange, possibly. Though one might argue that 'it' does, as 'it' is the vessel for collections ... I had planned that it was only that, a vessel, and not an agent of prost[A]itution ... an interesting idea nonetheless!

PB: Curiously the term 'procurement' relates to both the process of delivering a building, and of course the service that a pimp provides; namely the 'procurement of the services of a sex worker']>>

Many governments have made the act of prostitution illegal, pushing it into back alleys and hideaways, criminalizing the values and exchanges, rather than regulating them. The uBRO-SSv is proposed as an officially regulated alternative, one that contributes to the economic growth of its location. No more shadows [other than the ones it casts upon the ground plane]. No more hiding. No more illicit dwelling.

The Ministry of Whore[2]culture allows freedom of expression and for personal interest to flourish becoming, perhaps, the first non-gender specific lodging for the profession. Previously brothels have typically assumed a female worker and male customer. Here, the veils of forced identity are removed, allowing for the sexual act to occur between two consenting adults of any gender identity or preference. It allows for independent contractors and union-driven workers alike.

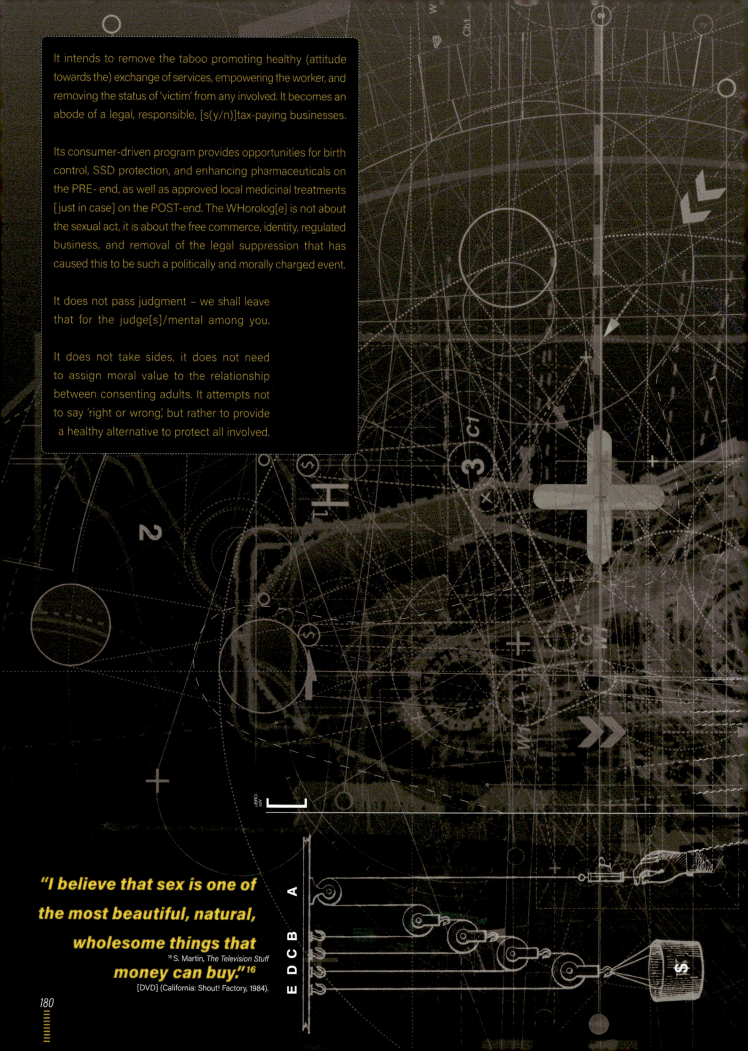

It intends to remove the taboo promoting healthy (attitude towards the) exchange of services, empowering the worker, and removing the status of 'victim' from any involved. It becomes an abode of a legal, responsible, [s(y/n)]tax-paying businesses.

Its consumer-driven program provides opportunities for birth control, SSD protection, and enhancing pharmaceuticals on the PRE- end, as well as approved local medicinal treatments [just in case] on the POST-end. The WHorolog[e] is not about the sexual act, it is about the free commerce, identity, regulated business, and removal of the legal suppression that has caused this to be such a politically and morally charged event.

It does not pass judgment – we shall leave that for the judge[s]/mental among you.

It does not take sides, it does not need to assign moral value to the relationship between consenting adults. It attempts not to say 'right or wrong', but rather to provide a healthy alternative to protect all involved.

"I believe that sex is one of the most beautiful, natural, wholesome things that money can buy."[16]

[16] S. Martin, *The Television Stuff* [DVD] (California: Shout! Factory, 1984).

"If you are not buying the product, you are the product"
(Beetle, B 2010)[15]

If nobody wants to sell sex, it is a crime to force anyone to do so. But when men or women do want to sell their bodies, they should have that full right without encountering punishment or discrimination. If the client behaves decently, the relationship between the sex buyer and the sex seller must be considered a purely private transaction.

NILS JOHAN RINGDAL

The dual project explores the following conditions and principles:

+ A set of [s]explicit architectural entities or conditions.

+ A series of drawings that both explore and express the unpacking of those entities as autonomous Conditions.

+ A set of emergent atmospheres arrive – drawing data [which is not the object data] that result FROM the drawing being unpacked.

+ A series of Taxonometric data reservoirs are developed – a situation labeled as *speculative chronologies*.

+ The shadow-caster conditions of the chronologies become machines and devices that never were … creating conditions that are yet to be …

+ The shadows are simply recordings of events that have 'just' transpired, only milliseconds before … a prior documentation of a yet-to-be condition. They are in essence synthetic and crafted pasts projecting highly fabricated futures into a single [graphic] event.

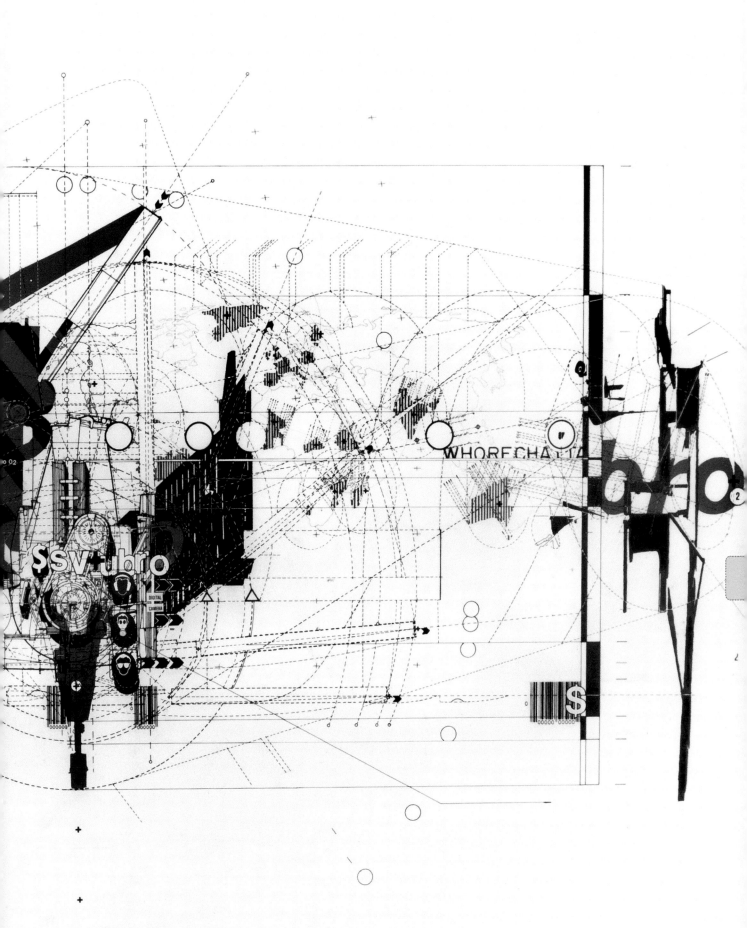

uBRO

The device and its representation (drawing), establish, accept, and record the conceit that shadows can act as scanners, tracing the surfaces of sites and contexts.

> "the shadow in the fiscal sense represents the covering up of the business trade from government entities: a stamp of 'non-approval.'"

The bird's-eye view was selected because of the easily recognizable tracking of shadows as object delineators. This was also deemed appropriate for the uBro's condition of program driven movement – it rotates based on physical/fiscal functional conditions.

2 shadow ranges + kinetic strategies

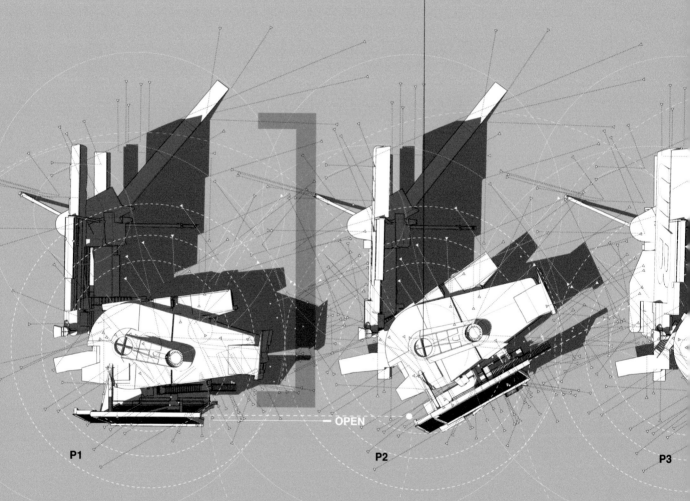

P1   P2   OPEN   P3

EMPTY

Here, the drawing tracks the significant program positions and uses the distortion of the residue found between these positions to deposit planometric reservoirs of ink, the architect's device for demonstrating the obstruction of environmental illumination. The drawing serves to document multiple circumstances, chronologies, and loci – framing the temporal nature of these [typically] segregated subjects.

The brothel itself, semi-independent of the drawings that both generate it and are produced by it, has a different set of descriptors. It is not [as] concerned with the reservoirs of ink that are the shadow-scanning metric, instead it is concerned with surveying a different phenomenon, the [s]exchange.

"Oh Brothel, Where Art Thou?"

"I remember a shadow, living in the shade of your greatness." (Odinson, 2012)[17]

CLOSED

P1 P2 P3 P4 P5   **P4**   **P5**

OCCUPIED

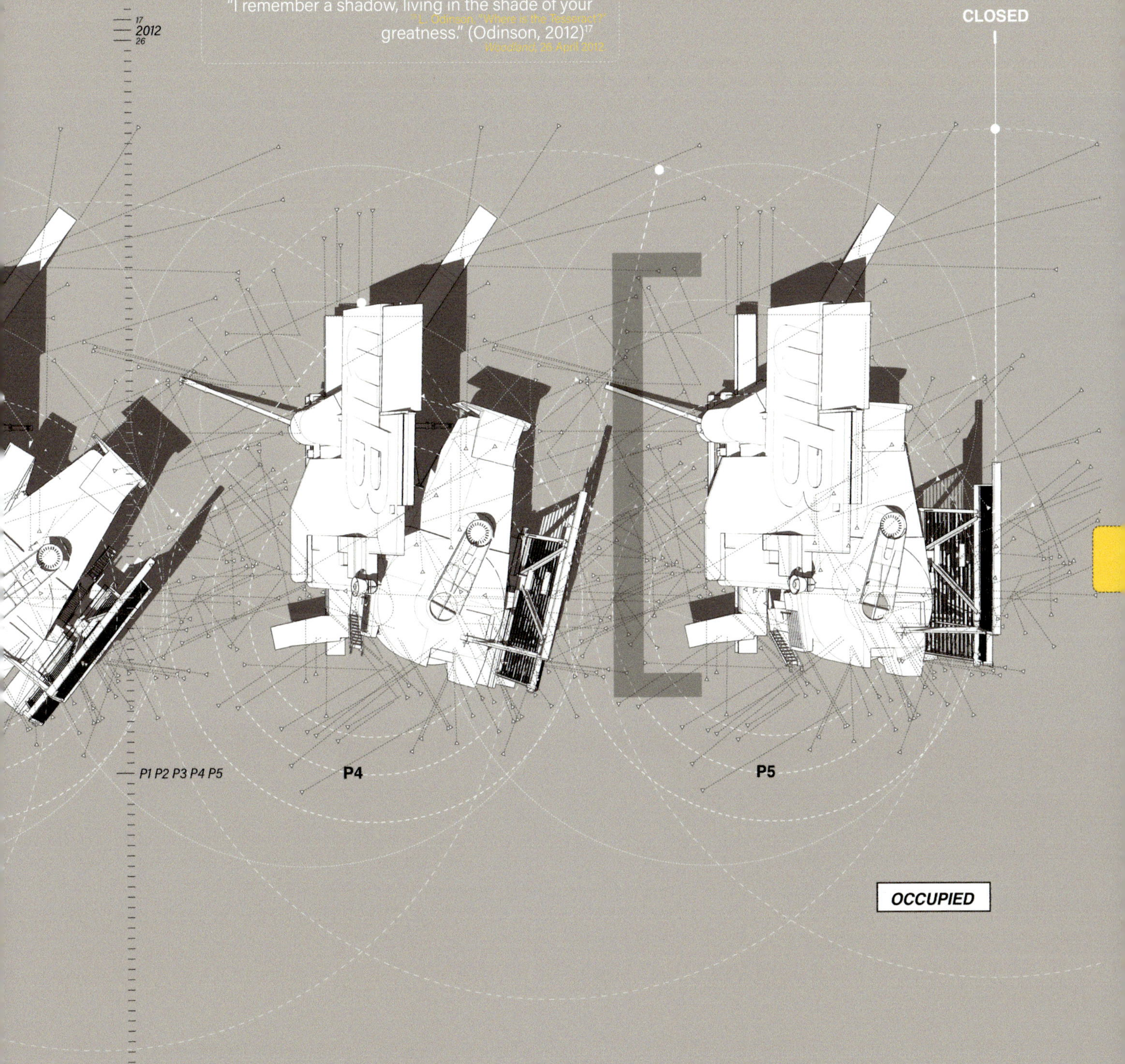

Sequencing diagram/ap. Pulsating geometries.

Topography Scanners and SS.V(D)s

The plan has traditionally been used for calculating, projecting, testing, and documenting the shadow as a response to an architectural proposition. Shade is a peculiar phenomenon in the architectural drawing. Many, if not all entities in this drawing typology, are meant to show 'what is/will be there' ... *there* being an incredibly elusive and metaphysical place [where is the 'there' of a plan? a projected or potential reality] Shadows, however, represent 'that which is not there', or at least that which is partially hidden by the removal of light, obscured by the synthetic assembly of the construction hypothesis.

A shadow is the result of the failed journey of light rays traveling 92.2 trillion miles, only to be denied at the last moment of their journey. However tragic, it provides one of the most poetic devices of the plan. The transitory nature of the shadow is typically suppressed or condensed into a singular moment of time, due to the static nature of traditional architectural depiction. The topography scanner measures/records/observes the condition of the double negative the removal/denial of light, and the impermanent fluctuating pathways that it traces along both horizontal and vertical surfaces. It is topographical in that the behavior of the shadow, the removal and therefore the negation of a thing, scans both [w]HOR[i]ZONTALly with the VERT[i]CALly. This condition, though generated by the project [architecture], is exclusively a function of the drawing [the uBro-ssv(d)], which is a residue of the project. There is a delicious irony that the act of removal/erasure [sun/light] is 'rendered' via the densest application/addition of graphic information [solid black].

These Taxonometric Reservoirs become repositories for the data generated through the action of drawing. They are the projected 'goal' of these drawings ... a set of architectural conditions, or machines that are conglomerations of previously drawn components. They are replicators, with a touch of editor built in. They strive to become at once both autonomous emergent conditions whilst simultaneously being integrated components of the host drawing.

+ + +

<<"Which brings us at last to the moment of truth, wherein the fundamental flaw is ultimately expressed, and the anomaly revealed as both beginning, and end."
(Architect, [MA-tricks]2003).[18]>>

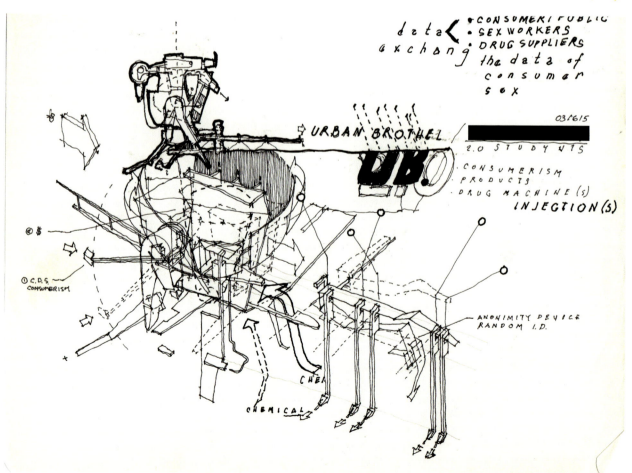

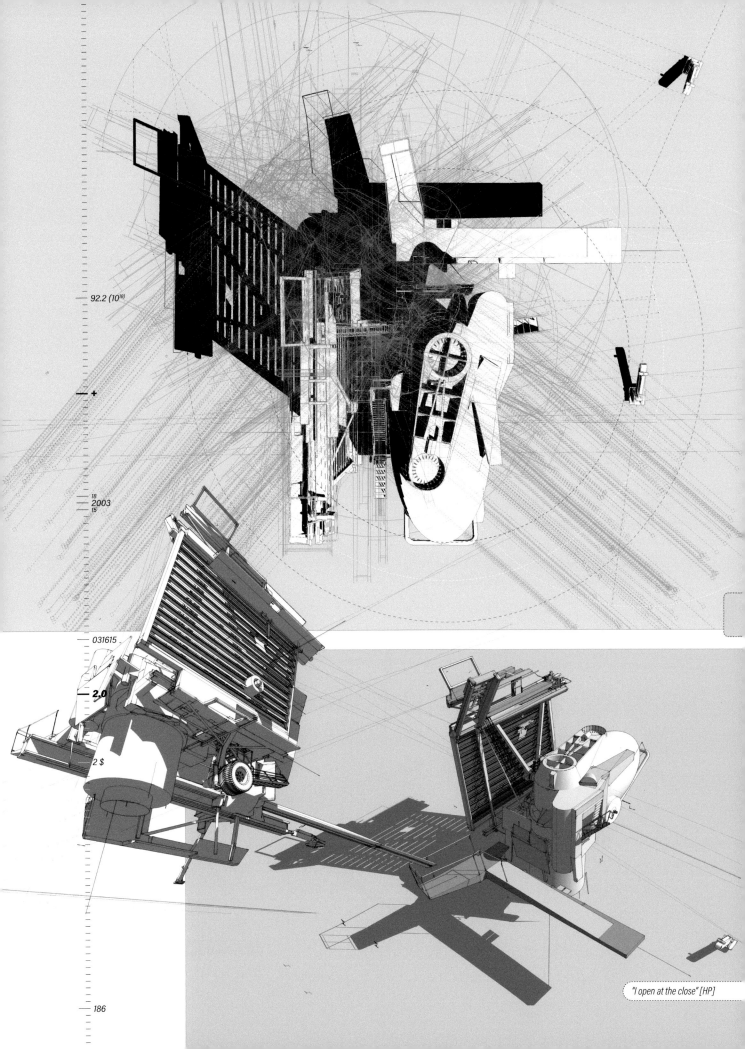

The M[I]nis(TRY) ☺ of [W]horolog(e)ical STuDies

The intention is that the building should record the duration of fiscal exchanges within the transaction window. Pre-, Intra- and post-climA[C/x]tic currency indicators [PCCI] "Oh My" (Takei, 2013),[19] tells the story of the financial implications for each participant, their physical [and therefore financial] requirements giving new meaning to 'pay-per-view'], and their contribution to the broader economy. Although never constructed, the architecture would inscribe a drawing onto the landscape, and then onto the façade of the building itself, becoming its own drawing mechanism and its own presenter.

[19] G. Takei, "Oh My," 22 February 2013, https://www.youtube.com/watch?v=6nSKkwzwdW4

Original P.R. mast – inhabiting the red light

> "peek-a-boo, I see you ..." (Churchill, 1934).[20]
>
> "I spy, with my little eye ..." (Jefferson, 1801).[21]

[20] W. Churchill, "We lie within a few minutes striking distance ...," London, 16 November 1934.
[21] T. Jefferson, "Inaugural Address," Washington, DC, 4 March 1801.

The experimental and hermeneutic nature of this drawing typology allows for these entities, which normally exist while in tandem, to be isolated graphic commands and imprints.

> "'Sex workers have to be hyper, hyper social-media-literate,' says P.J. Sage, a cam model and sex work researcher. 'At least 50 percent of your time is spent promoting and marketing.'"(*Wired*, 2018)[22]

[22] E.G. Ellis, "Social Media is Reshaping Sex Work – But Also Threatening It," 18 March 2018, https://www.wired.com/story/sex-work-social-media/

> "Sociologist Angela Jones has identified five 'affordances' the internet gives sex workers – and chief among them is 'reduced risk of bodily harm.' Sex workers often face extreme bodily risk, and the internet provides life-saving distance".[23]

[23] Ibid.

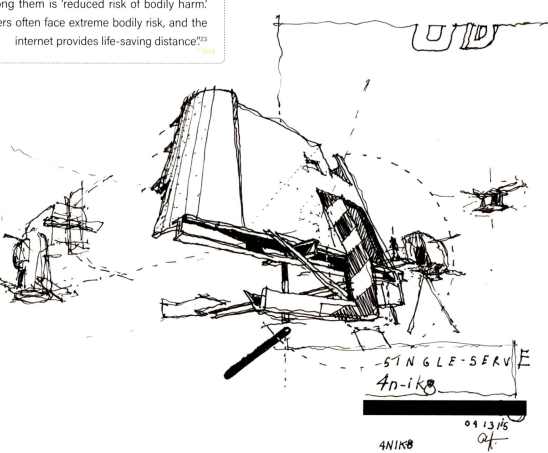

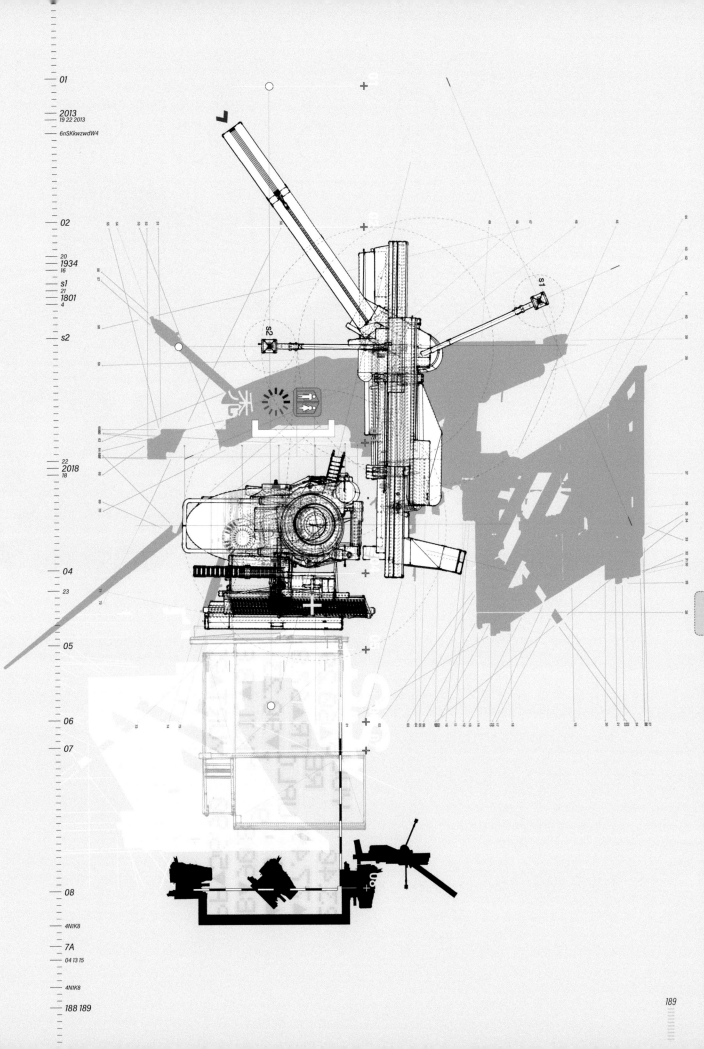

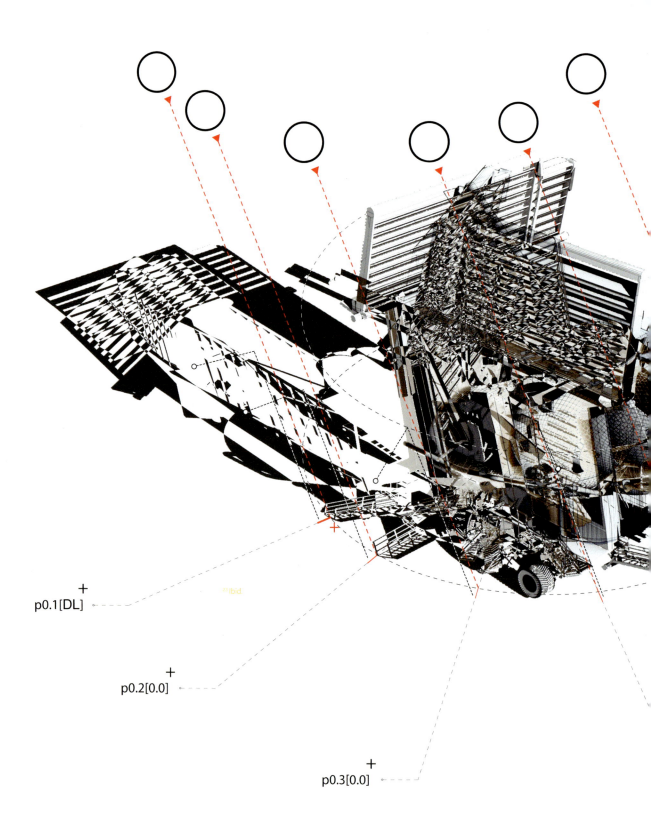

p0.1[DL]

p0.2[0.0]

p0.3[0.0]

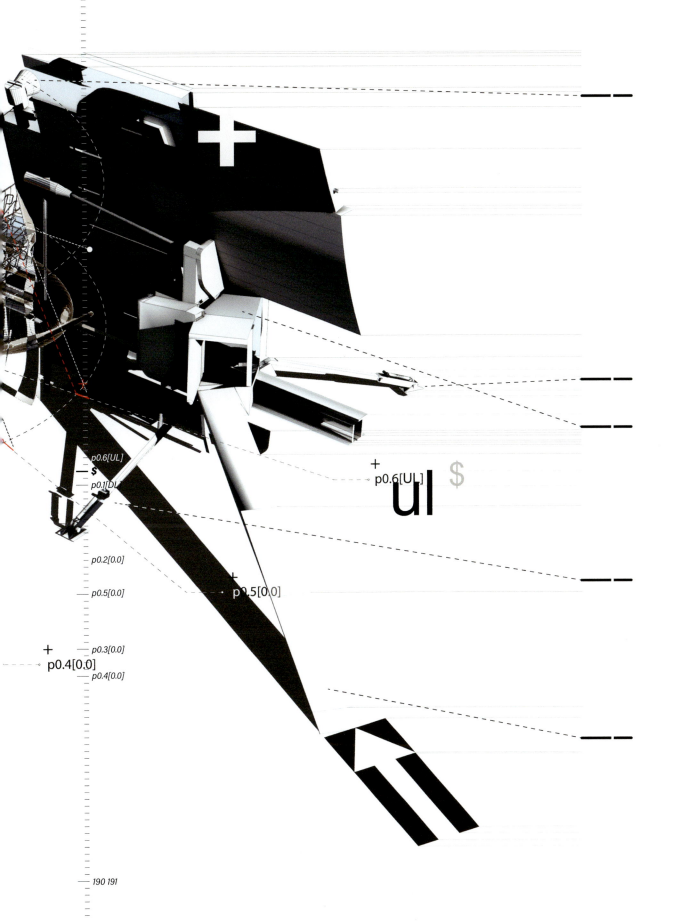

SS.V[D]

The 'single serve variant': a commentary on both the consumerism of the [s]exchange and a nod to the disposability of CONsumer product[s].

The mono-portion an analogy to consumer foodstuffs as well as our tendency toward 'flavor-of-the-month' technological delivery vessels. This tangential experiment explores the tailoring of an industry toward the ideal of the CONsumer, making constructs that create isolating paranoia through the implication of categorization of *difference*. The 'flavor-of-the-month' accentuates the constant need for CONsumer-driven apathy, and the thrust of an immediate need for personal satis[fact]ion. The uBRO serves the singular, as opposed to tradition brothels offering a variety of workers all at the same convenient location. Mass helpings vs. single servings

> "Um, he's sick. My best friend's sister's boyfriend's brother's girlfriend heard from this guy who knows this kid who's going with a girl who saw Ferris pass out at 31 Flavors last night" (Adamley, 1987).[24]
> *S. Adamley, "Registration" [Speech]*
> *Glenbrook North High School, 11 June 1987.*

In this drawing, Trajectory Residues [uBro-ssv], the experiment was established to serve as a metric for the constant shifting between horizontal and vertical hybrid moments of a shadow's mutable paths. The result is a drawing of a drawing (device), an artifact classified by its own ontology. The document becomes a systemic metric of interiority. Shadow casters and planes of light-blocked impregnation are recorded and mapped over changed chronological markers, etched upon the plane of denotation/detonation [Barthes]. ✚

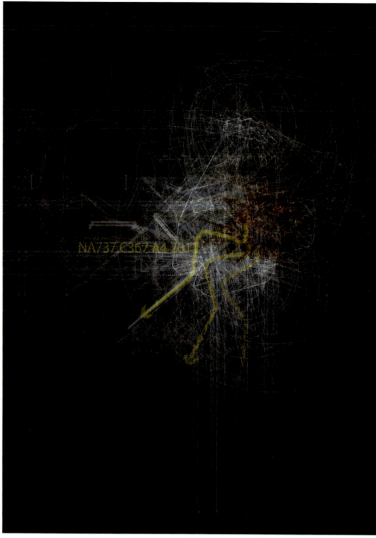

Projection cones and fiscal mappings

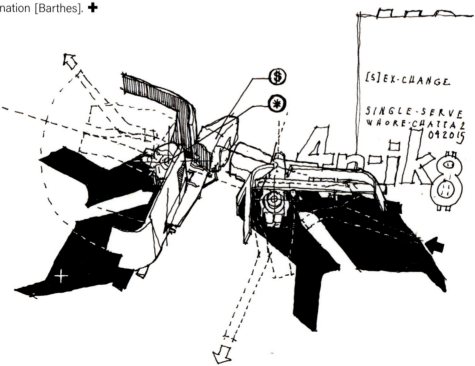

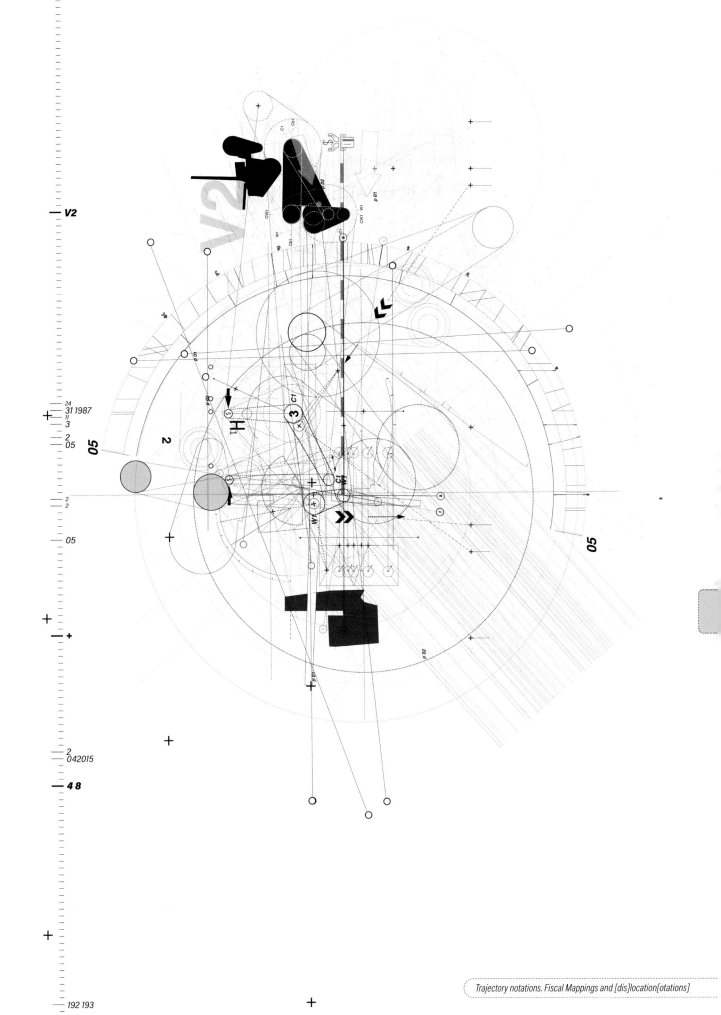

Trajectory notations. Fiscal Mappings and [dis]location[otations]

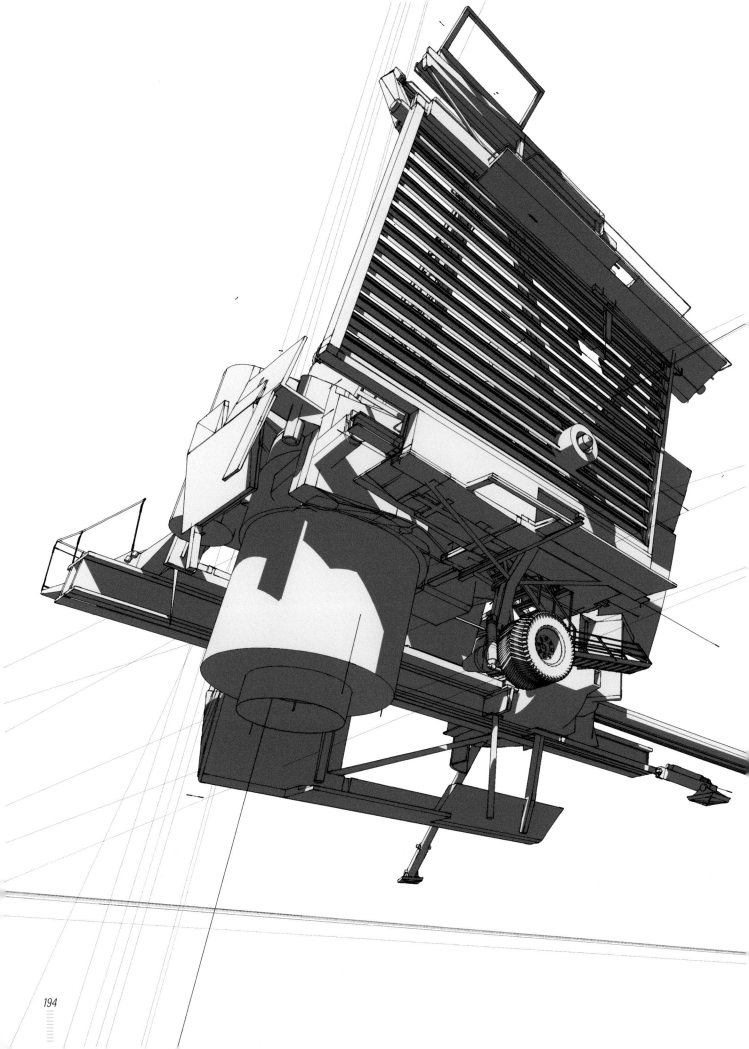

"These Taxonometric Reservoirs become repositories for the data generated through the action of drawing. They are the projected "goal" of these drawings ... a set of architectural conditions, or machines that are conglomerations of previously drawn components. They are replicators, with a touch of editor built in. They strive to become at once both autonomous emergent conditions whilst simultaneously being integrated components of the host drawing."

Fiscalanguages. Active skin component.

Calibrating Space
Nat Chard
Professor of Experimental Design, The Bartlett School of Architecture, London

Before photography, the scientific community drew on a range of artistic skills to accurately represent the matter under discussion. The medical world relied on figurative and visceral wax models of dissected bodies to reveal how our interiors worked and skillfully cast and painted wax moulages to identify the various symptoms of diseases on our skin. The care in these constructions was matched by the various methods of reproducing anatomical drawings. Zoology and botany had similarly refined methods of representation that were usurped by the figurative veracity of the photograph. The advent of photography offered a new and precise pictorial opportunity to register the circumstance of matter in place and time. This capacity made the new medium an ideal accomplice for both inquisitive scientists and, as a consequence of the medium's apparent veracity, those who had the expertise to manipulate the process to persuade others of phenomena on the margins of credibility, especially in spirit photography.

While photography provided a reliable method of reproducing what we could observe, it could also probe into territories at or beyond our margins of perception. Photographs taken through microscopes or telescopes made these territories more accessible, yet it was the scales of time, both of the instant and duration, that photography revealed in a completely new way. When Arthur Mason Worthington[25] was able to catch the splash of a drop of liquid with photography it revealed worlds he had not been able to access fully through his drawings (made from his afterimages following a flash). This extra perceptual capacity of the medium opened up the presence of a new temporal spatiality – one that we could not access directly but where we trusted the mode of representation enough to believe it to be a reality that we could form a composite with our regular perception.

In addition to accurately recording the literal and figurative, scientific photography was revealing new territories in other ways. In the process of making these spatio-temporal enquiries, the protagonists of this new frontier were also inventing new physical spaces to help tease out further realms. In Eadweard Muybridge's[26] photographic field at Palo Alto he constructed a calibrated space that appeared in the images as a background grid so as to register the positional difference in each sequential frame he captured of humans or animals in motion.

Étienne Jules Marey[27], an almost exact contemporary[28] to Muybridge, also calibrated the object with abstract registrations on key human limbs so that their positional difference would register in multiple exposure photographs. To make this reductive isolation work, he built spaces of darkness that would combine enough light on the subject's registration marks with sufficient darkness in which the subject's black outfit could disappear.

In Muybridge's operational field the space is made for the scope of the cameras, and it is calibrated for their understanding of the world. In Mareys' Collège de France[29] set-up the object to be examined is modified to reveal isolated and specific traits while the world within which it operates is erased, so that the occupants occupy an absence, again in a way that makes sense for the camera more than for us as observers.

In these constructions the precise abstraction of the subject and context along with a means of capturing an instant or high-speed stream of instances provides the scientist with a selective insight into the behavior of something in time. These events happen somewhere and have traits that are recognizable in particular terms to the scientist, but to the rest of us the degree of abstraction of these places and their objects might leave us wondering about their codes and terms of reference. These sites are charged with iconographic and spatial meaning that is so dense they need a temporal inspection that is beyond our own reach.

[25] Arthur Mason Worthington (1852–1916), British physicist studying fluid mechanics who at first drew and then photographed the splash of a drop revealed through a high-speed flash.

[26] Eadweard Muybridge (1830–1904), British photographer who undertook most of his work in the United States.

[27] Étienne-Jules Marey (1830–1904), French physiologist who developed a range of cameras specific to his lines of inquiry.

[28] Marey and Muybridge were born a month apart and died a week apart.

[29] Marey was a professor at the Collège de France, Paris.

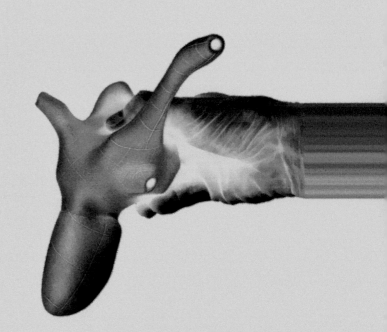

No wonder we find them so captivating as our imaginations feverishly ferment the plausibility of their formations. The graphical character and definition of these spaces and their occupants (animal or mechanical) is familiar from the scientific world of graphs and the conventions of engineering drawings. The reductive simplicity and clarity for those initiated with the code invests these objects and sites with the authority of rational thought and reason. Several generations of architects have cleverly borrowed the language of objective thought to substantiate all manner of inventions (both in terms of the way architecture is drawn and how it is physically present). Here we could include poetic allusion to the mechanical and industrial rationality in early modern and constructivist work, but for the purposes of this discussion the 1987 Pamphlet Architecture (No.12) publication *Building Machines* presented a combination of straightforward registration of buildings that are sited in abstracted fields of operation, annotated with keys alluding to mechanical and scientific manuals. The drawings of Neil Denari[30] and Wes Jones[31] are particularly rich and provocative in describing something in an apparently objective manner yet siting it in fields of calibration that suggest something more is going on. Some of Bryan Cantley's drawings fit into this practice – for instance when he uses the familiar and comforting order of a financial ledger (and by association the whole realm of generic registration) as the context to some if his buildings. What I would like to discuss here, however, is where his contexts wear the cloak of the language of reason but subvert its terms and take us unwittingly into unfamiliar worlds, in such a way that the initial appearance encourages us to trust him enough to follow him up to the point where, on closer inspection, we are lost in an unfamiliar and sometimes unsettling territory. The context that seemed to make sense of his architecture has sneakily turned the whole conversation.

Marey and Muybridge built inquisitive fields, mostly to study the physiology of humans and other animals.

> "The graphical character and definition of these spaces and their occupants (animal or mechanical) is familiar from the scientific world of graphs and the conventions of engineering drawings."

Since then many other types of laboratory have been built with abstract calibrated subjects and contexts, often to simulate conditions that are hard to access without pre-testing. Examples would include many of the set-ups for the Apollo space program, car crash test laboratories, wind tunnels, and ship hull testing tanks. Typically, in these places there are parallel occupancies – control and observational perches for humans but mainly for other sorts of bodies such as cars, 'planes' or boats. The outside of the buildings that house these events are often unsettling. Although there are traces of human occupation, these are secondary to the larger but mysterious internal program. I am thinking here of buildings such as Albert Kahn's[32] 1937 test cells for the United Aircraft Corporation to test their Pratt and Whitney engines (East Hartford, Connecticut) where a variety of door sizes, an access ladder for the roof and some drainpipes are the only familiar clues to the content within, other than the subdivision of the massive cells. Conversely the 1948 16-foot high-speed wind tunnel at the NACA's Moffat Field, California reveals all its bowels yet remains almost entirely mysterious about what is going on inside.

In many of Bryan Cantley's drawings the buildings follow this pattern. There are very few sections, so we have to imagine their interiors. There are sometimes hints to human occupation but mostly suggestions of something other. The logic of this otherness is reminiscent of the wind tunnel or the test cells, or perhaps the crank case or gear housing of a 1950s motorbike yet with a (mysterious) logic that we have not yet deciphered. The geometric origin of this logic is normally registered to tease us further, but without explanation.

I first came across Cantley's work in San Francisco MOCA, where some of his models are part of the permanent collection. These models rehearse many of the formal traits of his later work – large volumes that appear specific to a hidden interior and made out of individually simple forms that are composed to create the enigmas discussed earlier, an apparent formal transparency of a skin shrink wrapping something strange inside. This assembly is qualified by a series of more articulate pieces on the surface that suggest that practical things are taking place inside the building that need contact with the outside or need room beyond the logic of the enclosure. In the models these are typically highly programmatic elements taken from plastic construction kits, and this can be seen again in his more recent Ozonic Bladder Anomaly model. These accomplice accretions animate the simpler volumes suggesting greater complexities and elaborate operations taking place inside. In the computer rendering of the Cosmo project such additional pieces are bespoke to the design and give a more measured range of scales to further provoke our imagination. While the form of these buildings might recall some enigmatic research institutes, their graphical notation on their skins learns from the bodies under inspection within them – the registrations placed on cars to identify the progression of their deformation in a crash; the black and white marks (for black and white film) on space rockets to help identify their movements in the air; the marks on Marey's bodies; the tufts of wool on the wind tunnel test models – so that Cantley's buildings both conceal their content but present themselves as if they expect to be inspected. Sometimes this graphical identification characterizes the whole body of the building (as in the Fiducial Shifters or the Palimpsestuous Relationships while in others the marks are highly selective, like Marey's registrations but also recalling the registration pins that the Italian Sculptor Antonio Canova (1757–1822) used on his plaster models to identify critical surfaces or the acutely judged marks made by the British painter Euan Uglow (1932–2000) on both his subjects and their context (in both the paintings and his studio walls). We see these sorts of marks on the Ozone Metric Anomaly and the model for the Syntaxonome and Syntaxomometric Drawings.

Cantley's calibrated architectural bodies then sit in calibrated space. The world has been taken away, rather in the way that the 'planes sit in the wind tunnel or the cars in the crash test laboratory, with everything other than the selected terms of the context erased. Except where the context provides an intimate host for his buildings (such as the Palimpsestuous Relationships) we are not given a figurative register of the place. Instead, we see the project in a calibrated field where the calibrations appear synonymous with those on the buildings (again, in the same way the marks on the crash test cars register with those within the space of the laboratory and its equipment). These are not pictorial worlds, where we might, for instance, see material or formal resonances between the architecture and where it sits. Neither, in most cases, is it a cartographic world, with situating grids or contours. Instead, it is a world that discusses sensibilities outside our normal reach, coded and framed in a way that requires another level or form of access – in the way that Marey or Muybridge could divine physiological attributes with their cameras that we could not perceive normally.

Just in the way that the crash test laboratory ignores the pictorial aspects that surround our cars and sees the world in terms of its attributes for accidents, the context for Cantley's architecture is also a realm beyond our normal perception. On first inspection his calibrations appear to make sense, in the way we are familiar with in the scientific laboratories. The codes appear familiar and comfortingly explanatory. Yet when we look closer they are quite the opposite. If we look at his Authorship Devices there is a familiar locational grid at a slight angle to the page. To one side there are setting-out registrations on another axis, yet their connecting lines stop before they reach the item they qualify. If we try to find a corresponding axis to qualify one of these setting out points, the various setting-out lines in other directions live by different rules and terms. If we were reading a map it would be like having an X coordinate, perhaps a sample of time and a line of poetry to locate ourselves. We are led halfway across the abyss and then left to our own imaginative devices. In another drawing in the series what appear as setting out lines become enmeshed with those that would normally connect a key with its component to make a territory where there is an appearance of making sense but the means of making that sense is beyond our reach.

"... it is a world that discusses sensibilities outside our normal reach, coded and framed in a way that requires another level or form of access ..."

The plan of the UBRO complex locates the parts of the building with what appears to be a more conventional pairing of axes, yet these are of such density and interwoven with additional axes to the extent that makes them hard to decipher. When we look closer these lines qualify a projection that sits over the plan but intersects with registrations for the plan, like the ghosts in spirit photography where the camera can detect the pictorial form of an invisible haunting. If we return to the Fiducial Shifter, a stand-alone orphan on sit-almost-anywhere legs, the setting out, keys, and annotation conforms to familiar norms, even if these are not consummated with values. There is even a typographic setting out drawing for the number two that is painted on the side of the Shifter. The whole ensemble of registration and object is framed by a background figure that sits so innocently in cream behind the Shifter. It is at this point that we realize the rug has been pulled, for its perimeter suggests a performance beyond graphical framing. Its figure might at first sight be read literally, perhaps as a neighboring firewall, as part of its base aligns with the feet of the Shifter to suggest a ground line, but this location of ground is not confirmed anywhere else. If we flip the figure to ground – as a void in which the Shifter might sit – this does not work either, for parts of the device sit beyond its limits. To the right of this cream figure is a large arrow with a twisted vector. Again, the recognition of a familiar graphical device is at first legible, yet the arrow's infill is a multitude of vectors, reminiscent of the traces in a bubble chamber.

How the cream figure and the arrow qualify the space of the shifter and its calibrations is not in the realm of the conventional registration between building and context, just as the crash test laboratory is not how we normally understand a street, of how Marey or Muybridge's photographic fields pictorially relate to the context in which the activities they record typically take place. Bryan Cantley's drawings are akin to the plates that emerge from the photographic and film cameras from these laboratories. His buildings and their context are calibrated with registrations that might only make sense through a similar sort of registration from a camera that is sensitive to spatialities outside of our normal grasp. His drawings are not so much propositional as they are registrations of circumstances and sensibilities we have already missed.

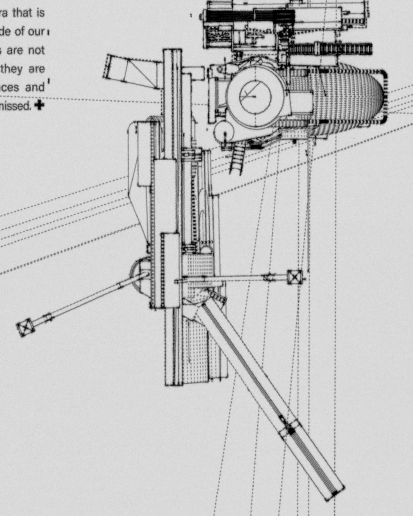

+ Towards a s[Y/N]thetic Reality

Peter J Baldwin + Bryan Cantley

Senior Lecturer in Architecture, University of Lincoln, UK

Professor of Design Theory, CSUF

The past 60 years have seen a period of technological advancement previously unparalleled in human history. The invention of the silicon microchip in the late 1950s and the subsequent development of the personal computer (as we know it today) in the early 1970s sparked a cultural revolution, fundamentally changing our relationship with technology and its presence in our daily lives, altering not just the way we occupy our time but the very environments we inhabit.

In the 30 or so years since Architecture first took its digital turn (Carpo, 2013),[33] what was once a source of inspiration and perhaps fascination has become as synonymous with architectural design as the Rotring pens, and Mayline drawing boards that the use of CAD software has for the most part replaced. With the emergence of ever more sophisticated digital tooling we, as designers, are increasingly distanced from the influences of materiality, tactility, and atmosphere, that are inherently part of the of the construction and behavior of an analogue model or drawing. If the medium is indeed the message (McLuhan, 1967)[34] then it is inescapable that a change in the media of production would fundamentally alter not only the architecture produced, but also the way that architecture is occupied and understood. As the virtual environment becomes ever more pervasive and immersive and our detachment from the physical grows, it brings with it, a subtle yet critical change of inflection, a shift of intent from the creation of atmosphere to an intention to create a representation of spatiality.

[33] M. Carpo (ed.), *The Digital Turn in Architecture: 1992–2012* (New York: Wiley, 2013).

[34] M. McLuhan, "This is Marshall McLuhan: The Medium is the Message," New York, NBC.

This essay explores the rise of simulation within the architectural design project as our primary means of communication, speculating on where our current trajectory may lead before offering an alternative premise, rooted in the notion that the architectural design process need not be separate(d) from the architecture that it produces, extrapolating this idea to its ultimate conclusion the inhabitable drawing.

Generative Architectural Notations

"Architects do not make buildings, they make a range of different types of representation that may be used in the construction of buildings, or they may be used in a number of other ways to create a wide variety of spatial possibilities" (Clear, 2013).[35]

[35] N. Clear, "Drawing Time," in N. Spiller, (ed.) "Drawing Architecture", *Architectural Design* 255 (2013), pp. 70–9.

Drawing has long held a central place within the practice of architecture, indeed both Robin Evans and Nic Clear both make compelling arguments that the drawing is the primary (perhaps only) output of the architectural design process (ignoring for a moment the emergence of new hybrid design build agencies, etc.). Yet however persuasive these arguments are they only tell half the story, drawing is not only a method of communication, a set of instructions for construction or assembly; it is the process by or through which we are able to gain a deeper understanding of the many, often homogenous influences and factors which impact the design proposal.

In this way drawing has, traditionally, been understood as a speculative arena within which observations, inspirations, and intuitions can meet and interact, and manifest (Spiller, 2013).[36] Through this generative graphical process, ideas and hypotheses can be developed, tested and countered. The act(ion) of Drawing allows for criticality and reflection rather than endless speculative cogitation.

> *"Through [a] generative graphical process, ideas and hypotheses can be developed, tested and countered. The act(ion) of Drawing allows for criticality and reflection rather than endless speculative cogitation."*

[36] N. Spiller (ed.). "Drawing Architecture", *Architectural Design* 255 (London: John Wiley & Sons, 2013).

The dualistic nature of self-critique requires that the Architect fulfills two parallel roles:

Draw-er:

The Drawer, the person generating the drawn information, through a process of annotation and denotation. This creative act is often subjective and often instinctual.

Read-or:

The Read-or (a portmanteau of Reader and Author, inspired by Roland Barthes' seminal text[37] which transfers the creation of the unity of meaning of any given text to the reader) who reviews and tests the information seeking to detect faults in the logic of the design proposal through repeated re-readings of the project from a metaphorical critical distance.

[37] A reference to "The Death of the Author", in R. Barthes and S. Heath, *Image Music Text* (New York: Hill and Wang, 1977).

With the rise of the rendered image however there has been a compression of critical distance (Jamieson, 1997).[38] This distance rather than a physical space (in his conceptualization) is a position of cerebral occupancy in which information gathered from various media sources is processed and where serendipitous interactions occur, through which we gain a deeper understanding, by comparing, contrasting, and cross referencing new information against our prior knowledge, experience, and understanding, an essential imperative within the design process. The effect of the image, however, is to trick us into assuming we have engaged, that we have achieved instantaneous understanding.

[38] F. Jameson, *Postmodernism, or, the Cultural Logic of Late Capitalism* (Durham, NC: Duke University Press, 1991).

Toward a s[y/n]thetic media

> "The Media represents world that is more real than reality that we can experience. People lose the ability to distinguish between reality and fantasy. They also begin to engage with the fantasy without realizing what it really is. They seek happiness and fulfilment through the simulacra of reality and avoid the contact/interaction with the real world" (Baudrillard, 1994).[39]

[39] J. Baudrillard, *Simulacra and Simulation*, trans. S.F. Glaser (Ann Arbor: University of Michigan Press, 1994).

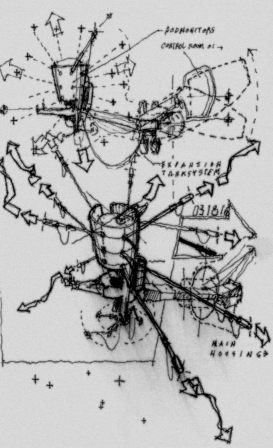

Whilst on the surface the argument for drawing vs image might appear to be semantic, the alteration of intent fundamentally alters the purpose and role of visual information in the design process. Rendered as an image, the drawing becomes an exercise in illustration rather than a tool and a process for understanding architectural opportunity and how it might be brought into being.

Just as the proliferation of the photographic image fundamentally changed our relationship with Architecture and its representation (buildings began to be designed to look good in photographs), the emergence of the rendering as the primary means of dissemination of an architectural possibility to a public audience has altered architectural design thinking. There has been a marked cultural shift within the design studio toward a dominance of the digital image (most often shown on screen) as the sole means of developing an architectural proposal. The inevitable consequence of this is that a building must look 'worthy' in/as a rendering. This feeds back into the design process – buildings are now designed to look good in renderings. Tragically buildings generated in this manner often fail to manifest the perfect image they can so readily project in the sublime simulacrum of the virtual. One need only scroll through Pinterest or Instagram to witness the saturation of the architectural image on these platforms, countless images, often hyper realistic until a closer inspection reveals structural inadequacies, impossible geometries, and spatial sequencing errors.

Yet even this is only the tip of the iceberg, thanks to Virtual Reality, these simulated architectures are no longer confined to two Dimensions, the visual has begun to extend into the realm of deep fakery. Buildings are presented as immersive fictions, preferable (and far more perfect) than the reality, a powerful device for selling, but a falsehood, unburdened by the passage of time, the overlay of infrastructure, always a perpetual perfect summer's day, occupied by perfectly photogenic people, simulations that are "practically perfect in every way" (Poppins, 1910).[40]

[40] M. Poppins, "Measuring Up," Conversation with Banks Children, 27 August 1910.

> "Isn't it all 'fake'? Or might it be argued that 'theoretical' architecture is fake, while the real is 'real'?" (Gumby, 1974).[41]

[41] R.J. Gumby, "Deepfakes," RIBA Annual Lectures, Portland Place, London, 3 September 1974.

Toward a synthetic medium

As social media[42] increasingly becomes our social medium[43] and our emersion within an augmented reality becomes increasingly complete, will we begin to seek out, to construct or to have constructed a synthetic reality which sites our individual world view?

[42] A means of mass communication.

[43] The intervening substance through which sensory impressions are conveyed or physical forces are transmitted.

> "It is the world that I have pulled over your eyes to blind you from the truth" (Le Corbusier, 1947).[44]

Perhaps this is architectures final conceit? That our personal environment, will be a series of entirely constructed, augmented and occupiable renderings of a bespoke reality, a revisionist's fantasy filtered through rose tinted spectacles in which historicism replaces history, and perception surpasses truth; much like Wash-35, described in Philip K. Dick's "Now Wait for Last Year" (in which Virgil Ackerman, a 300-year-old gazillionaire reconstructs an 'à la mode retro' of his childhood home Washington City in 1935).[45]

[44] Le Corbusier, "Shallow Realities," International Lectures, Architectural Association, London, 18 December 1947.

[45] P.K. Dick, *Now Wait for Last Year* (New York: Doubleday, 1966).

Will we find ourselves unable to function in the desert of the real? Perhaps a more perverse fate awaits? Unable (or unwilling) to distinguish the real from the simulacrum in which we find ourselves caught, trapped between the fear of consequence and the desire of a life unburdened, unable to unplug, perhaps fearful that the act of disconnection is itself only a simulation.

Will we ever stop and ask who is constructing this simulacrum? We are told that information is tracked and monitored for our safety, our privacy and protection, yet we never question who, if anyone polices this, and indeed who polices them: *"Quis custodiet ipsos custodes?"* (Juvenal, 1992).[46]

For all of the obvious danger of this condition, we are complicit, willingly embracing the warmth of vindication that a homogenous world view brings, we no longer have to think, to be critical, we are freed from the heavy burden of cogitation, coddled in our 'perfect world' a shallow reality sustained by a thickening crust of data, the soma of our times.

[46] Juvenal, *The Satires*, trans. N. Rudd (Oxford: Oxford University Press, 1992).

> "When you control the mail, you control INFORMATION!" (Newman, 1997).[47]

[47] Seinfeld, (1997) [DVD] Series 9, Part part 5 (New York: NBC, 1997).

We no longer care if our 'perfect world' aligns with anyone else's. What was once a community-based condition, is now singular, a voice of one. That voice used to be part of a chorus, even if it was occasionally out of tune. This begs the question, can our bespoke realities sync with those of others?

> "There is no 'you/u' in SoC[i]al Med>I<[a/um], just an 'I' and 'me' …>> er <<[U]m?" (Quimby, 1994).[48]

[48] J. Quimby, "Vote Quimby," Springfield, 15 May 1994.

> "He that keeps nor crust nor [simula]crum[B], weary of all shall want some" (Shakespeare, 1606).[49]

[49] W. Shakespeare, *King Lear* (1606) London: n.s.

[IN]habitable drawing:

If a drawing is CONstructed, and there is no one around to read it …

In 2005, Marcos Novak produced a seminal essay titled "Trans Terra Form: Liquid Architectures and the Loss of Inscription"[50] within which he describes the current trend within the arts towards an exchange between otherwise binary conditions. Architecture, music, and cinema trade their dominant characteristic through a coincidence of opposites, architecture, noted as being "the most solid of arts" becomes liquid and so on. Coining the term 'Intermediums' – Novak explores the resulting notion that a fluid architecture would no longer be a singular condition, but one that could be reconfigured in response to user/occupier needs and demands.

[50] M. Novak, "Trans Terra Form: Liquid Architectures and the Loss of Inscription," http://h2o-arquitectura.blogspot.com/2005/12/trans-terra-form-liquid-architectures.html.

Though he does not address it in his original paper, in our current cookie driven virtual environment, it is intriguing to consider the possibility that these responses may be prompted by prior preferences and interactions, or by a gestalt data profile of the two.

Perhaps the next step in this line of thinking is an inversion? Might it be reasonable to suggest that these internal structures might be influenced by external factors and influences?

> *"…the inhabitable drawing conceptualizes Architecture as the ultimate social medi[a/um], no longer confined to the physical … and proposes a new synthetic reality, in which the drawing becomes an occupiable environment."*

This sounds decidedly familiar and might be seen as analogous to the interplay between internal and external influences as well as the personal preferences that inform the dialogue between states of Draw-er and Read-or within the architectural design process.

The Inhabitable Drawing [I.D.] is an experimental graphic typology, encountered in varying forms within this book which explores (and it might be argued exploits) this tangential line of thought, positing that the drawing, once a preface to the built world might now become its interface, a way of negotiating, navigating, and engaging with each other's synthetic realities.

Both literal and figurative, the inhabitable drawing conceptualizes Architecture as the ultimate social medi[a/um], no longer confined to the physical, exploits the potential of virtual and augmented reality technology, and proposes a new synthetic reality, in which the drawing becomes an occupiable environment.

Many of the projects that deploy this type of drawing do not imagine that the occupant of the Inhabitable Drawing is human, for example the Syntaxonomes self-generating drawings are occupied by the architecture that they serve to generate, Cosmo's mappings are infected by the viral phages themselves, and the Tree Hugger's mappings are generated by its own zone of occupancy.

This begs the question; must the drawing be physical to be inhabitable? The answer is assuredly not, perhaps the question is if the drawing is not real, then how might it be inhabited? DeLanda[51] might suggest that this is a question of Actualization. We might consider his definition of the Virtual; real but not actual this then is a matter of the source of the data; external source of data vs. an internal set of data responses.

[51] M. DeLanda, *Assemblage Theory* (Edinburgh: Edinburgh University Press, 2016).

This new condition transforms from an Intermedia to an Entermedia, as the proposition rests on the viability and experiential anomalies found within VR – a medium that requires sensory, if not spatial, immersion. Imagine being, according to your physical and visual receptors and recorders, fully absorbed into an experimental drawing ...

The I.D. offers a new territory and agency for architectural intervention. Much like Carroll's Wonderland in which he describes a series of totems that when activated (in this case eaten or drunk) performed transformative functions,

altering the scale, context, and orientation of the occupant or the environment (we are never quite certain which). 'Eat Me' and 'Drink Me' are the documented instructions, however the labels do not offer any clarity as to what the outcome of the consumption might be.

'Draw Me' might be understood as the function of interface, the sync-ing of the I.D with a contextual, environmental trigger or cookie, prompting a recalibration and reconfiguration in response to an external stimulus.

This response is intended as a trigger, a prompt for renewed criticality. Much like Alice as she chases the white rabbit, the occupier is forced to engage with new or alternative perspectives, both literally and metaphorically, to reorientate themselves relative to the current mode of the drawing.

To say that the I.D. is simply an interactive drawing would be an awkward reduction; it would imply that the viewer / occupier could arrange compositional elements at will via a set of commands or controls. The Draw Me takes these many levels deeper – it is not so much a map as it is an immersive environment with never-repeatable outcomes.

This proposal shifts the notion of authorship, proposing that the Intermedia and the Entermedia have a reciprocal and dynamic correspondence. We may choose how we respond to the stimuli, but no longer can we deny their existence ...

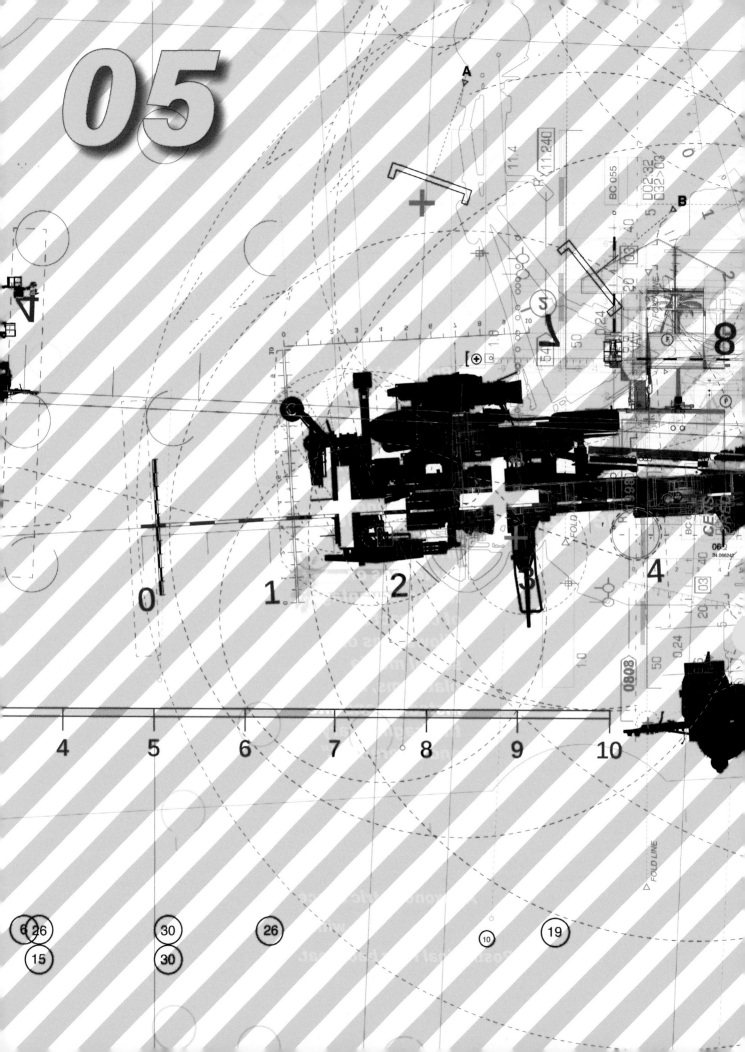

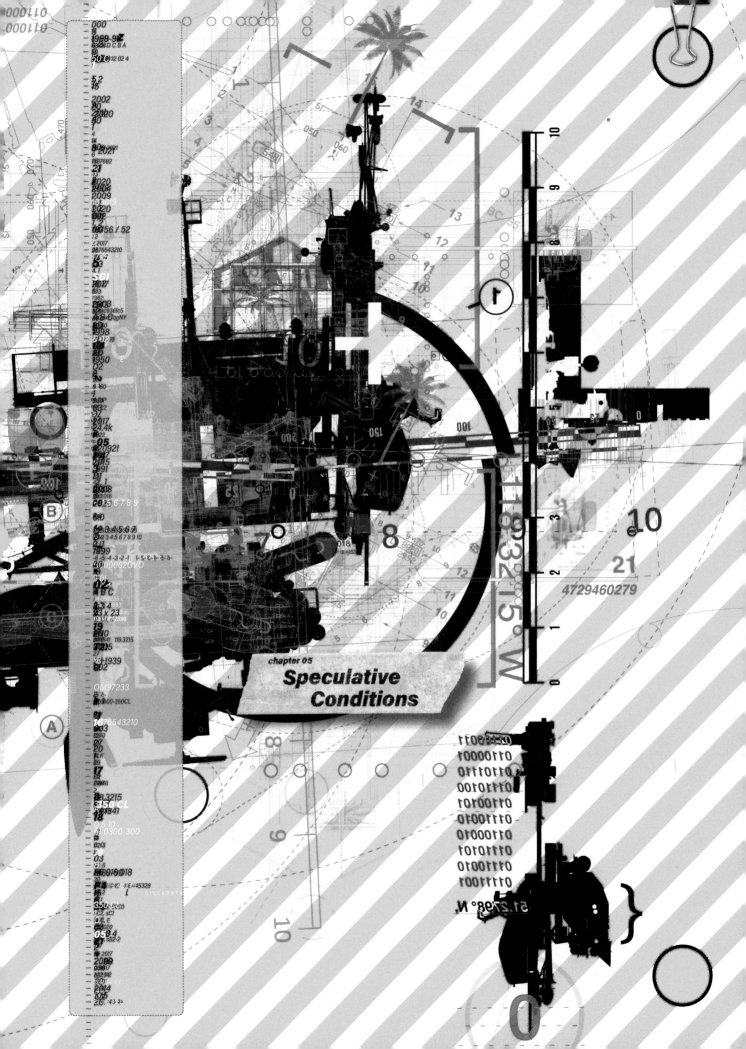

chapter 05
Speculative Conditions

S(y/n)taxo[G]nome + (taxon objects)

An architecture that informs/constructs its satellite dialogue as well as its synthetic context[s]. The Syntaxonome occupies the space/state between the entity and its construction[s].

Con-text(ual maneuvers in the dark)

"And so art is everywhere, since artifice is at the very heart of reality. And so art is dead, not only because its critical transcendence is gone, but because reality itself, entirely impregnated by an aesthetic which is inseparable from its own structure, has been confused with its own image ..." (Baudrillard, 1983).[1]

[1] J. Baudrillard, *Simulations* (Semiotext(e)/Cambridge, MA: MIT Press, 1983).

Baudrillard proposed that the dominance of electronic media and digital technologies would have a profound effect on language and meaning. Detaching subject from object, the constant stream of information, would eventually render the division between appearance and reality indiscernible.

"The single biggest problem in communication is the illusion that it has taken place ..." (Whyte, 1950).[2]

[2] W.H. Whyte, "Is Anybody Listening?" *Fortune Magazine* (New York, 1950), p. 74.

The consequential reduction/compression of social and political issues and spaces is at a critical juncture. It follows that architecture must address not only

the phenomena of the disappearance

itself, but

medi(a/um) of obfuscation

as well.

Communication manifesto[pographies]

Historical (de)Relic(te)s

The project is developed from two parallel ideas, the communique housing and a drawing apparatus. A transcription device based on pseudo-political ramifications of the inner/inter office communication[s], combined with architectural tools of expression/documentation.

There is, historically at least, an [anti]-social hierarchy that exists within the office environment [architectural and other] that is illustrated perfectly from the in[t]ner office memo (pr/e/mail), passed around, often in plain view through the office mail run (those were the days – for younger readers there once existed in larger companies and offices an internal postal service, that distributed both external and internal communications in paper copy), subordinates were often aware of, yet explicitly excluded from, the information in these secretive documents, creating and reinforcing the void within extreme office tiered politics.

These 'clandestine' documents carried a social sting, tangibly manifesting their exclusivity through the graphic demarcations; somewhat akin to the warning stripes of the Vespidae or OSHA[zard striping] standards. 'No step' is replaced by 'no read'.

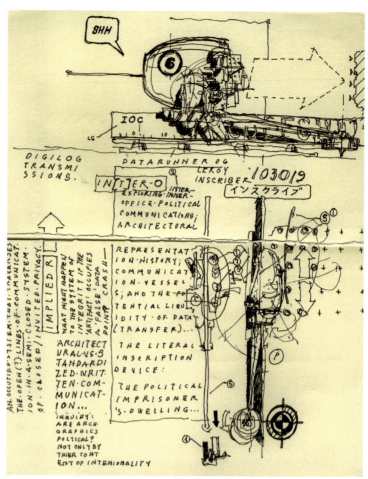

DATArunner sketch

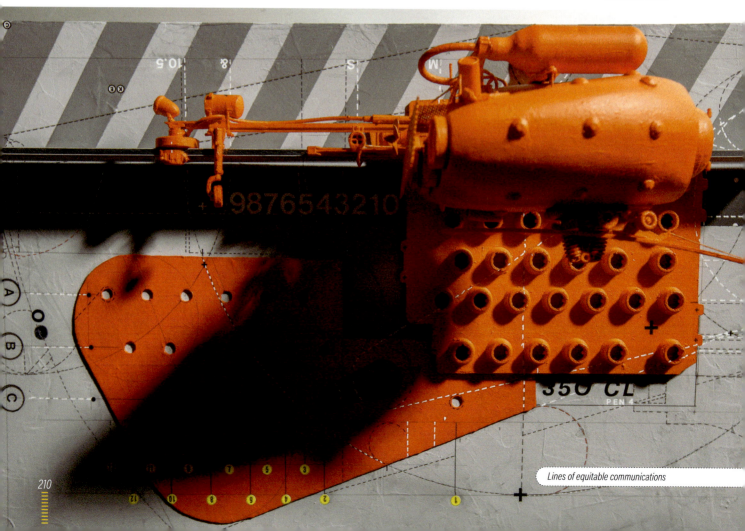

Lines of equitable communications

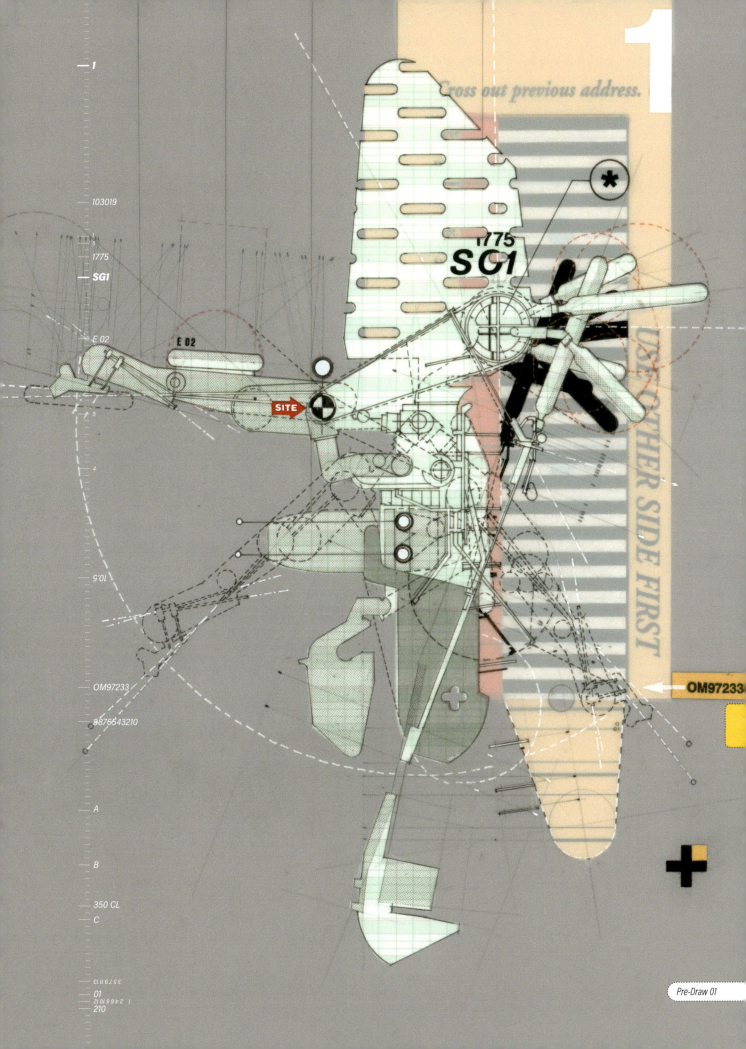

Pro[b]ject

The project began through an exploration of the relationships and behavioral codes that reside in the artifact, in the delivery mechanism, and the connotations of [its] graphic commun[e]ications. This became an opportunity to see if these residual capacities might fold back onto the dimensional reality of the mechanism, potentially breaching unknown territories ...

Receiving, processing, and propagating lines of communication ...
lines in the sand ...
party lines ...

> Polit[e]ical projectioning. If a tree falls in the proverbial woods, and no one [person] is around to hear it, can the silent reverberation/percussion be absorbed back into the tree/forest, altering it somehow? If the categorized lines of communication are immediately flattened, could it imply a restructuring of the social order?

The project asks the question: *"If a system could approach transparency in the process of its construction, then [could/would] that system be without an implied/immediate hierarchy?"*

The underlying premise being that this transparency would allow the potential for all the levels and relationships within a system to be known. Allowing for an understanding their interactions before a hierarchy is imposed. Such is the nature of the Syntaxonome. We might label it as an equalizer ... It becomes a curious circumstance, possessing the ability to demarcate and eradicate order simultaneously;
It becomes a mechanism of epigenetic reciprocity.

Rarely has the equalization of established hierarchical systems been under such interrogation. If the Syntaxonome is a machine for illuminating the internal or constituent parts [or DNA] and external/formal conversations that constitute a unified structure, then the implication might be that [an/the] architect has the same [opportunity/responsibility].

> "There are certainly correlations and intimations at the analogy of the auth-or, the read-or, and the observ-or co-existing, if not being parts of the same whole"
> (Terwilliger, 1999).[3]
> R. Terwilliger, "Animations and Imitations", Inaugural Lecture, Springfield University, 31 October 1999.

A Taxonometric dance with a Postliminal Fuzz backbeat.

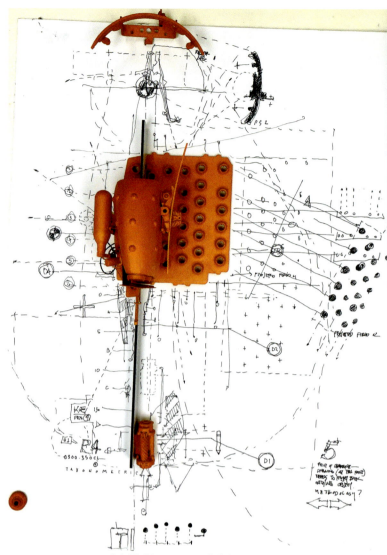

Point[s] of departure – organic dialogue between medium[s]

Communication breakdown. Analog data sets

Core extrusions and Data-Architectures

OOObject

An architecture that informs/constructs a satellite dialogue and its synthetic context[s], the Syntaxonome occupies the space/state between the entity and its construction[s], presented as a syllepsis or perhaps a syllepsis/n't.

Early graphic prototypes of the Syntaxonome explored the idea of a flattening of the partisan organizational structure through an uncensored broadcast of a[o]pposite project data. The syntax of its taxonomy [the structure of an internal grammar] is observed with reference to the orthographic projection system. The premise of the project is to explore the possibility of an architecture that can project its own graphic notation/annotation system, at the time of its construction, incorporating this graphic data as a part the compositional strategy.

The Taxonometric Reservoirs within this project become repositories of notational data generated through the action of drawing, a speculative projection of assumptions. These are the [dr]a[w]mbitions of the project and its residual graphic output: to generate a set of architectural conditions/machines/configurations and harvested conglomerations of previously drawn components. These are replicators, with a touch of self-editor. For the purpose of this project, this circumstance, the entirety of the dimensioned form [object and base, impregnation media and receptacle] are considered to be the Reservoir. This is an opportunity to bridge the situational media[s] that are traditionally found in the architectural project.

These are one half of the equation; they are the two[and-a-half]Dimensional repositories that allow for, receive, and generate not[at]ional data from a given architectural entity (which forms the other half of the equation). They are projections of the 'call.' ... The objective is to reproject [creating a semi-infinite feedback loop] the graphic knowledge back onto the 3D form, generating a system of hosts/parasites that will [eventually] result in the original condition becoming informed/deformed by its own genomic datasets. Input and output are increasingly blurred, triggered by a systemic oscillation between broadcast and reception.

The Syntaxonome becomes archetyp(ic/al) rather than a singular formal event.

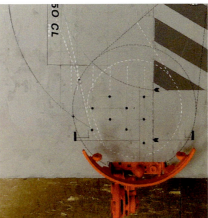

Receptor membrane/percussive sensor *Reciprocity indicators* *[No]menclature buildouts*

This project occupies a paradoxical condition that springs from the media logics built into this new typology. The formal presentation of the Syntaxonome, the 3D model and the 2D drawings, are both hot media. They engage singular senses and demand little [physical] interaction with the read-or/observ-or. The systemic relationships of media-to-media are, however, cold in that they require greater interaction with each other. This is a uniQ(UE) condition of the architectural representational world, where the two main typologies of communication are required to form a coactive, corequisite, and co-dependent relationship.

Meta object-zones emerge input, output, stay put. A bit of Lilliput. Denotated planes, detonated.

Elevational Aspirations. Signal 01

CONclusion

The Syntaxonome could be considered a reflection of 'real-IS[n't]m', where the conscious and subconscious experience the representation of the artifact/fiction and its [external] representation , simultaneously ... the syllepsis/n't.

The project exists in both one-way and reciprocal states. Simultaneously hot and cold. This project, is a phase-hopper, a trimmer that constantly denotes its current period by referring to its other phase.

Whilst one might argue that any given architectural project must refer to its media [models and drawings] in order to be understood as a whole, this is unusual in that its mode of reference constantly switches between host and parasite and back again, neither component is thought to be its own [unabridged] media.

Sesquizygotically chimerical: the whole is constructed of the two [un]related mediums, each of which shares the majority of the others DNA, yet each is validated autonomously. This is an example of OOOscillative causality. The residues are exclusive in the sense that each removes the other from the initial broadcast, though this removal is determined from the transition from model > drawing. The emergence of the drawing, as a residue of the model, establishes a hidden condition of the model, rendering it a cloaked situation ... ✚

Analog notes, scribbles, scripts and diagrams. "Drawdel (Mayne, T) and Phygital (Smout Allen)" projection sketches. Using the Taxonometric Object as a drawing device, trying to inhabit the space between the drawing and the artifact. Chicken or egg? Paper or plastic? Pornotation[s]?

Semantic readers/syntax scanners

Line[r] Notes:
Data runner [2020]. Get in line. Lines of communication/political lines.

Sequence distributions, phrasing complexities, and a catalogue of [N]Options.

Destruction of universal flatness.
Surface scanning.
Hierarchy-tamping.

Annotated anointings. Anointed annotations?

No postage necessary if
mailed in the United States.
co-Axial Terminus Receiver.

Analog inefficiency and imprecision in all its glory.

Playing the numbers. Marching orders. Communication breakdown. Transmission repair. 8675309.

Grounding. Data Runner. Composed of: expressing … exploiting … feeding [off of] … existing [within] … the tools, methods, and residues of disciplinary-specific and politically motivated lines of communication. Looking for clues at the scene of the crime. Investigation of the object as a site/sight for investigative/speculative drawing sequences.

ß

[N]Au[T]obiographically metaphoric enshroudment?

Thinking about methods of graphic communication and the vehicles that love them. Open LINES of communication with specific systems of dissemination. Drawings making drawings … drawings making models … models making drawings … models making models … who is making the architecture [and where is it located?]

The differentiation between architectural objects and architectural models – the subject of a line of communication and its vehicle of delivery.

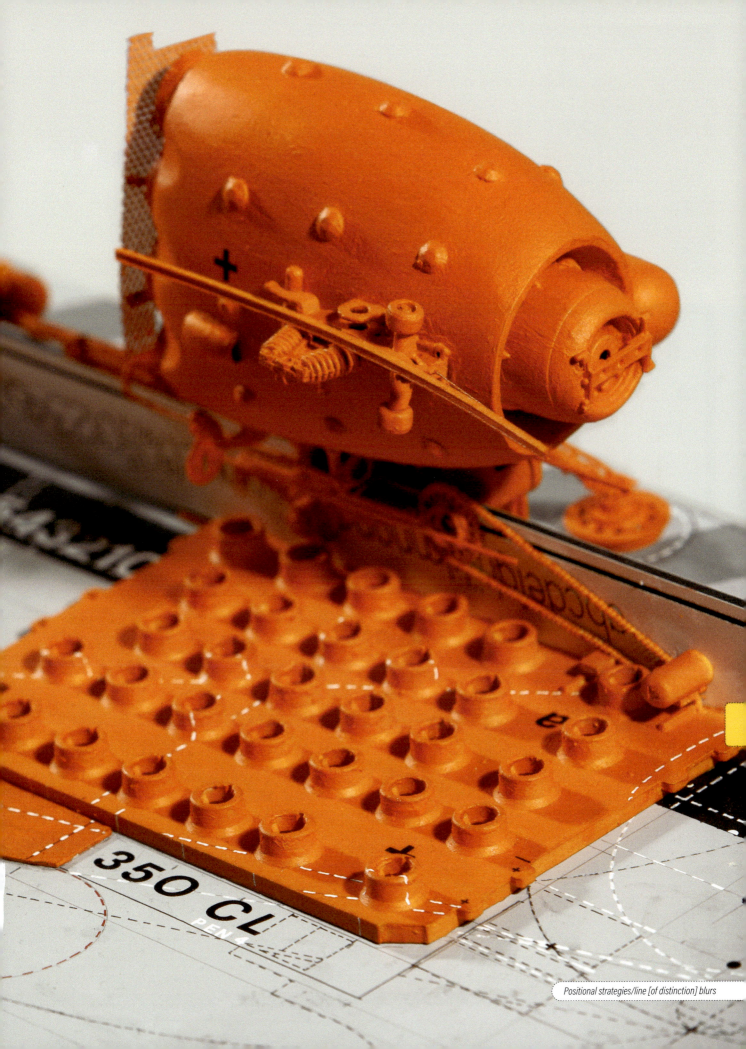

Positional strategies/line [of distinction] blurs

Self-reflexive aerials

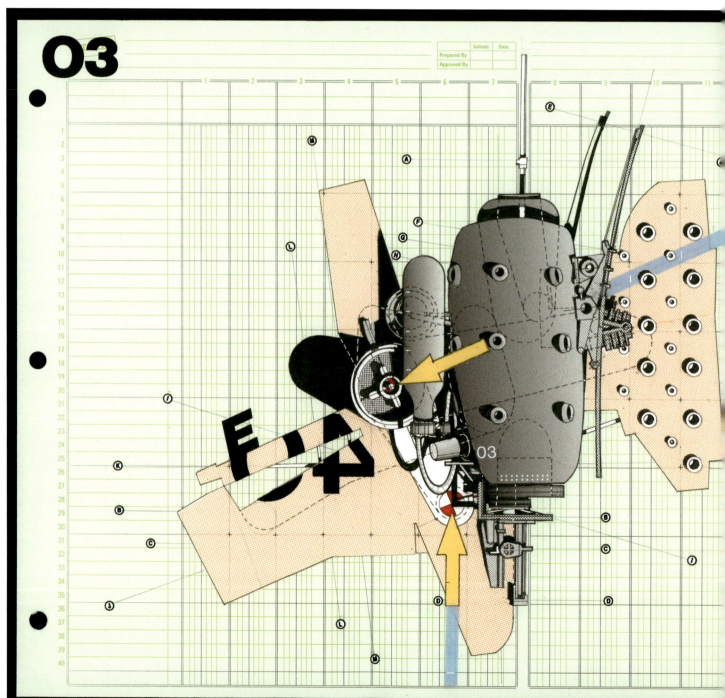

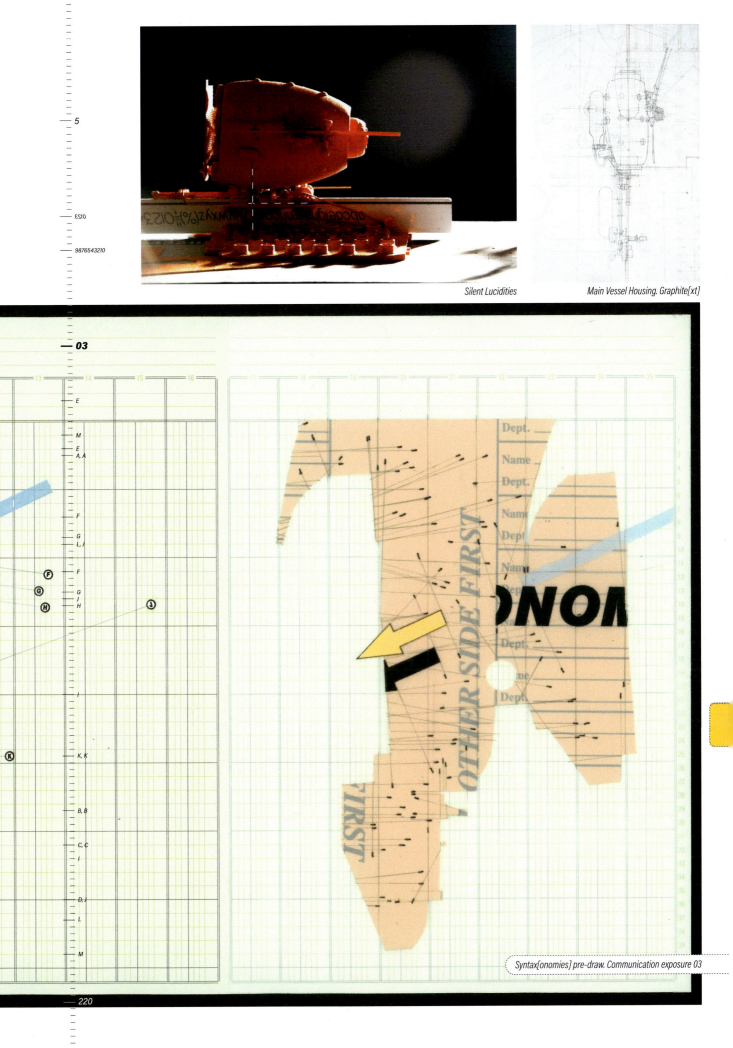

Silent Lucidities *Main Vessel Housing. Graphite[xt]*

Syntax[onomies] pre-draw. Communication exposure 03

Transmission diagramming. Projection m/node

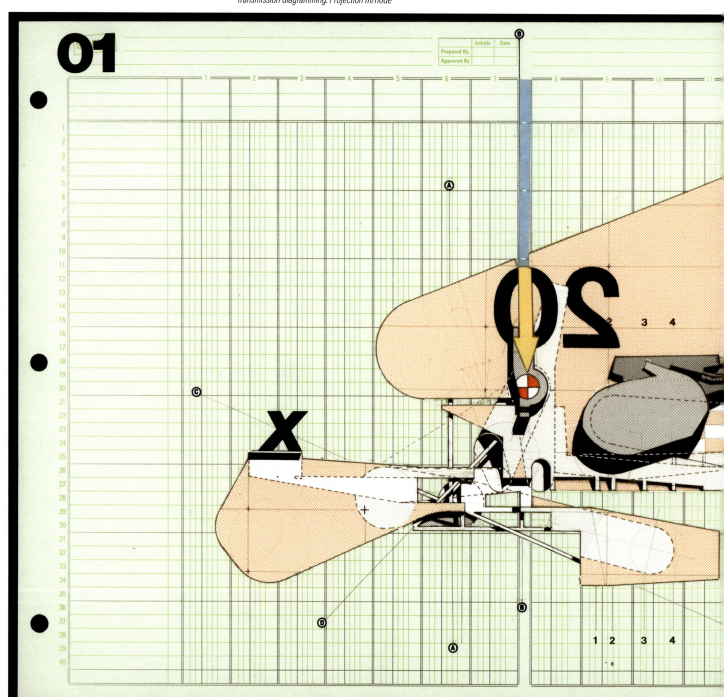

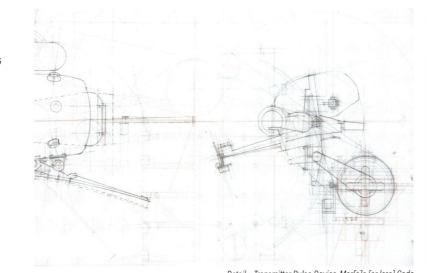

Detail – Transmitter Pulse Device. Mor[s]e [or less] Code

Pre-Draw 07

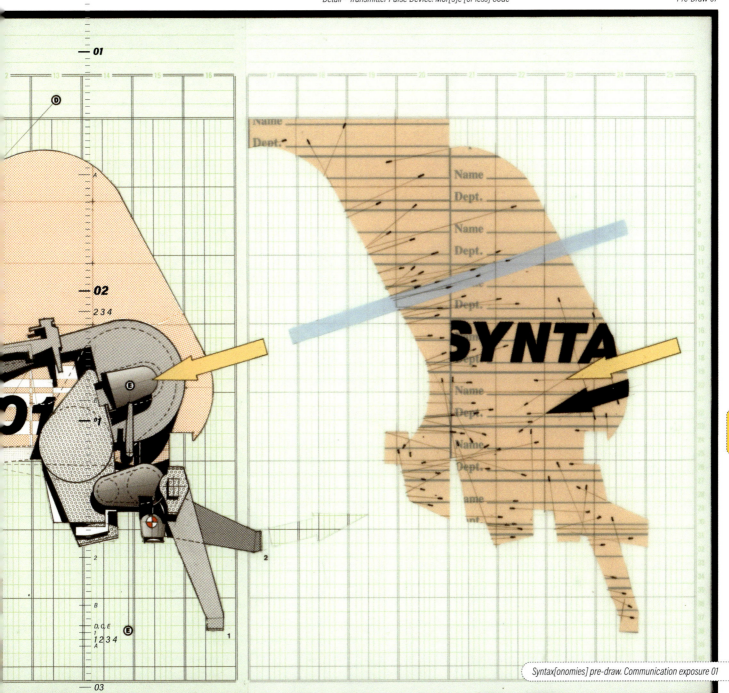

Syntax[onomies] pre-draw. Communication exposure 01

20220202_02[4]

Martin Summers
*Professor of Architecture,
University of Kentucky College of Architecture*

Framed as a method of enquiry, the act of designing or making is a non-linear process translation and discovery that takes internalized and often subconscious ideas and manifests them as a physical or virtual output. It is an optimistic attempt to give form to the designer's innermost thoughts and motivations and communicate those complex and often idiosyncratic concepts to the world. The resultant artifact is often only one of many attempts to reveal something that alludes translation or evolves through that very act of making, yet it strives to communicate through a multi-directional flow of information. To the external audience it attempts to clarify ideas and intentions of the designer whilst simultaneously communicating emergent ideas (and questions) initially not considered to the designer. At its best, design is a passionate, obsessive, and personal quest that reveals truths about our collective experience.

These projects often begin with a hunch, a nagging question, or an unresolved idea which establishes a trajectory or framework for the exploration, allowing the initial motivation to be explored and through which other ideas can emerge or surface. The space of inquiry becomes a mechanism or process for the designer(s) to engage with(in) an agreed set of expectations regarding how things might progress within that framework. As one gains control over their own process or a team stabilizes a specific workflow and direction, one can observe and analyze the artifacts of production, identifying new ideas that are now revealed. It is the critical act of reflection and introspective analysis that is most important to the evolutionary path of the idea, because the analysis allows one to see anew the translation of that idea and test its potential while often revealing multiple paths of possible inquiry.

Requesting User Input [-]

Many of us have experienced the limitations of language (spoken, written, visual) in communicating the inherent complexity of ideas, often requiring us to approximate ideas through tangential glimpses. If we accept this, then what is being lost in translation through this text to you?[5] I find writing a difficult medium through which to communicate layered ideas concisely. Must it be concise?[5] Forgive a moment of anecdotal indulgence, but the question must be asked: "Where does this anxiety with writing come from?" Maybe a grade school English class that I really didn't enjoy? Or perhaps the introduction to basic computer programming on a Commodore 64, another language to master and wrestle with. Frustrations with the syntactical precision required to achieve a result on screen warring with excitement at the possibilities it offered. Is this the origin of my text-based anxiety?

Not all text and language frustrated me. Finding pleasure in 'Choose Your Own Adventure' books that produced an open-ended space of discovery. These appealed to my intuition and was a path of least resistance, like these musings in the face of writing now?[6] Those books used notations to communicate without drawing singular conclusions, allowing parallel realities to exist simultaneously. We now take for granted this simultaneity and rarely admire digital media's ability to embed information within information – containers that contain containers, embedded spaces? Maybe it is not anxiety, but frustration? A perceived responsibility to effectively communicate linearly a richly and layered non-linear space of design.

Re-focus! Spatial simultaneity, information embedded in information? Construction Drawing, constructed drawings? Bryan's texts challenge the linear nature of communication like his designed artifacts. Rather than forcing his thoughts into complete sentences or taking advantage of character allowances on social media platforms, he instead leans into the fragmentary and referential.

He describes the artifact or object indirectly by that which is adjacent and further shrouds its origins in mystery. He is designing social constructs that accept and encourage the intertwining of physical and virtual space. He is using disciplinary techniques to make a virtual mirror within the

> *"Bryan's texts challenge the linear nature of communication like his designed artifacts. Rather than forcing his thoughts into complete sentences or taking advantage of character allowances on social media platforms, he instead leans into the fragmentary and referential."*

[4] The title is the date and version number of the last iteration of the text, with some slight artistic liberty on what constitutes final.

[5] Yes, it must. I'm working on the 39th version at the moment to get it to work within the word count required by the book layout.

[6] "This interactivity was a valuable storytelling device – it both harnessed the kids' attention and took advantage of their innate creativity." J. Rossen, "A Brief History Of 'Choose Your Own Adventure,'" 10 April 2014, https://www.mentalfloss.com/article/56160/brief-history-choose-your-own-adventure

[7] M. Carpo, *The Second Digital Turn: Design Beyond Intelligence* (Cambridge, MA: MIT Press, 2017), pp. 143–4.

artifacts of his production. In a strange way, his mostly analog process anticipates the digital space of search and result made possible by HTML while revealing the gaps and spaces between.[7] Maybe I should just relax about the writing process and see what unfolds? Maybe I just did? Isn't the medium the massage?[8]

Media, Medium, Massage, Misreading, and Misdirection

We are, as a species, good at adaptation. Our very survival makes this evident and we require it in this moment to face multiple, existential crises. Most of us have adapted to the requirements of the COVID-19 pandemic, a disruption to norms that occurred almost overnight. A worldwide social experiment. The 'new normal' that once occupied the space of fantasy has made our mediated reality more present.[9] Information and the promulgation of disinformation in this reality produces its own type of pandemic.[10] Virulent information gestates within the virtual medium's collective intelligence and spreads the virus (corrupting instructions) via a social media constructed to produce algorithmic intensities.[11] Opaque algorithms that a recent Facebook whistle-blower noted are good for profits, not society. While collective intelligence can provide valuable statistically driven approximations, it can also lead to catastrophic amplifications of error.[12] A gap has opened between information and fact that has been exploited by some to catastrophic effect and a staggering loss of life. Disinformation has been weaponized to erode any sense of clarity or truth and increase 'alternative facts.'[13] These are amplified through various media echo chambers (Social Amp[s]). Bryan's beautifully constructed projects and their disciplinary notational systems point toward this inherent conflict [in] direct communication and the flattening of the virtual and the real. Subtly woven into his architectural notations are indicators of intentional misdirection that allude to missing references or warning about the embedded potential demise of the object, space, and culture. Though Bryan would say that he is not visionary as he is often very humble and self-deprecating, the social performance and media manipulation in his work can now be seen as predictive of, or alluding to, this new and often destabilized multi-media communication landscape. He deftly uses his skill to expose what is lost in translation and heightened by its transmutation through media shifting. He reveals what we take for granted or are not observant enough to see, opening new territories for conceptual exploration that do not offer definitive answers but help us prepare for their emergence.

Indeterminacy and the Spaces Between

As stated before, introspective analysis and reflection are critical to the evolution of an idea and the growth of the designer engaged in the design process. To analyze requires a disciplinary type of 'reading' of the specific qualities of the artifact and a body of knowledge through which to interpret what is communicated; it is often as mysterious and personal as the process itself. The very attempt at analysis, translation, or interpretation is an architectural Schrödinger's cat where intent expresses itself in sometimes contradictory patterns. Regardless of its transmutability, the act of analysis fundamentally assumes that something is being communicated, and that the analyst has the ability or knowledge to decipher this content. This is true for both the designer in the process and the external observer attempting to understand the artifact. Each designed artifact is naturally incomplete, indeterminate, and distanced from an observer who is external to the process of production. The designer of the artifact has their own distance from the object's source, requiring an intensive, introspective analysis to tease out preconscious motivations manifested through the design process. Analysis in some ways is an attempt at divining a 'truth' from the artifact, a clarity in communication that the artifact expresses (ideal or perfect) even if the external observer doesn't fully understand the nuance of the language nor the architect their own deeper motivations. It is at this point in the analysis that a keen observer/architect sees that another distancing or gap has opened. A chasm so deep that it reconfigures the pursuit. A thick space between. A liminal space that has altered the way one sees enough that the pursuit of 'truth' naturally brings about its opposite.[14] The potential for new forms of misdirection, obfuscation, imperfection, and error, producing tensions that make this gap explicit and allow one to revel in its vastness. This gap between intent and reception can be frustrating or productive, suppressed or exposed, rejected or revered. It is the latter of these dichotomies where I would position the work of Bryan Cantley and where we share certain affinities. The body of work is an optimistic affirmation of imperfection as a productive space to reveal truths about our shared and flawed human experience.

Theatrical Objects

Bryan Cantley's oeuvre designs a subversive and uncanny space of simulation that uses the standardized graphic notations of construction drawings combined with the aesthetic of kitbashed machines to ground us in the near familiar. He then slowly defamiliarizes the space through theatrical mutations where new social and programmatic hybrids form, double meanings resonate, fields and flows of information are denoted, and mechanical processes inscribe social spaces with latent potential transformations. He is using the medium of representation to design spaces that no longer carry the weight of building instructions – "Instructions for the construction that were not transferred."[15] The overtly theatrical, aesthetic objects work with the notational systems to propose unexpected yet plausible tasks within the world it is actively designing. Notations reveal virtual processes that in[en]form the social constructs with a productive friction, highlighting programmatic mutations that the objects and their written description allude to but never fully manifest. The informational fields give the atmosphere presence, but do not clarify the architectural objects' specificity, pointing instead to an active context in dialogue with its operations and performance. The theatrical object is constructing and remaking the site of its own performance, feeding itself with fuel that our senses cannot detect and performing its duties in a way that makes tangible this virtual space. Bryan brings our focus back to the media and the medium, a space where the real and the virtual strangely flatten. A type of social 'digital twin' critiqued within traditional analog techniques. Iterations of the specific project don't refer to an ideal, previous, or future object, but instead, use media shifting to construct new parallel worlds within the specific media of its making. Each designed artifact produces a representational illusion to the external world while constructing multiple interiors within the media that are even stranger.[16] The media serves as a mirror that might make us more aware of what we consider 'real.' The gap between the object and its representation are collapsed onto each other, making the designed artifact and its media a containing object of significant value.[17] He focuses us back on the medium and a new object has emerged. ✢

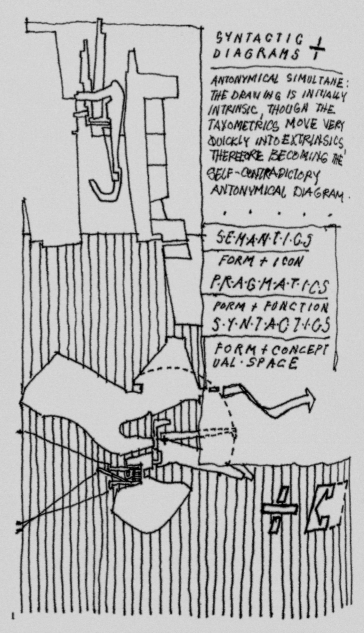

[14] "An attribute that Broeckmann highlights is that 'malfunction and failure are not signs of improper production. On the contrary, they indicate the active production of the 'accidental potential' in any product.' Virilio says that 'the innovation of the ship already entailed the innovation of the shipwreck. The invention of the steam engine, the locomotive, also entailed the invention of derailment, the rail disaster.' The invention of new technology also implies its modes of failure." M. Austin and G. Perin, "Drawing the Glitch," in F. Migayrou, L. Pearson, L. Allen, and B. Sheil (eds), *Drawing Futures* (London: UCL Press, 2016), p. 16.

[15] Bryan Cantley and Eric Owen Moss: Form:uLA. Gallery Talk, 10 October 2014, https://www.youtube.com/watch?v=x9xMVM2ihXc

[16] I find it revealing that we rarely if ever have access to the interior of the architectural objects Bryan constructs. This idea is reinforced through direct knowledge because I worked with one of my students to remodel a few of Bryan's Sketch Up models in Rhino 3D so that we could make them watertight and 3D printable. In that process, it was clear that specific detail in the interior didn't really exist, a model made for its exterior surface representation. The interior in his drawings typically is only alluded to through wireframe or X-ray views that tend to reveal the performative exterior surface of the object, the complexity of lines as aesthetic shown through layered and mediated views. In most cases the exterior constructed surfaces leave traces of the specific techniques of the media – model (physical or digital), drawing, collage, and rendering.

[17] Of note here is the container containing containers, or the idea of objects nested within objects. The contents of the various media construct their own "worlds within worlds" while also making present the individual architectural artifact as an object. Media shifting exposes the artifact to its own process of revisions that makes present the oeuvre, as a much larger constructed world or object that Bryan has constructed.

Camera Noxoculo

An invitation/exhibition from the Yale School of Architecture, this 'tomb' explores the [con]temporary 'death' of the architect/self in the moment of convergent photographic processes.

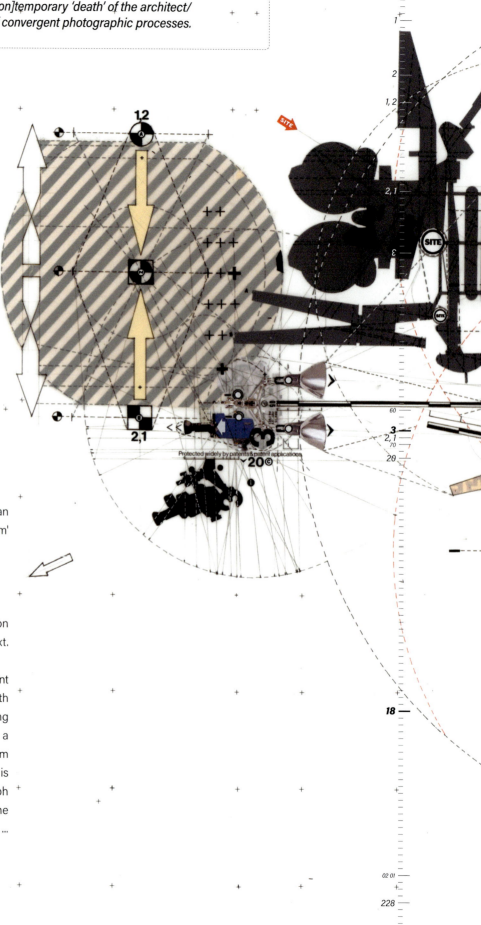

CONTEXT

"(A)long with poets and gravediggers, architects belong to a very small group of people who might be expected to take a professional interest in how they are memorialized after death. And many architects have indeed designed their own tombs, from Mimar Sinan to Le Corbusier.

The exhibition presents tombs that architects design for themselves, in the past and the present, as a starting point in a conversation about memory and death in Architecture. What do we as architects choose to remember and honor – and how?" (Tryon, 2019)[18]

J. Tryon, "In Memoriam: Invitation to Participate," Email to Bryan Cantley, 19 September 2019.

This project was developed in response to an invitation to contribute to the 'In Memoriam' Exhibition held by the Yale School of Architecture. The exhibition invited 32 Architects to each design their own tomb, asking contributors to consider the nature of commemoration and memorial in a contemporary context.

Taking the work of Roland Barthes as a point of departure, this proposal considers Death in abstraction; that it marks the passing of something as much as it considers a literal death. Through the Inherent dualism of the selfie (in which the photographer is simultaneously author of the photograph and the subject of the photograph) the camera becomes analogous to the tomb …

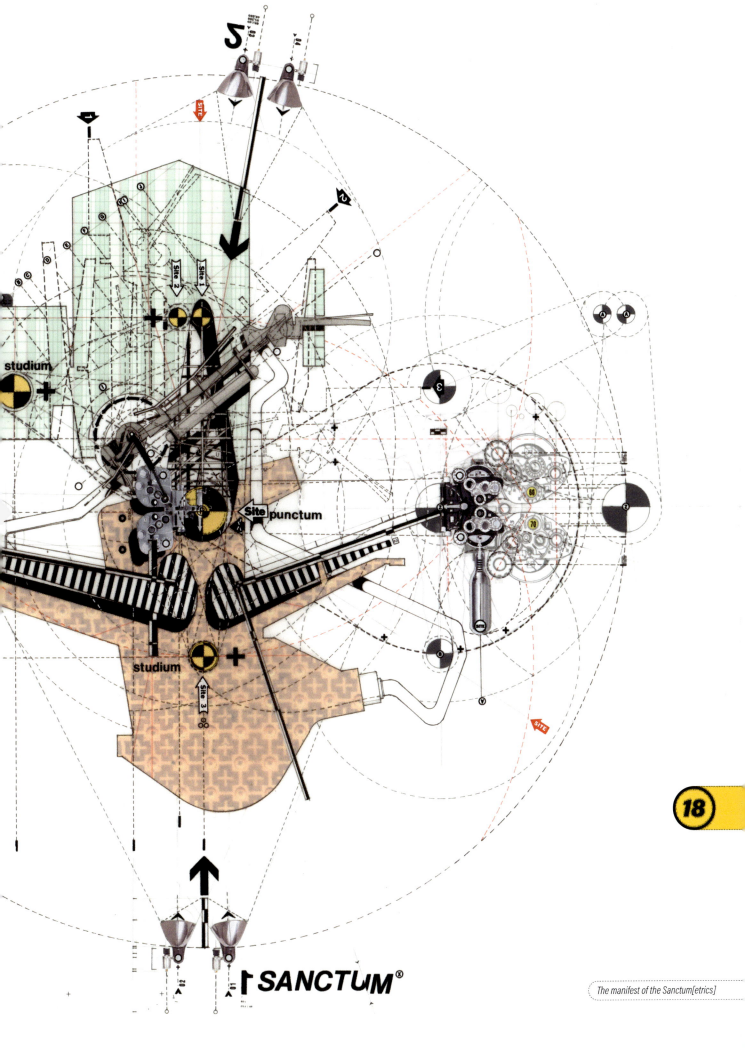

The manifest of the Sanctum[etrics]

 **La petite mort**

"An expression meaning 'the temporary loss and/or weakening of consciousness' and in modern usage refers specifically to 'the sensation of post orgasm as likened to death'" (Wikipedia, 2021).[19]

[19] "La petite mort," https://en.wikipedia.org/wiki/La_petite_mort. Accessed 11 November 2019.

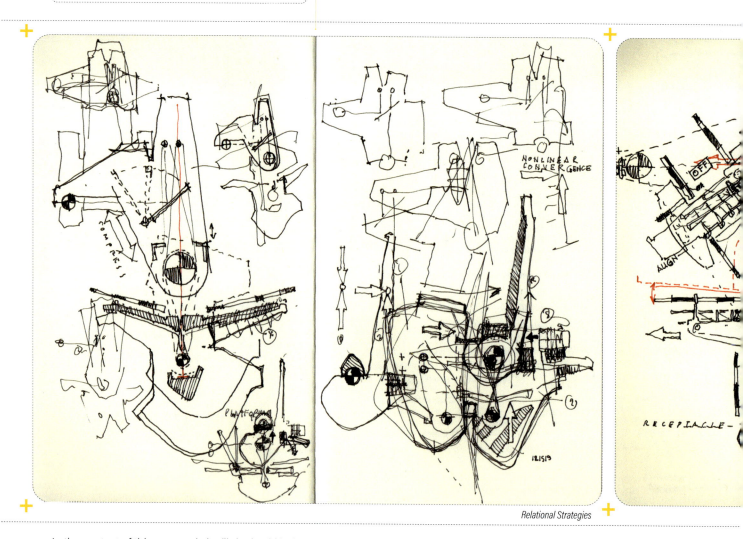

Relational Strategies

In the context of this proposal, the 'little death' is the momentary disorientation, the loss of consciousness/awareness that occurs in the instant of the POST camera 'flash.' For this generation the 'selfie' becomes a death, captured as a digital image.

A time-sensitive condition of loss/separation.

A range of denoted chron-illogical possibilities …

If [a temporary] death [of the self-] is achieved via the act[ion] of taking a selfie [photograph], then the camera becomes the vehicle for its interment, the tomb. This raises the possibility that a similar condition might to occur between the architect and the[ir] drawing.

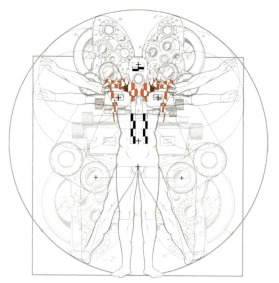

230

② Drawing [as] the Everlasting Mo[MEme]nt

If we accept that:

A ·········> the photograph is an oxymoronic 'everlasting moment', and

B ·········> and that the photograph = marks the death of the photographic subject, it extends that:

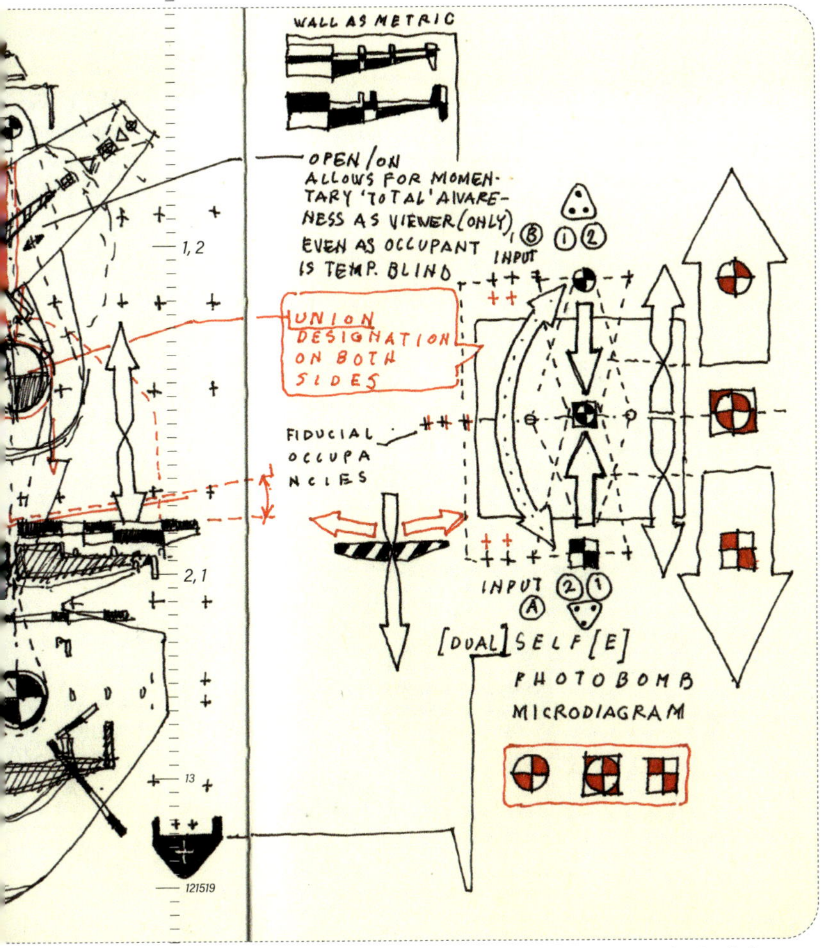

Photobomb diagram

₁**IF** the selfie is the beginning of the death of the photograph[ic/ed] self ...

₂**AND** the drawing is related to the photo/image both are representations of another event/object/entity/condition/space ...

₃**THEN** might we assume that the drawing and the photographic image represent everlasting moments, or selective 'recordings' of a moment never-to-be-again + always present through a visual reference?

The plane of denotation, detonated ...

TYPE 12 The PhotoGRAPH[ic] Self[ie]

Camera Lucida – An optical device that merges the image of a 'scene' with the artist's hand. The author/photographer sees both the scene and the drawing surface as simultaneous events – a simultaneous double exposure.

Camera Obscura – An optical device that projects an image in real through a small pinhole or lens into a darkened chamber.

+ Studium, Punctum, and [the] Sanctum – the '-ums' have it ... The Studium serves as not only the intention of the photographer/drawer/voyeur, but also provides awareness that allows discovery. The elements present are to be uncovered, examined, and [re]understood.

The Punctum is the element[s] that emerges from the 'scene'. It leaves an imprint on the viewer, the receptacle for the intentions and inferences of the subject matter, they are the page on which the inscription is written.

The Sanctum is the holding cell for all [here] that is sacred or desired.

In the Self-[e], the moment/space of discovery, the elements composing the image cross paths, as the subject/object of the image the self, in the given con-text become one with the viewing of the image by both the simultaneous photographer, subject, and reader/voyeur.

TYPE 13 + Fiducial Markers

Objects placed in/on the 'field of view' of an IMAGING SYSTEM which appear in the produced image, often for use as a point of reference or mark of measurement. They 'prove' that an event transpired, by their empirical nature and factual existence.

These markers may be placed into/onto:

> **the imaging subject itself**
[a crash test dummy, the Apollo moon landing photographs], or

> **on the reticle of any optical instrument itself**
[arguable that the drawing, and therefore the drawing surface itself, is a type of optical instrument].

MEDIA LOGICS

One might argue that since the 'death', and therefore the emergence of the tomb [created automatically at the time of a thing's death] happen in the same, instantaneous, moment [the *flash*], that the object in the drawing then demonstrates the 'snap' of the photo lens, and are therefore an honest rendering of that 'everlasting moment.'

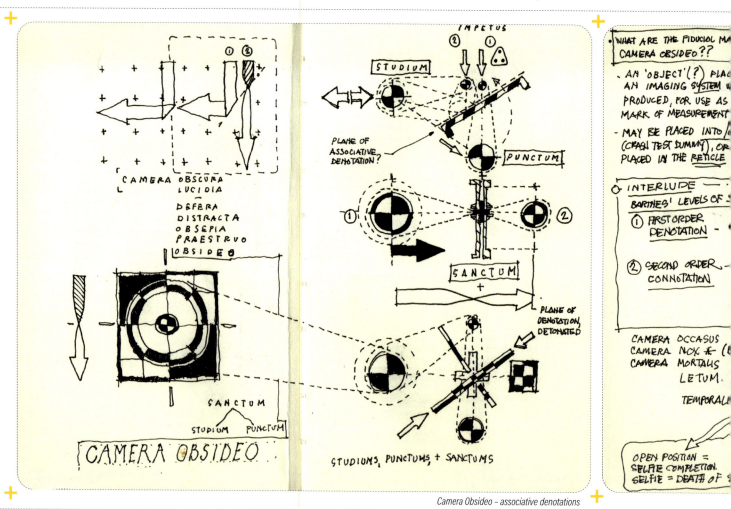

Camera Obsideo – associative denotations

③ Drawing/Apparatus concept

₁**Two cameras** [Obscura + Lucida] are locked into position centered on the occupant [the Self-[e] ... through their alignment the two-sided/dual selfie is created, where the [momentary] death of the self occurs ...

₂**The con-struct** only exists as a diagram of the workings of the idea of the two cameras [O+L]

₃**The PROJECT** therefore, the Camera Noxoculo, "occurs" in the moment of alignment[s]. The Taxonometric Residues [Postliminal Fuzz] are/become the evidence of both previous and future tombs. Perpetual Tombage[isms].

The tomb exists as/in the *flash*, the residual information that lasts forever ... this can only be discussed/documented in the temporality/infinity of an image, or in this case, the drawing.

The two-sided Self-[e] documents the expiry and preserves the image of the moment of death – asking perhaps if the idea of tomb is the image or the moment.

<<[**PB**: *or perhaps a super-positioning of both*]>>

④ The Self-[e] Photobomb

How does the idea of self-photobombing evolve? The two-sided selfie is the residue of the self-photobomb. It becomes:

The *flash[bulb]* causes both temporary blindness/death. A momentary blocking out/erasure of all fore-, mid-, and background components/spatial indicators. The tomb here then operates as a CONDITION OF SUSPENDED ERASURE – the death of recognition, awareness, spatial insertion, community/environmental participation, depth perception, and to some degree, consciousness …

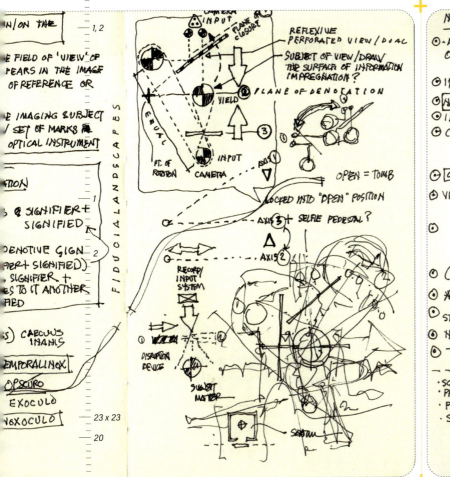

Fiducial Marker interludes

\>\> a choreographed condition of [dual] 'self-awareness';

\>\> the simultaneous death-of-author/photographer and the encapsulation of the tomb/everlasting moment;

\>\> a change of the orientation of both the occupant/subject and the photographer/voyeur;

\>\> a manifestation of focal points and the creation of a '4th' plane, [the pre-ground, also known traditionally as the picture-plane], but one that is unique to the condition in that it is occupiable, and that it freely exchanges with the background plane as the Camera Noxoculo rotates/exchanges its roll.

This points back to the fading tomb … The instant death comes on suddenly and semi-violently but does not suggest a termination of the sepulcher. In this instance, the tomb disappears as eyesight [Eyesite? i-site?] slowly returns, bringing with it the awareness of occupational and spatial identity.

5. Fiducial Anonymity in the age / condition of the Self-[e]

Is the selfie (image) a circumstance of self ... selflessness ... or is it a fictitious self? If the latter, through the production of synthetic conditions of reality [synthetic reality, dare we label this SR?] – then we might argue that it is a condition of fiducial anonymity. Obscurity via the surgical removal of the self from true spatial occupancy.

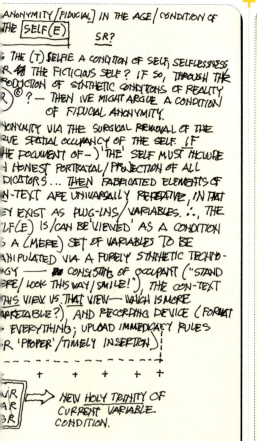

Fiducial Anonymity

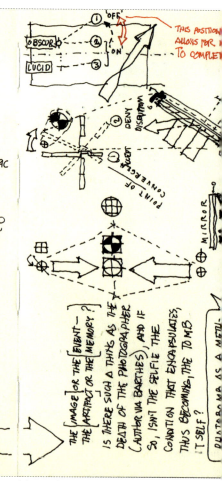

The tomb is created at the moment of self-loss

If [the documentation of-] the self must include an honest portrayal/projection of all indicators, then the fabricated elements of the context are universally cyclic, they exist as plug-ins. Therefore, the Self[ie] can be 'viewed' as a condition of a set of variables to be manipulated through a purely synthetic technology:

Occupant ... ["stand here/look this way/smile!"]

Con-Text ... ["this view versus that view" ... which is more 'marketable'?], and

Recording Device ... [format is everything; upload immediacy rules].

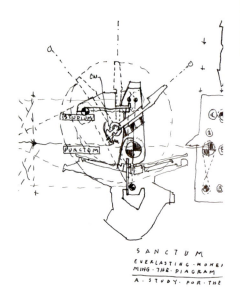

Everlasting Moment diagram 1

This proposal for the Camera Noxoculo can only be regarded/discussed/experienced as a drawing, a set of intentions and positions, although is it set up to mimic various spatial occupancies derived from a planar organization of choreographed moves, operations, and placements.

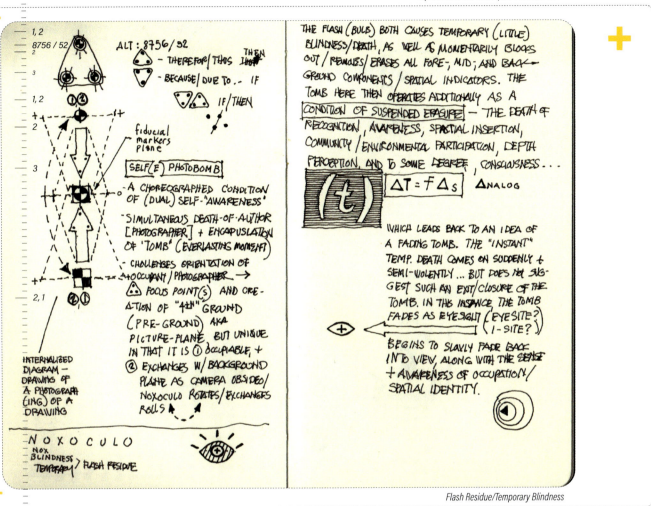

Flash Residue/Temporary Blindness

A drawing of a drawing, a diagram of a diagram, it compresses the notion of image/drawing of a flat event, allowing for [its] many readings, just like as its cousin the text.

The tomb, therefore, is rendered through the [temporary] death of architecture (object) through the establishment of the drawing. ✚

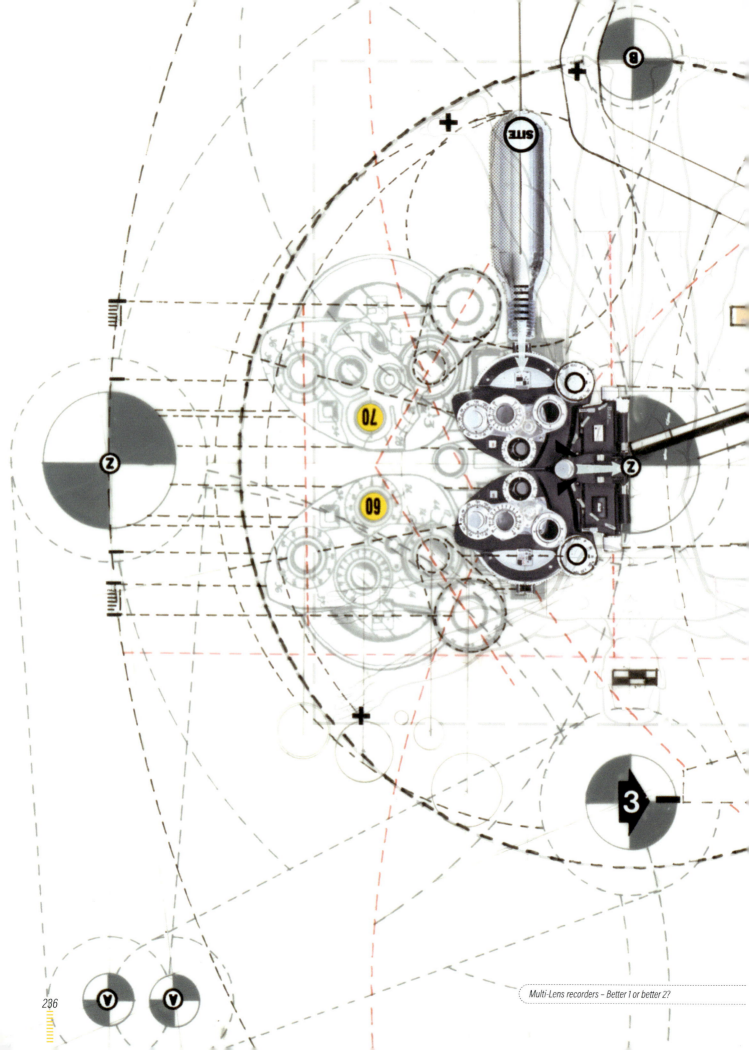

Multi-Lens recorders – Better 1 or better 2?

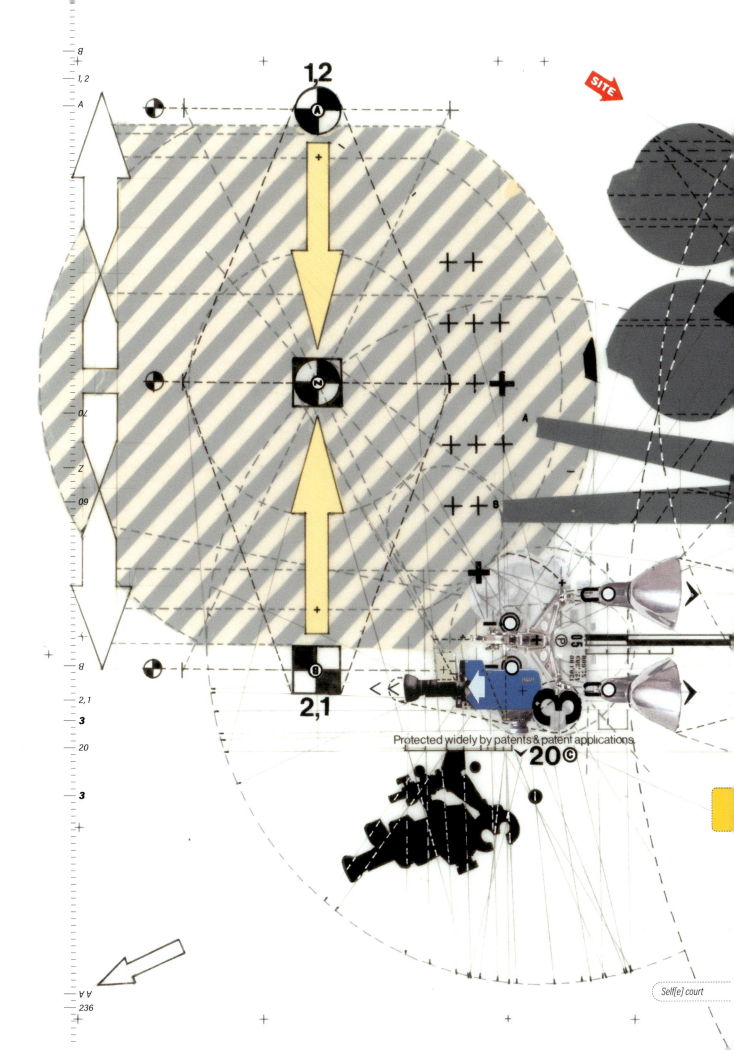

Self[e] court

H[n]otel-CA

An exploration of the closed architectural system that was the Los Angeles seen/scene.

"Come work with us ... forever, and ever ..."

(an) **LA Story** – reflections on the purportedly historic system of segregation within the Los Angeles architectural scene. This project is framed as exploration of a system that was predicated on being able to withstand the "financial burden of inclusion" a system that sustained inequities of access for those not financially independent. Those not attending the best schools and those not able to work for free, were not able to participate on a level playing field.

The project does not intend to make an ethical argument: its scope is far too limited and reductive for that; it is after all based on the perceptions and recollections of the author some 30 years prior to this publication; instead it might be viewed as a set of anecdotal contextual observations, a cathartic attempt to decode a set of recollections ... this project might on some level be seen as a type of therapy [aren't they all?]

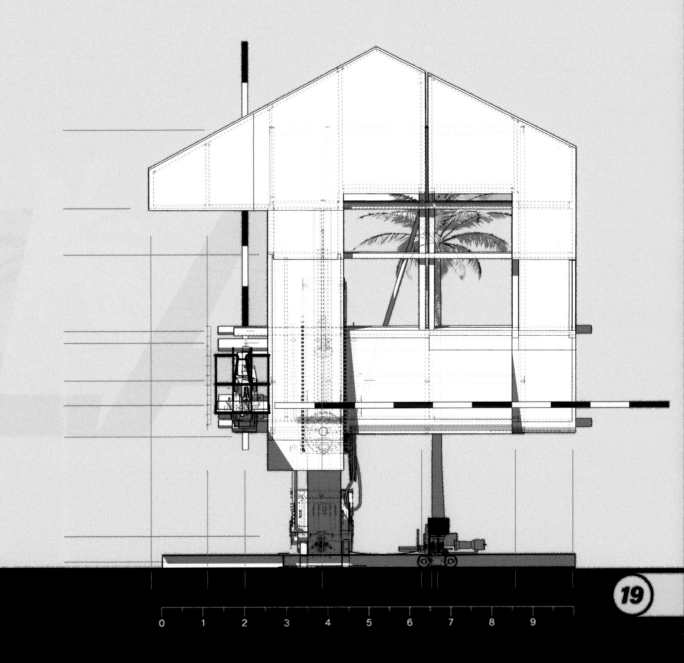

Anti-elevation: the inability of initiating pursuit

DESCRIPTION

The project has three distinct sections, none of which might be thought of as a conclusion ... instead, these subdivisions might be thought of as alterative/parallel timelines than separate elements. These components, in the chronological order of appearance/development, are:

– the SEgregation ENgine [**SEEN**],
– the FAçade MEchanism [**FAME**],
– and the architectural i-COn DEvice [**i-CODE**].

Each of these elements can, be understood as an autonomous condition surrounding the main conceptual structure. Much like the dynamic between employer and intern, the pieces and their relational strategies are still unclear. It's difficult to play a game without (all players) knowing the rules.

"I'd like to play a game ..." (Jigsaw, 2004).[20]

[20] Jigsaw, "I want to play a game," New Jersey, 1 October 2004, https://youtu.be/TwJFdFI8Kt8

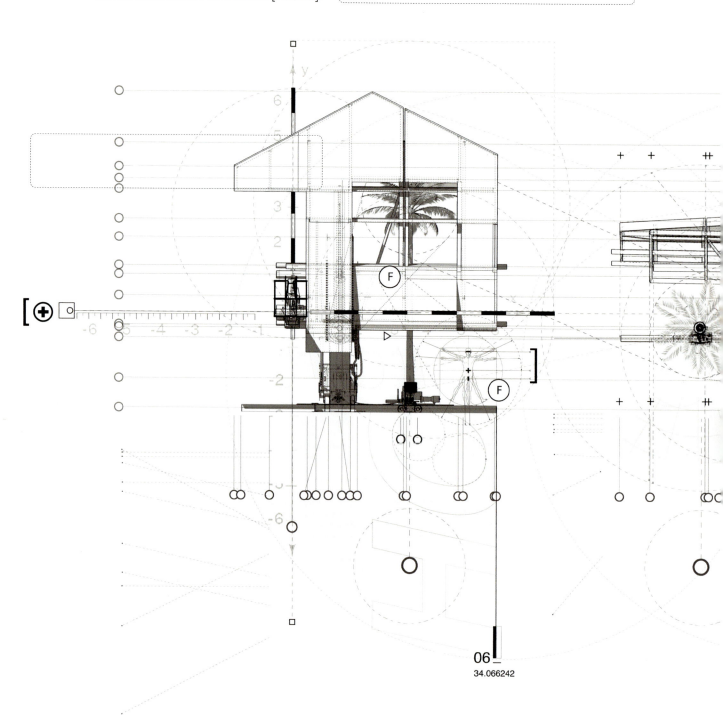

06
34.066242

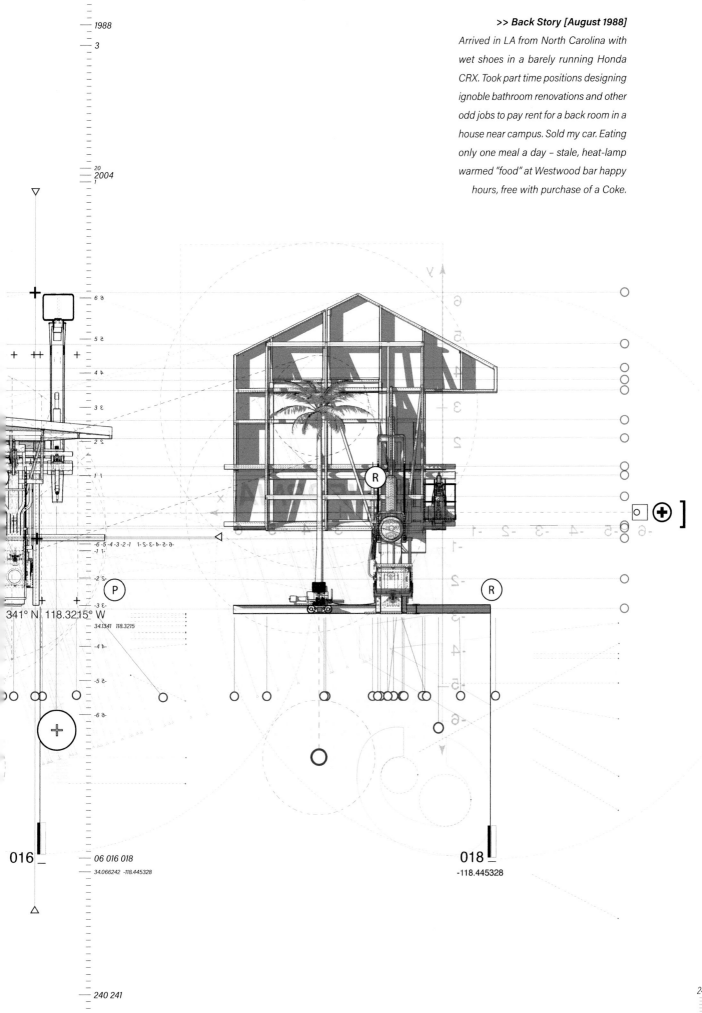

>> **Back Story [August 1988]**

Arrived in LA from North Carolina with wet shoes in a barely running Honda CRX. Took part time positions designing ignoble bathroom renovations and other odd jobs to pay rent for a back room in a house near campus. Sold my car. Eating only one meal a day – stale, heat-lamp warmed "food" at Westwood bar happy hours, free with purchase of a Coke.

>> *Back Story [1988-90]*

Chasing multiple part-time jobs in-between classes, I realize that I cannot compete with privileged classmates that do not have to work during their schooling. Survived on GENERIC ramen from Ralph's and inedible vending machine soup at North Campus.

The SEEN

The SEgregration ENgine is the origin of the project, an edited/abandoned phase, it explored a literal exclusionary system based on the recognition, filtration, and segregation of the architectural graduate. Their access to the inner workings of the profession was dependent on their [financial] ability (perhaps a biproduct/runoff of the entertainment industry philosophy that Los Angeles itself embodies, as much as a conscious disciplinary affectation).

The circular cadence kept the remuneration dependent from engaging with the inner circle. Much akin to the art of Aikido [where the self is conceptually considered to be the exact center of a spherical universe] turning all intrusions/advances away past the rotating center point of the sphere. The intern in this case could always apply work/force to the system, but the resultant spin would keep the line of attack off center. Pushing a ball causes it to rotate, thus deflecting the force away from the center.

34.1341°

>> *Back Story [1989-90]*

Working on freelance projects from 12:00–3:00 a.m. every night to purchase supplies for school. Up at 5:00 am everyday making bologna sandwiches to avoid hyped lunch fees on campus. Introduced to the evils of coffee by a delirious classmate, the first one was free...

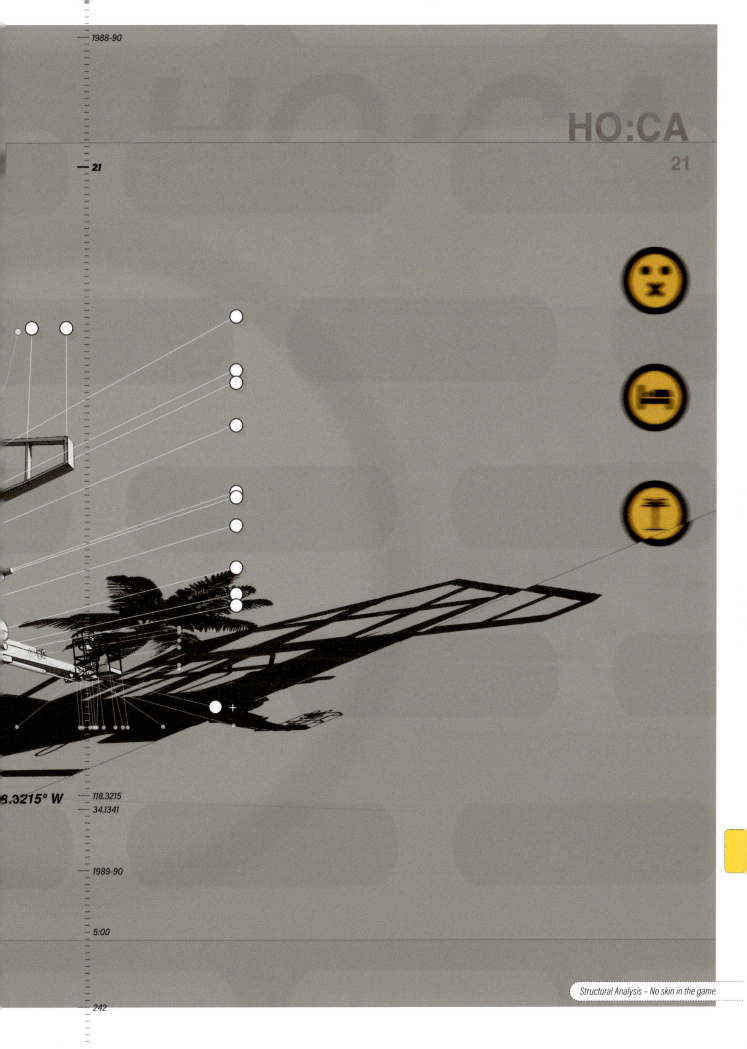

Structural Analysis – No skin in the game

>> *Back Story [1989]*

Passing on thesis advisors who required outside payment to serve as mentors and consultants. Rent or Thesis? Self-Leveling Bootstraps became a working metaphor. Shopping in the 'used supply' bin at Flax Art in Westwood for affordable provisions. Involved in intimate relationship with used Letraset sheets [60 percent off!]. Discovered all-you-can-eat breadsticks with salad purchase at Olive Garden.

"Palms were useful in selling Hollywood as a new Mecca, just as they had sold Los Angeles as a desert Eden; the desert realm turned up often in early films in which desert sheiks seduced virtuous-turned-lusty maidens. In the same way, Los Angeles went from Victorian virtue to Hollywood vice: sexiness on screen was an instant hit, and the earliest film fantasies came from the hot, palmy desert" (Dailey, 2014).[21]

V. Dailey, "Piety and Perversity: The Palms of Los Angeles," *Los Angeles Review of Books*, 14 July 2012, https://v2.lareviewofbooks.org/article/piety-perversity-palms-los-angeles/

Communication Breakdown – Chorographical score

FAME

The FAçade Mechanism, a distillation of the physicality of architecture to a representation of a pitched roof building, perhaps [a/the] most instantly recognizable of icon of (domestic) architectural identity. The discipline and profession are indistinguishable from the outside, the perspective of the student. *The Building*, with its attendant symbolic political baggage, summons all, not revealing itself as an inequity machine until the prospect is already consumed by its deviations. Within this construct, there are five primary conditions: the [non]occupancy reservoir, the armature of exclusion, the impenetrable façade membrane, the LA Palm Icon, and the overall condition of the imposed view.

₁ The reservoir, a viewing platform, is the manifestation of the isolation mode. It separated, the renumeration dependent from the inner community of the Los Angeles Architectural elite. It was the only place from which to glimpse *Shangri-LA*. The reservoir is an extension of the exclusion arm.

₂ The armature of exclusion controls the level of participation, or access, into the inner circle. It is a control mechanism, one that requires the unknowing participation of the inhabitants, transforming them from occupant to voyeur. Analogous to a teeter-totter, only lifting the voyeur to the point of 'insertion' when it is balanced by the counterweight of its own pneumatic engine.

₃ Of the five conditions, the Façade membrane is the most recognizable, and most difficult to engage – the membrane of architectural empowerment. The 'sloped-roof building', the graphic icon[ization] and residue of the architectural discipline is constructed as an ironically a thin component, despite its immeasurable theoretical and emblematic complexity. It is the veneer through which we can view the profession, and through which the profession examines the viewer. It becomes the frame for the restricted view, teasing equitable admission. It is the glass ceiling, turned on its horizontal axis. Polished and slick on one side, it reveals its crude and workaday assemblage on the other, a figure of total contradiction.

> "The greater the decrease in the social significance of an art form, the sharper the distinction between criticism and enjoyment by the public. The conventional is uncritically enjoyed, and the truly new is criticized with aversion" (Benjamin, 2015).[22]
>
> [22] W. Benjamin, *Illuminations: Essays and Reflections* (London: Penguin, 2015).

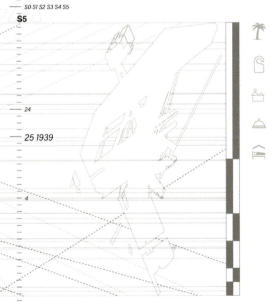

> *"Pay no attention to the man behind the curtain ..."*[24]
>
> [24] O. Diggs, "Oz has spoken," *Emerald City, Land of Oz*, 25 August 1939.

₄ The Palm tree, the only other living organism, represents the emblem of Los Angeles – a synthetic, curated landscape, a symbol of paradise originally planted by the Victorians. They are transplants, non-native but inhabit a faux oasis *(f[au]asis?)*. It is the unobtainable goal, the archetypal carrot before the horse, the allure of admission. It works closely with the Façade, to produce the circumstance of the inaccessible conclusion.

₅ It is only by occupying the reservoir, suspended by the armature of exclusion, forced to look at but never able to touch the tree, that the circuit is completed, the narrative becomes its own one-way feedback loop.

> "Just as the Victorians had allowed themselves to be seduced by their own constructions of Orientalism, so too did more modern Los Angeles residents fall under the embellished foreign allure of the palm tree" (Mueller, 2016).[23]
>
> [23] N. Mueller, "How The Palm Tree Came To Southern California," *Garden Collage*, 21 January 2016, https://gardencollage.com/wander/gardens-parks/palm-trees/

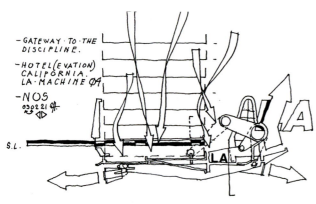

LA Gateway sketch – Hotel[evation]

>> Back Story [1990–91]

Came to realize that I could not support both myself and my creative visions simultaneously. Understanding where I fit in within the economic pecking order and financial drive of Los Angeles. Began a series of theoretical explorations in my sketchbooks during many late hours at laundromats and 7-Eleven parking lots. The seeds of Form:uLA were planted alongside the smell of vending machine detergent and the landscape of automat 'meals'.

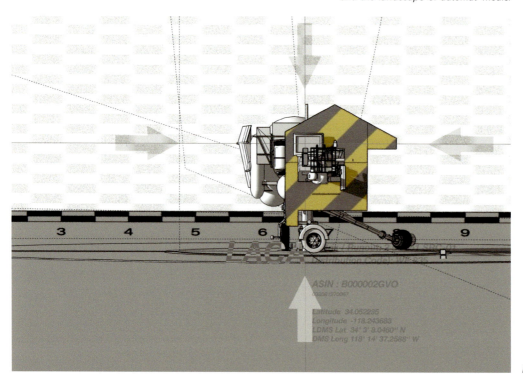

LA machine

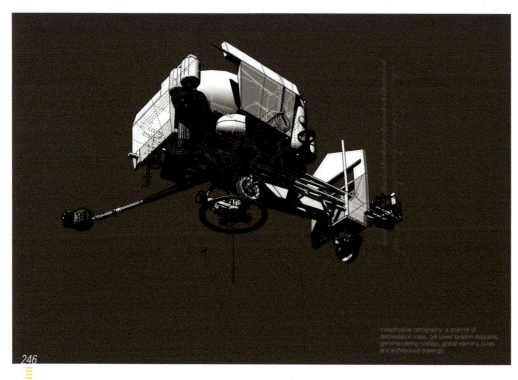

Shangri-LA device

i-CODE

Comprised of an evolving set of tangential projects, the iCOn Device is the radical, de-generate offspring of the H[n]otell. It attempts to describe the process of representing the mechanism of architecture as a series of semi-graphic iCONs.

Each device reduces and illustrates commonly/publicly accessible symbols of architecture and employs them as part of an academic construct. They become the delivery mechanisms of architectural language and meaning.

They are, on some level a revisiting, of the Primitive Hut [the *Hut-el California*? The *MO[REorless]tel*? The *Less-is[mo]tell*? The *Mo[re]-tell*?]. They examine and express the relationship between the architectural icon, its graphic reduction, its presentation, and its meaning to both the general public [consumers of architecture] and architects [producers (and consumers) of architectural theory]. They are, in a sense, the sirens of the architectural profession, promising an accessible future that is in fact impassable.

> "A motel is where you give up good dollars for bad quarters" (Youngman, n.d.).[25]
>
> [25] H. Youngman (n.d.), "Quotes About Motels," 23 July 2021, https://www.azquotes.com/quote/1337682.

Becoming vehicles for architectural theory and "its validity as a reminder of the original and therefore essential meaning of all building for people: that is, of architecture" (Germann, 1974),[26] there architectural emblems and fundamental components: the column, the beam, a window/door, an arch, the rotunda, and the stairway are mated to mechanical delivery systems, mediums of meaning and conveyance.

[26] G. Germann, "On Adams House in Paradise: The idea of the Primitive Hut in Architectural History by Joseph Rykwert" *Journal of the Society of Architectural Historians* 33, no. 3 (October 1974).

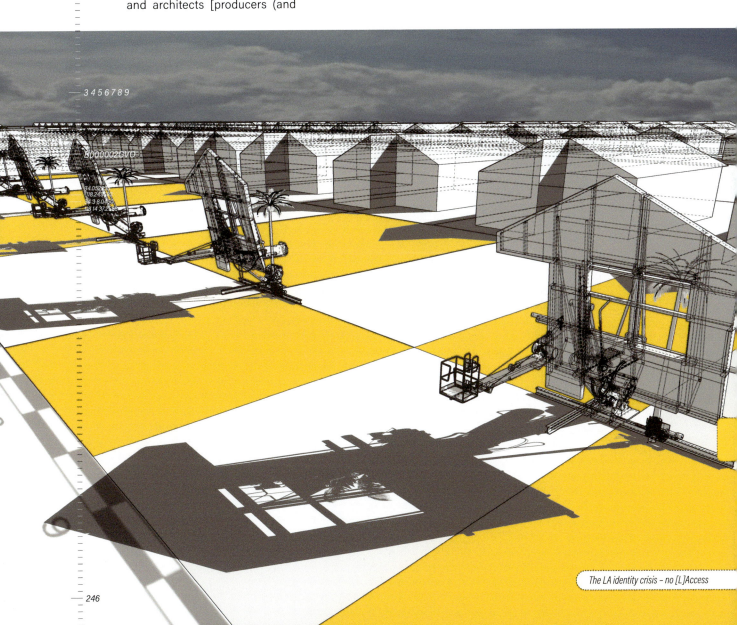

The LA identity crisis – no [L]Access

Early study of domestic skin [LA]nguage

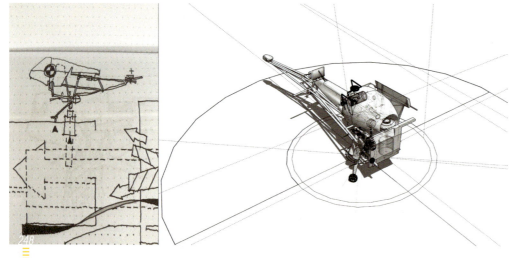

Center of a spherical universe – Aikido aspirations

The CoL[A]umn

The CoL[A]umn is a unique being; it serves as a beacon of the visible structure of architecture. It has the unique ability to perform in a group vernacular and an autonomous setting. Just as the bowling pin, it stands not only as part of an ensemble, a presentation of unity; it carries just as much content when displayed as a singular entity. Indeed, it might even be said that when presented in the singular form there are still connotations of a group identity. As much as any of the fundamental architectural elements, it can convey its core meanings; structure, aesthetic, and intent without having to rely on its insertion into an architectural context. In its documented format, also speaks to the ordering system of the classical elements. It can play a game of spatial hide-and-seek with its insertion context, but also may announce the stability and ceremony of the protected institution hiding behind a repetitive mask.

"Bowling is not a sport, because you have to rent the shoes" (Carlin, 2002).[27]

[27] G. Carlin, *Napalm & Silly Putty* (New York: Hyperion, 2002).

The column in this case is represented as a singular entity installed upon a mobile platform, capable of being moved into formation alongside its mimicked brethren to offer shared subtexts. It is connoted notation, annotated upon its itinerant podium.

"Greek architecture taught me that the column is where the light is not, and the space between is where the light is. It is a matter of no-light, light, no-light, light. A column and a column bring light between them" (Kahn, 2003).[28]

[28] L. Kahn, *Louis Kahn: Essential Texts*, ed. R. Twombly (New York: W.W. Norton & Co, 2003).

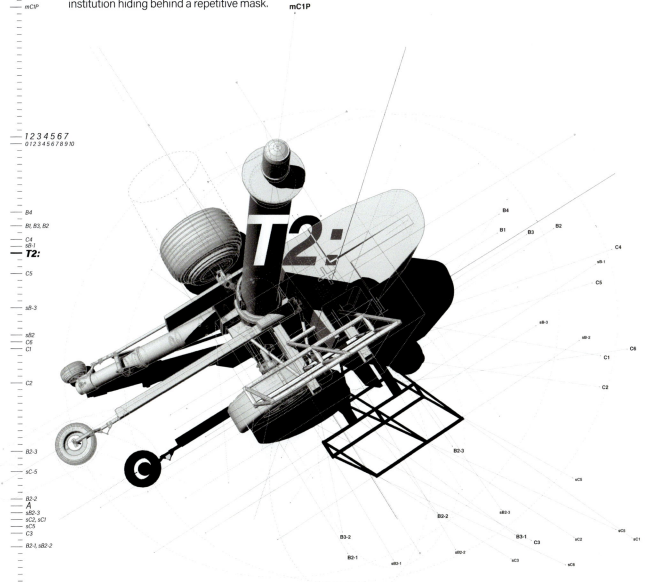

The Column[otation] - the mobility of static reasoning

CON-clusion

This project has [mis]behaved quite similarly to many others, a set of non-linear system of observances, adjustments, critiques, and rebirths. Most of the **seen** component was jettisoned to distil the apparatuses critical to the proposal. Whereas most endeavors in the studio go through rigorous and considerable editing, they do not typically involve a revolution, rather the evolution through erasure. This entity, perhaps because of its rich symbolic content, values the judgments of extreme deletions, where necessary, to produce a series of viable conceptual offspring. Amp[utation]s become legitimate hosts, abortions new DNA, and expurgations alternative conversations pathways to the multiplicity of the design narrative and the architectural opportunities.

$$A < B \because C$$

A – The architectural intern, the student, the newly graduated designer. A transplant into the newly discovered discipline.

B – Admission to the discipline and community. The utopia of knowledge turned into application.

C – The glass façade, the tease and false promise of open access. In one instance, the architectural graduate cannot afford to work for free – their familial situation and financial condition do not compute with the cost of living in Los Angeles. They are forced to take employment at less glamorous offices, along with part-time work to make ends meet, thus unwittingly assisting in the construction of the invisible fascia, affirming the pedigree requirements of the profession. It is the incarnation of the 'who-you-know' state. It ultimately becomes the trap of immense time and fiscal investments, ones that prevent the intern from pursuing other professional pathways. ✚

"In the end, success is not about who you know, it's about you know who" (Breault, n.d.).[29]

[29] R. Breault (n.d.), "Quotes About Success," 3 February 2021, https://www.azquotes.com/quote/21948

>> *Back Story [1990]*

Started a small firm with colleagues, understanding the unbalanced mathematical residuals of small project fees combined with overhead costs. Moving car every three hours to avoid Santa Monica parking fees.

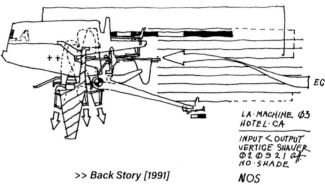

LA Machine sketch – vertice shaver

>> *Back Story [1991]*

Moving to Orange County, living with relatives to secure a fiscal future where I might start chipping away at my overwhelming student loan debt. Wondering quite a bit at academic, creative, and professional opportunities I passed up in order to pay for provisions. Putting Form:uLA on hold while I danced through the corporate architecture field. Still designing odd renovations here and there to add to my kingdom of riches. Driving a delivery truck of camper-shell window frame extrusions to offset rent.

>> *Back Story [1992]*

Tenure-track position at CSUF, began unpacking and re-examining Form:uLA as a theoretical studio ...

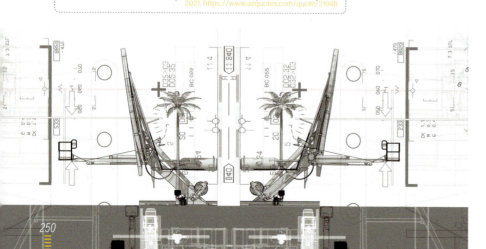

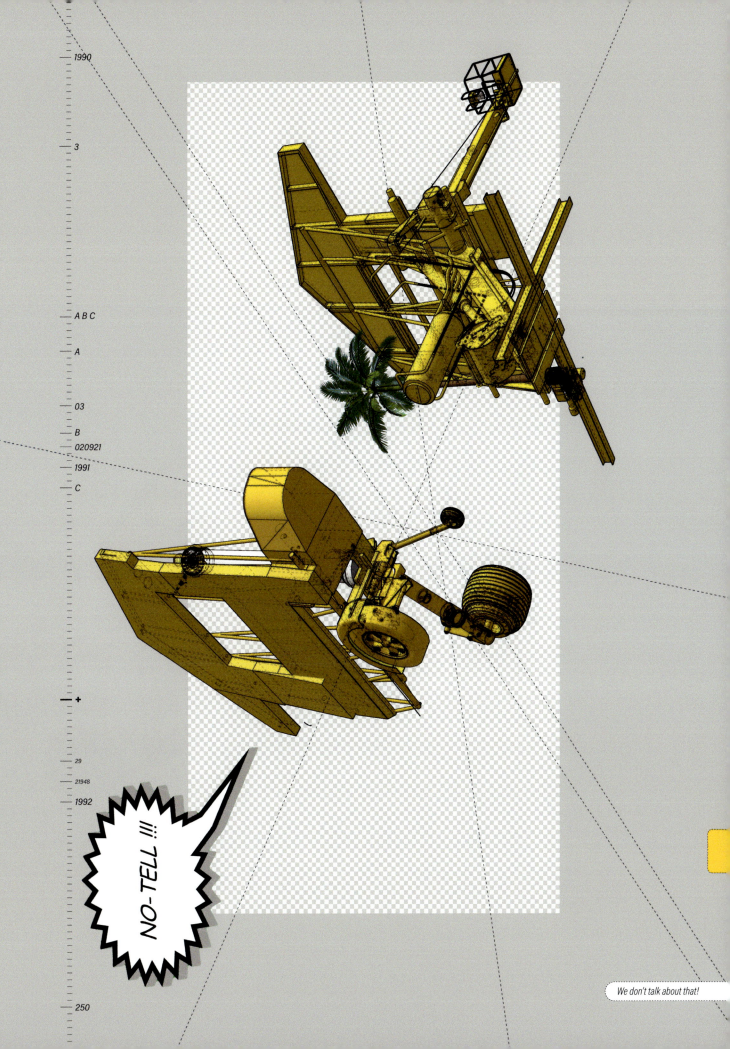

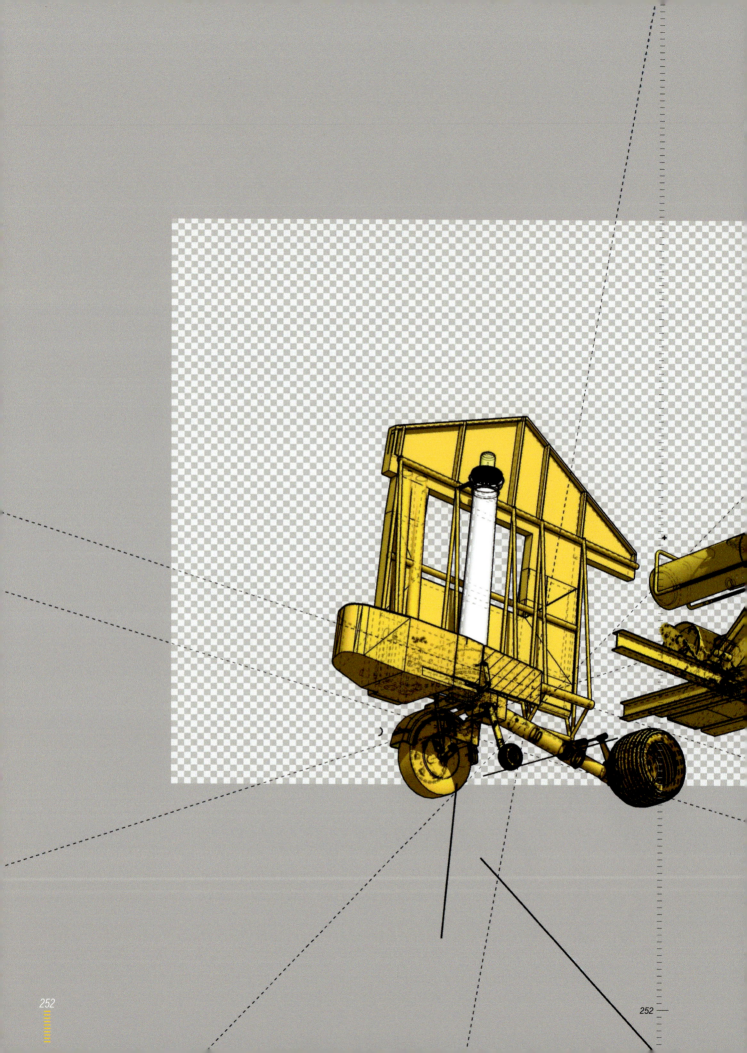

Onomatopoe[s]i[s]a

DomestiC-19

A proposal for the new dwelling in a current-pandemic world [2020], and its implications with soc[i]al interfaces, the redefinition of public spaces, and the nature of architecture as filter.

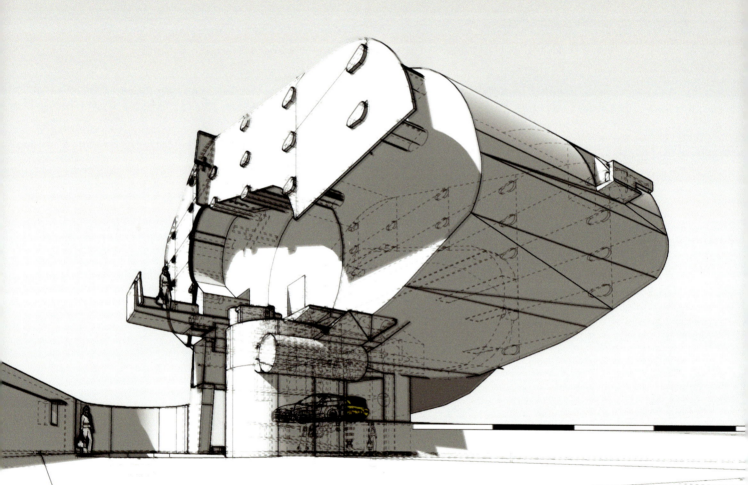

"In big cities around the world, people eyed each other warily over face masks, moving to the edges of the sidewalk, hugging the entryway to buildings, letting the elevator pass rather than join other passengers in a confined space. ... Meanwhile, hundreds of millions of people, including many architects, were confronting the inadequacies of their own domestic spaces: small apartments, clustered around empty event spaces and workout rooms that weren't safe to use, with laundry available only in the basement. Open-plan suburban houses, with vast interiors, lacked sufficient partitions to keep people with the virus apart from those without it. As weeks of isolation turned into months, and as the fear of a rise in infections grew with the approach of summer, these inadequacies seemed to forge a new consensus, not fully articulated but widely felt: Architecture is about rights, about air, about equal access to the necessities of life" (Kennicott, 2020).[30]

[30] P. Kennicott, "The pandemic has shown us what future architecture could be," *Washington Post*, 13 July 2020, https://www.washingtonpost.com/magazine/2020/07/13/pandemic-has-shown-us-what-future-architecture-could-be/

This project is a response to "lock-down." The mandatory social and spatial isolation that many faced in the early days of 2020, the result of the sudden, horrific, and global impact of COVID-19. The project explores the [re]definition of architectural interactions; the way we (as a society) temporarily[?!] redefined our social interfaces and physical space.

This project does not seek to address construction costs and socio-economic equalities (not to say that these are not significant issues), rather it concerns itself with the adaptions and alterations to the program of traditional domestic zoning typologies. It explores issues of an intra (and post) Covid domestic condition, where physical isolation, social segregation, cognizant air filtering, and the home delivery service serve as a primary conditions of social engagement and human interaction.

001

002

003

Courtyard as decompression of social space

[Components]
YARD/FILTER

"The origins of the suburban garden tradition can be traced in part to the early writings of influential landscape gardener Andrew Jackson Downing, who in 1865 was one of the first writers to promote a national landscape aesthetic to a wide audience. He set the stage for what has evolved into a traditional American front yard aesthetic" (Colston Burrell, 1995).[31]

"According to NASA, there are about 40 million acres of turf grass in the US – lawn, in a sense, is our largest crop" (Borrelli, 2017).[32]

The front lawn was originally intended as a communal, egalitarian space in North America, but like egalitarianism itself, that proved to be more an ideal than an actual. Suburban living became synonymous with a cultish conformity, as Ernest Hemingway supposedly said, the suburb was "full of wide lawns and narrow minds" (Borrelli, 2017).[33]

"Get off my lawn" (Kowalski, 2008).[34]

The front yard, once a semi-public gathering space, becomes an apparatus of mechanical segregation and sequestration – a spatial and architectural filter. It shifts from a place of *transitionary assembly* to a place of *transitionary exclusion.* Where it had traditionally hosted friendly exchanges and intimate conversations between neighbors and members of the community, a place of ceremony and curation, it became a buffer zone, a bulwarked fortress of medical 'necessity'. Still open to the sky, and still a prologue to the domestic façade, whilst the point of access moved from the front door to a walled perimeter, a gated palisade. The point of entry, the threshold was decompressed from inches to *yards* providing the only condition that seemed to prevent viral spread – the aloofness of unpopulated [air]space. Of course, this space became politicized as neighbors were often pitted against each other based on their 'beliefs' in the science behind filtration and of communicable disease infections.

"Social distancing, also called 'physical distancing,' means keeping a safe space between yourself and other people who are not from your household" (Centers for Disease Control and Prevention, 2020).[35]

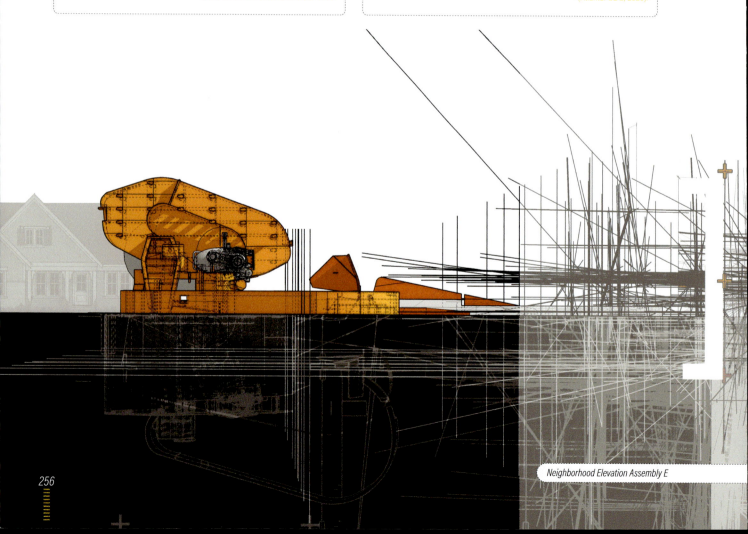

Neighborhood Elevation Assembly E

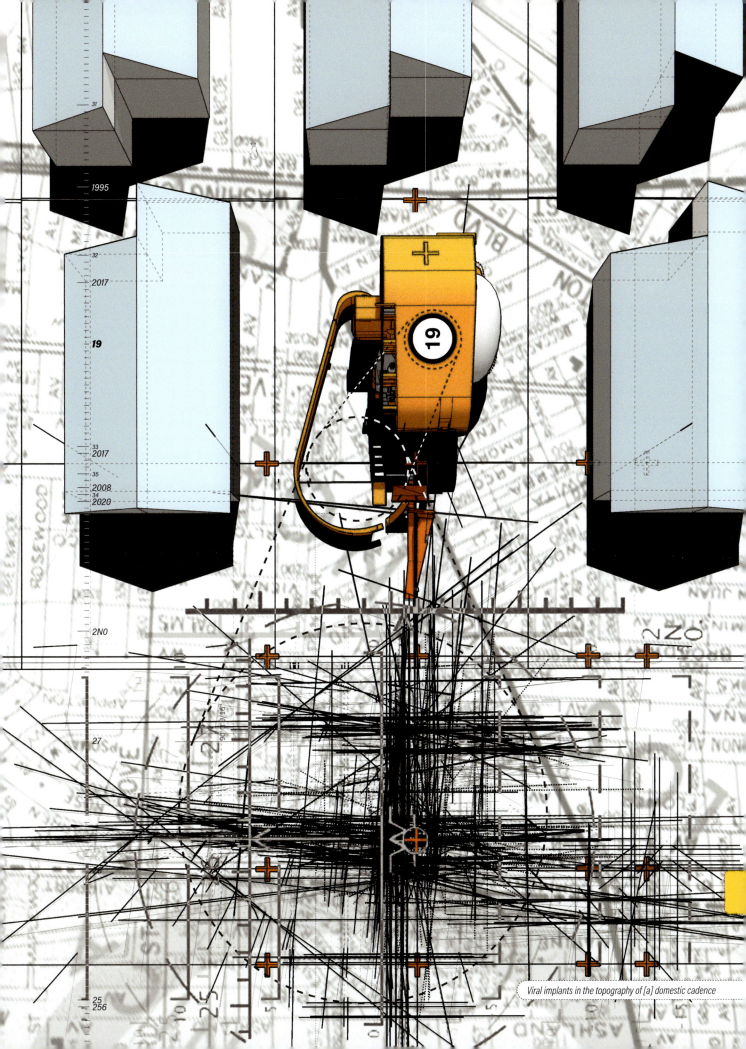

Viral implants in the topography of [a] domestic cadence

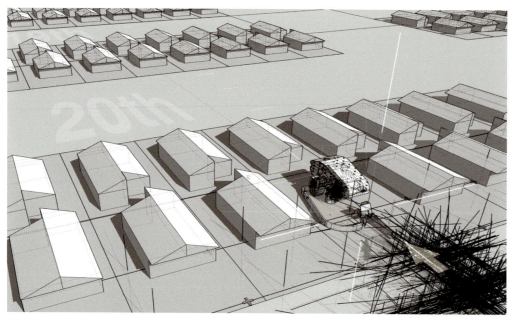

As the drone flies ...

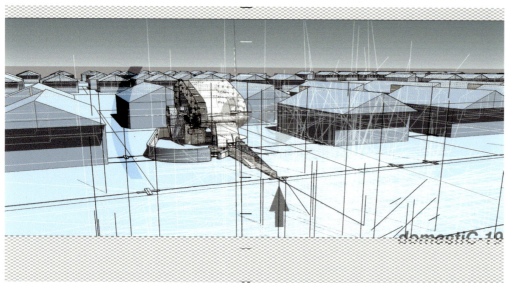

Point of entry – pixelated societies ...

Sub-[n]urbia/[Vir]eidenti[al]

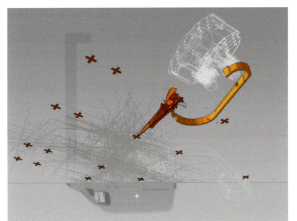

Delivery port as new social order

This space also endeavors to employ[deploy?] a potentially sun-drenched area. A response to the 2020 theory that it might help combat, or 'burn-off' the virus:

> "Coronaviruses on surfaces and objects naturally die within hours to days. Warmer temperatures and exposure to sunlight will reduce the time the virus survives on surfaces and objects" (Centers for Disease Control and Prevention, 2020).[36]

[36] Centers for Disease Control and Prevention, "Guidance for Disinfecting" (Atlanta: CDC, 2020).

Consequentially this volume of empty distance created a decompression zone. It became an externalized, [open] air-lock, assisting the destruction of the invading organisms. A virtual Temple to the Sun, a life-giving [or at least life-prolonging] entity in this narrative.

It became the *Longest Yard*.

> "By the 1950s, it's firmly rooted that a front lawn is a painting, a non-productive space" (Borrelli, 2017).[37]

[37] Borrelli, "The Front Lawn".

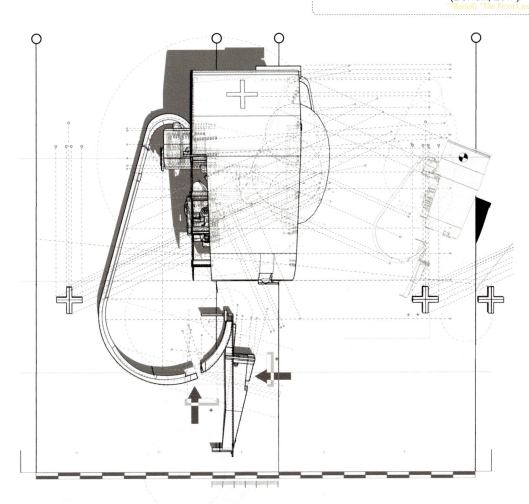

Plan[otation]-ing. Optics of metric[k]s

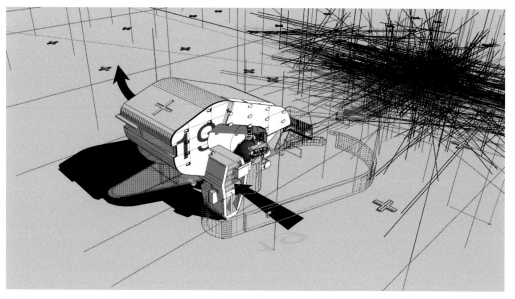

Standoff/Lockdown

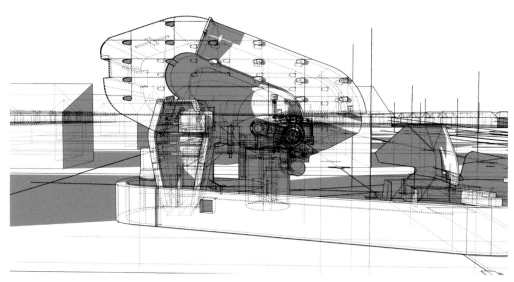

Air intake/exchange as an elevational tactic

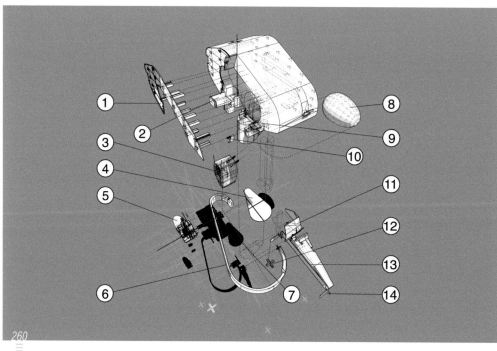

Segregated unions

DELIVERY PORT

The emergence of the perimeter wall as the new threshold forced the emergence of a secondary architectural condition, the [Amazon] Delivery port. Vast numbers of people compressed their normal spatial/commercial occupancy adopting the now ubiquitous home-delivery service. Consequentially increasing the revenue through an explosive growth of online shopping venues, yet another distinguishable fold in the architectural fabric – *removing the social from society, one package at a time*. For many Amazon or UberEats delivery drivers, this often became their primary source of human interaction forcing the evolution of an external delivery port as a new social environment.

The doorstep and porch where packages were once hand delivered evolved into an independent artifact that promoted the required physical distance. Prompting a new architectural element, the *drop box*, an air-lock configuration that occupied the perimeter of the site, becoming the new 'welcome mat' of the (post-)pandemic world, where that mat is imbued with a spatial and social viscosity.

"This is the Construct. It's our loading program. We can load anything, from clothing, to equipment, weapons, training simulations, anything we need" (Morpheus, 1999).[38]
[38] Morpheus, "You wanted to know what the Matrix is," *The Matrix*, 11 June 1999.

The Port became analogous to the confessional curtain, an occupant-operated device controlling degrees of interaction with would be *viral intruders*. Here, we pass(ed) judgment on our fellow humans, physically expanding the peephole surveillance system through many layers of front doors.

"You know, that's a kneeler ..." (Seinfeld, 1997).[39]
[39] Seinfeld, "The Yada Yada," Season 8, episode 19 (1997).

"*Kramer*: Newman and I are reversing the peepholes on our door. So you can see in.

Elaine: Why?

Newman: To prevent an ambush.

Kramer: Yeah, so now I can peek to see if anyone is waiting to jack me with a sock full of pennies.

Jerry: But then anyone can just look in and see you.

Kramer: Our policy is, we're comfortable with our bodies. You know, if someone wants to help themselves to an eyeful, well, we say, 'Enjoy the show.'

Elaine: I'm sorry I can't stay for the ... second act" (Seinfeld, 1998).[40]
[40] Seinfeld, "The Reverse Peephole," Season 9, episode 12, 1998.

It became a designated zone for the decontamination of packages and goods handled by others, a condition that emerged early in the pandemic taking over the wet rooms, entry halls and spare bedrooms of a wary population – creating a (national) programmatic and spatial shift. It became a metric of our worldly purchases, our purchasing power, and our ability to collect. It often became a way to feed and medicate ourselves and our families. A social and therefore, an architectural event. A portal through which we, quite literally, viewed and measured the [non]passing world.

"I can get you steroids, vitamins, greenies, anything you want. You name it. I'm the best hustler in the joint" (Caretaker, 2005).[41]
[41] Caretaker, "Caretaker meets Crew," Texas State Penitentiary, 27 May 2005.

Architecture as its own filtration device – the MASK [Metaphorical Architectural Signal Knowledge]

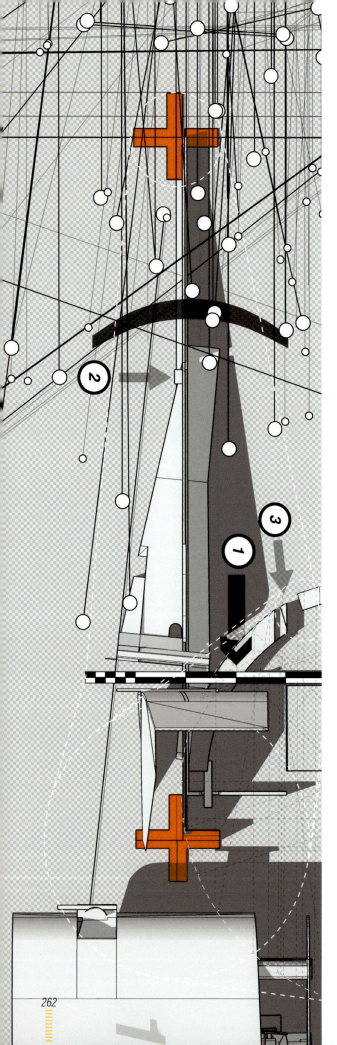

FILTER – AIR

The prototype also witnessed the emergence of the oversized air filtration system; no-longer furtive or hidden, it is articulated as a monolithic exchange unit, rather than a clandestine addendum, with an architectural identity, one that communicated one's desire [and ability] to live safely away from contagion. It replaces the multi-car garage as a symbol of domestic status. Never has the awareness of air handling offered such a unique an opportunity for architectural manifestation.

> "Hey, you're s'posed to be the fastest thing in the Valley man, but that can't be your ca(filte)r!"
> (Falafa, 1973).[42]

Air is extracted from the ducts and plenums of the private interior, a herald of physical responsibility, social consciousness, and political loyalties. It fortifies the idea of clean air, especially within one's own family, inverting the stronghold in on itself as relatives were often faced with intramural segregation.

> "Hello there – I'd like to talk you about ducts"
> (Central Services, 1985).[43]

Additionally, issues of air exchange, filtration, and light emittance become articulated in a colossal envelope of permeable mem[e]branes. Opposing façades of porous materials with operable louvers are intended to promote extreme cross ventilation and the absorption of the much-desired ultra-violet light, an attempt to neutralize potential infection, a climate-controlled collection of systems and [new] spatial taxonomies. Ironically it uses an open skin to discuss the closed nature of the project structuring. It talks about deep breathing in a time that encouraged shallow intake.

> "It was luxuries like air conditioning that brought down the Roman Empire. With air conditioning their windows were shut, they couldn't hear the barbarians coming" (Keillor, 2016).[44]

Can architecture become its own metric for filtration, its own exploration of isolation and porosity? Whilst the project itself was explored as a metA[rchitectural] condition – the drawings served as a speculative condition of buffering a [self] imposed distancing, asking if [an]architecture could become its own internal **annotated notation**? ✚

An act of [in]filtration[s]

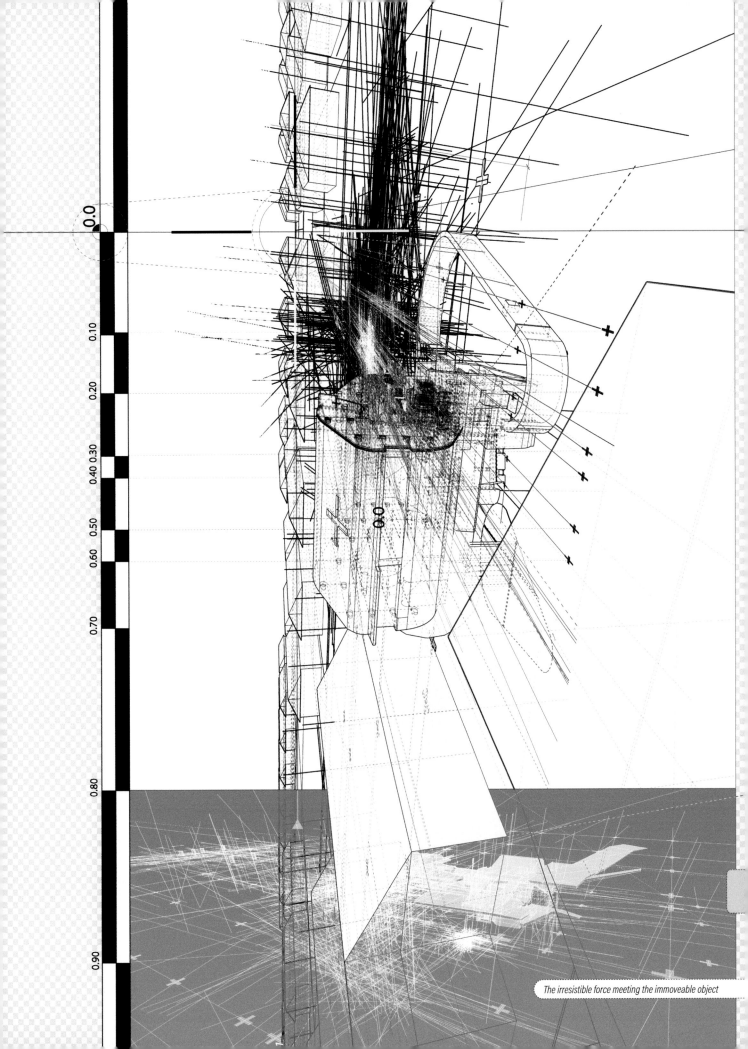

The irresistible force meeting the immoveable object

Eye, Hand, and Mind:
An interview with Bryan Cantley

Helen Castle
Publishing Director, RIBA

> "The pencil in the architect's hand is a bridge between the imagining mind and the image that appears on the sheet of paper" (Pallasmaa, 2009).[45]

[45] J. Pallasmaa, *The Thinking Hand: Existential and Embodied Architecture* (Chichester: Wiley), p. 17.

In Pallasmaa's classic book, *The Thinking Hand*, he highlights how the fusion of eye-hand-mind play a crucial role in creative work, most aptly in drawing.

At this moment when consumption of architectural drawings has shifted to social media, where visual images are viewed in a fast-paced, continuous feed at the speed of a like, there is incongruously a huge appetite for original work like Bryan Cantley's: artwork that expresses 'the thinking hand' with its embodied and existential qualities of dexterity and unique creative vision. At the time of writing Bryan has 24.4k followers on Instagram. This is a huge audience in architectural terms. It is tantamount to more than half the registered architects in the UK following him.

At RIBA, we regularly talk to architects and students about what they want more of in the journal – online and in print – and from our books. The resounding response is always more drawings and more about the underlying design process.[46]

It's as if the primacy of the visual, with the omniscience of the online image, has left designers with an insatiable yearning for what lies behind it: the individual handprint (whether analogue or digital) and greater insight into the thinking and making process.

[46] From January 2022, The RIBA Journal is adopting the tagline "Design in the Making" as part of an online content strategy that emphasizes the design process.

The best way to respond to this craving in academia and practice was to interview Bryan, in order to explore directly with him how his eye, hand, and mind converge in the drawing process. How does he employ observation, expression, technical process, imagination, and critical thought?

Eye: observation and expression

> "Drawing is a process of observation and expression, receiving and giving, at the same time. It is always a result of yet another kind of double perspective, a drawing looks simultaneously outwards and inwards, to the observed or imagined world, at the same time that it represents an object or vista in the real world, or in an imagined universe" (Pallasmaa, 2009).[47]

[47] The title is the date and version number of the last iteration of the text, with some slight artistic liberty on what constitutes final.

The visual quality of Bryan's work can perhaps best be characterized by duality. It draws on both observation and expression. It simultaneously explores the gritty specificity of the real world of iron and steel mechanical components while speculating on the possibilities of an imagined world. It is this that gives it its heightened sense of an alternative reality. In his Introduction, Neil Spiller adroitly describes it "as a visionary architectural tradition of machinic extreme dreams.

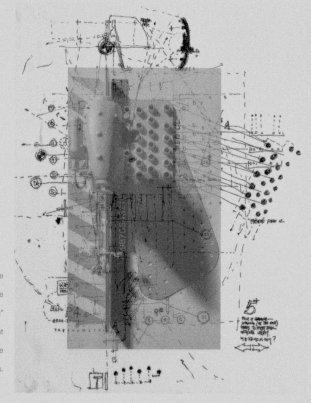

HC: So how did the process of observation and expression begin for Bryan?

BC: "It originally started as a set of observations and the explorations were not as much speculative as they were observations. And then at some point, I started to deconstruct the observation and started to reconstruct and reassemble and rethink the mechanical components. All of the drawings and certainly all of the projects rethink the internals and the externals of how machines and the machines' systems within the technology work."

"The projects all have circulation, and they have structure, and they have programme. The drawings do as well, but none of them necessarily looks like a traditional building or an architectural configuration, so it's been a sort of deconstruction and then a reconstruction of machine elements."

"The introduction of machine elements originally started from extreme observations growing up in a rural community in the South, in North Georgia, where I had access to a large host of machine forms to climb and play in as a child. I was influenced by these elements without an architectural metric. The farm and road construction equipment were large enough as a child for you to inhabit. They were the size of small houses."

"My dad was a textile worker. At times, he would take me into the plant. I remember climbing into one of the machines where they dyed massive amounts of fabric. These things were the size of small buildings, and it became a natural way for me to visually navigate and experience the machines."

"I had to, though, suppress all of that in my undergraduate education. It was only when I was a graduate at UCLA that the machines started showing up as elements within the buildings. Certainly not the building or not building components themselves. One of my professors, Doug MacLeod, said: 'You know your work, it reminds me a lot of this guy, Neil Denari. Much to my chagrin, I had not heard of Neil at that time. MacLeod showed me *Pamphlet Architecture #12*, featuring his work. It was a watershed moment for me.[48] It was the moment that I realized that buildings don't have to look like buildings that buildings could look and perform like machines. It was a breakthrough point. Mechanical components stopped becoming components or installations within the interior building and started to become the buildings or the architecture themselves."

[48] R. McCarter (ed.), *Pamphlet Architecture #12: Building Machines* (Princeton, NJ: Architectural Press, 1987). The publication features work by Neil Denari, Kaplan Krueger Scholz and Pfau Jones.

"I was raised around machines that both made other machines and that made architecture. Machines that were stripping the land for housing developments and building roads and machines that were making other machines to do those roles as well. For whatever reason that impregnated itself in me and all came to a head during that event, and at UCLA."

HC: Bryan goes on to explain why this underlying passion for the machinic lay stifled during undergraduate school:

BC: "It was in the mid-80s in the South, where architecture was taught a certain way and you had to learn the standards of architecture. I had to learn the rules before I could go back and start decoding them and kind of making them a bit of my own at UCLA."

HC: Given his own experiences, how does Bryan set out to nurture students' exploration of the given and self-expression? For him, it all depends on where students are in their education. As undergraduates, he encourages them to become sponges and to literally absorb everything. From architecture and from other disciplines. So, they understand the rules of how other disciplines are engaging – whether it's the rules of graphic design, painting, or fashion.

BC: "When students come towards the end of being undergraduates and start graduate school, I encourage them to do something similar to what I did and take those rules that they now understand and start carving out their own voice."

"As a musician, well a drummer! (The guy who likes to hang out with the musicians.) I often use the analogy of a cover band. As an undergraduate, you learn how to reproduce quite faithfully other people's sounds. In graduate school, you've stopped being a cover band and become original. You start writing and recording and then you start that journey all over again. You have to write your own rules and learn them. You have to figure out which ones are working, and which ones aren't. It's a perpetual learning curve."

"I've been in both kinds of bands. I've been in so many cover bands and probably four or five original bands, and it's a very similar thing. Unless you are one of the gifted ones you can't start as an original band."

Hand: analogue and digital technique

The rigor and unique creativity of Bryan's graphic technique is enthralling for any designer. The fact that he disparagingly describes it as a "boring, predictable process" is an indication of his critical drive and painstaking approach as much as his humility.

HC: So what are Bryan's typical steps when working on a drawing?

BC:

1. Writing and sketch booking: "A lot of the initial components with the drawing start with looking at related behaviors in sketchbooks before we even start getting into the form. I call them line politics."

2. Yellow trace: "With the trusted yellow trace, I start to look at formal relationships. It's a great medium because it behaves very much like the layers in Photoshop because you can draw layer #2 and then shift it to layer #4. This drastically changes relationships with everything above and below."

3. Large pencil geometry sheets: "I will typically do some pencil constructions of larger massing relationships, figuring out how components are going to start relating to each other within the geography of the page without becoming too set in their positions. I'll often do three or four of those large sheets."

4. Overlay sheets: "On the overlay sheets of DuraLar or Mylar polyester film, I do the inking process and shading. The shading is done fairly early, I don't use the shadows in their traditional sense: they are not generated from items. The absence of light on an object means they start to become their own formal components and reservoirs for conceptual and physical information. Giving the components the ability to start then relocating themselves. Not only on the X&Y, but also on the Z."

5. Introduction of other media: Occurs penultimately. It can be "paper or collage work or photographs or something else that might occur, such as multiple layers of Mylar at different levels."

6. Text and graphic information: "The pragmatics of the medium is that I'll put the letters, numbers, and graphic information on last. In the large part, they are done with the old transfer Letraset. They haven't been made for about 15 years and it can be hard to find stock. Now I am lucky if I get 20 percent usage out of it because most of the information won't come off the page. If you rub it slightly too hard then it picks up everything else that you've done. It's convoluted, but it's a pretty straightforward technical process that has a lot to do not only with the conceptual way that I'm thinking about the drawing, but also the physicality of the material palette that I use."

So where does the digital relate to this painstaking technique of hand drawing, layering, and collaging?

For Bryan, the digital is just another tool. Photoshop, for instance, taught him "to think of a drawing as a conceptual layering" which "translated to a physical layering." It "radically changed the way" that he was "constructing drawings." He now goes "back and forth between the two so fluidly, it's hard to sometimes isolate." Photoshop allows him to "generate different strategies about right versus left, up versus down, top versus bottom more rapidly" than if he sketches them out. He prints these tests out as a layer to trace or physically cut out.

Ultimately, though, Bryan regards himself and his process as "a victim of the chronology" of the analogue, even with the multi-layered drawings. When "you exact drawing information out of a model, there is no in-front-of or behind or on top that you can manipulate. It all becomes kind of mushed together". For Bryan, the drawing is a "singular event" with "foreground, mid-ground and background components." This is both "a challenge" and "liberation."

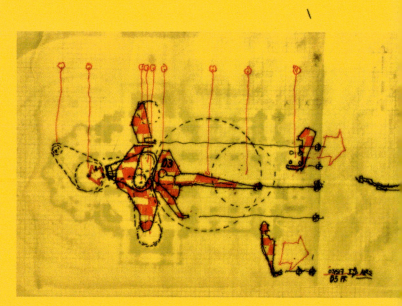

HC: So how does he take this approach to students who have grown up with a different digital tool set?

BC: "I'm an inventor and so I encourage students to take whatever tools they have at hand and use them to the best of their ability. Then to turn them upside down and to use them in ways that they wouldn't have, and then to find other tools that they wouldn't have thought of using before just to see where the speculation is going to take them. If you can, you need to get a student to embrace it by letting go of the safety net and venturing out into the areas of the unknown. They need to understand what the options might be, once they understand rule-based systems and which rules can be bent, and which can be broken."

The unconscious and thinking mind

HC: For Bryan the simultaneous engagement of the imaginative and thinking mind are key:

BC: "With drawing you have to engage both conduits [unconscious and critical] at the same time. There are parts of the drawing that are going to be analytical, particularly when you are finalizing, compressing and defining, and there's a large part of it that's going to be simultaneously moving in the opposite direction."

HC: The critical framing of each project from the outset provides a strong sense of intentionality.

As he explains:

BC: "Before I start a project or drawing, I write a set of rules or parameters – the issues that I want to deal with. They set out how things are going to behave, if a certain situation happens: if X then Y occurs."

Within these parameters, Bryan builds in the potential for a "generative set of responses. This challenges new rules to emerge as the drawing emerges. Often, they are in conflict with the original rules." This makes him "cognizant of writing a new emergent rule and how it might conflict with an original rule." It raises questions as to how to deal with 'the friction' and which one should come to the fore, which one should be undermined and which one rewritten. He provides the analogy of "writing a code for a project and then in the middle of coding the project writing it afresh."

For any designer or artist, a perennial quandary is knowing when to finish an artwork or project. For Bryan, it is also a conundrum, but best answered by "when the conscious and unconscious have answered the questions that have been posed, and they are somewhat resolved. Then a particular drawing is done for the time being and you move on to something else." It remains a dilemma as to "how one would strip the one from the other [conscious and unconscious] in the process of doing the drawing."

Synthesis

It is the imaginative and aesthetic qualities of Bryan's work that marks him out as a visionary architect. With its distinct style and machinic language, one of his images is recognizable at an immediate glance on screen. It is, however, the discipline and scrutiny of his process that are apparent when discussing his work with him: the union of eye, hand, and mind. His unique vision is as dependent on real-life observation as imaginative expression. His technique, though iterative, is highly structured in distinct steps, adhering to a clear 'chronology.' There is a keen synergy between the intentional and the instinctive in the creative process. For him invention resides in the tension of being both a rule-maker and rule-breaker. ✛

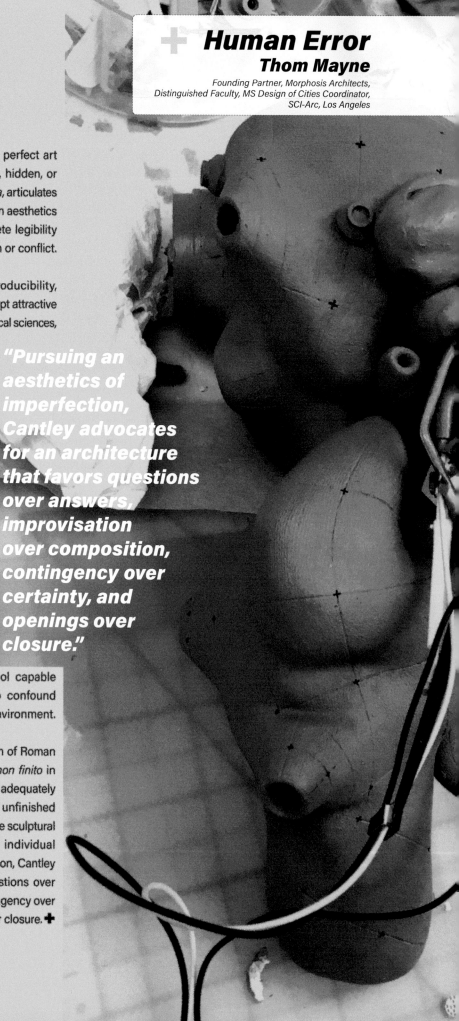

Human Error
Thom Mayne
Founding Partner, Morphosis Architects,
Distinguished Faculty, MS Design of Cities Coordinator,
SCI-Arc, Los Angeles

Alberti wrote that Rome had achieved such a perfect art of building that there was nothing mysterious, hidden, or unclear in its form. The treatise, *De re aedificatoria*, articulates a convention that continued to tyrannize Western aesthetics throughout modernity: the objective of complete legibility without the possibility of (mis)interpretation or conflict.

The *genericness* of perfection – its reproducibility, predictability, and universality – makes the concept attractive to contemporary modes of production. In the physical sciences, it proves useful as a wholly unreal standard utilized for theoretical purposes; however, perfection's transcendental quality can be violent, suppressing multiplicity, diversity, and change in the pursuit of ideals and resolution.

In the deliberately unresolved nature of his drawing experiments and building objects, Cantley uses subverted architectural processes as a way to think towards an alternative aesthetic driven by specificity instead of generality. Plan, section, and diagram – the classical devices of architectural representation – appear together in dialectical tension, generating new coherencies that reject the prescriptive intentionality of those drawing types. Juxtaposing the analogue and the digital, manual techniques resurface as the only tool capable of errors that are deft and dirty enough to confound the programmatic rationality of the digital environment.

"Pursuing an aesthetics of imperfection, Cantley advocates for an architecture that favors questions over answers, improvisation over composition, contingency over certainty, and openings over closure."

At the same time Alberti asserted the perfection of Roman building, Donatello introduced the concept of *non finito* in art – that the desires of the spirit could only be adequately expressed by the suggestive possibilities of unfinished sculpture. In their singularity and ambiguity, these sculptural objects newly engage the subjectivity of individual experience. Pursuing an aesthetics of imperfection, Cantley advocates for an architecture that favors questions over answers, improvisation over composition, contingency over certainty, and openings over closure.

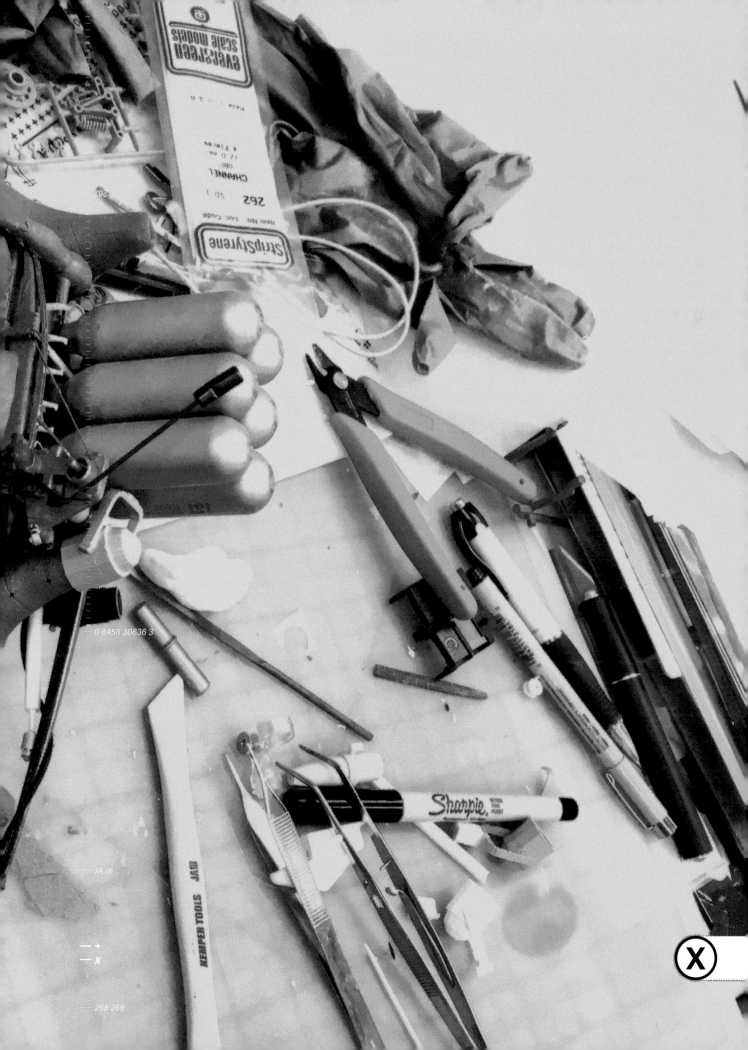

[Project Teams]

Initial concept layout strategies in collaboration with Christina Shin and Stray Dog Cafe
[Thank you Thom]

Alice [2.0]
Digital Model – Joey Dhindsa
Renderings – Joey Dhindsa + Bryan Cantley
Photography – Matt Gush

CSUF
Model – Kim Cantley + Bryan Cantley
Photography – Matt Gush
Renderings – Joey Dhindsa

Social AMPs 01, 02 + 03
Physical model – William Mills, Kim Cantley + Bryan Cantley
Photography – Matt Gush + Kevin O'Donnell
Renderings – Mike Amaya + Joey Dhindsa

COSMO
Renderings – Joey Dhindsa and Mike Amaya

Ozone Metric Anomaly
Digital model assistant – Megan Barnes
Photography – Matt Gush

Tree Hugger
Photography – Matt Gush

Camera
Invitation by Jerome Tryon/Yale

Syntaxonome
Photography – Matt Gush

'ME-di@ Logics + Being in the [k]now'
Editorial assistance – Eva Menuhin and Carrie Lane

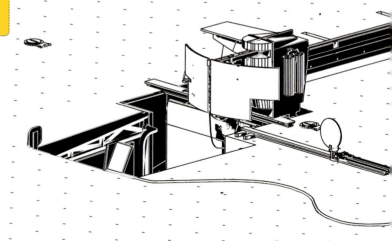

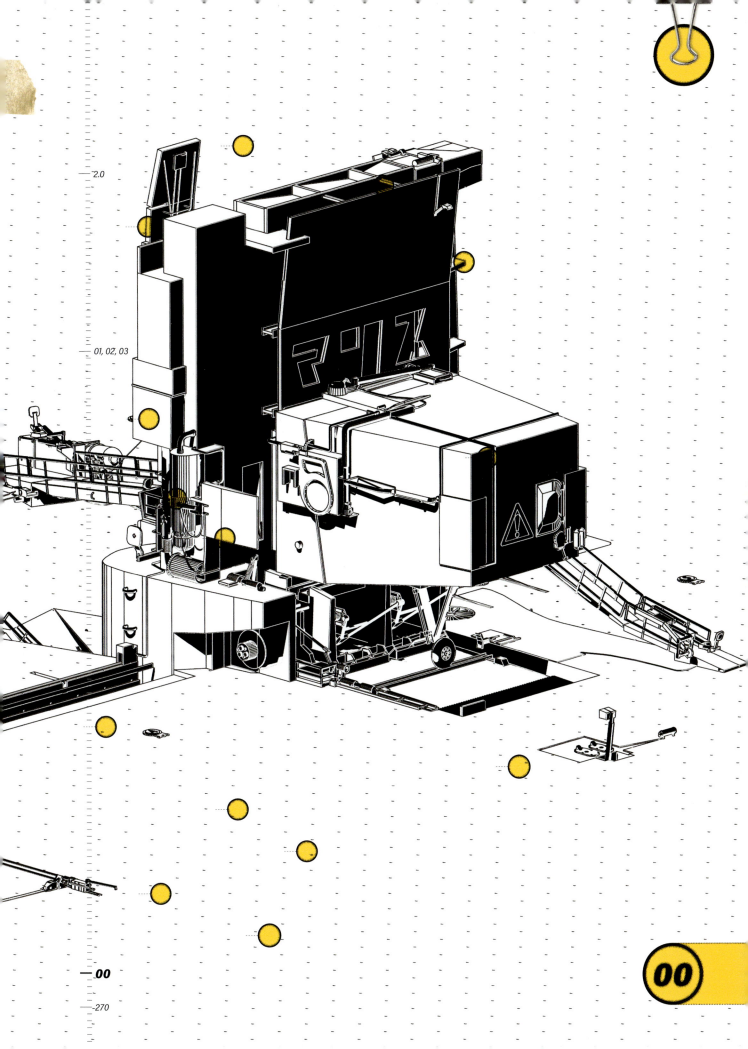

[Index]

Ackerman, James 52n24, 52-3
Ackerman, Virgil 204
'aesthetics of imperfection' 268
Alberti 268
'Alice in Wonderland' 15, 18n1, 19, 21n10, 35-6, 37n14, 38, 205
Altheide, David 20
analogue 150-1, 264, 266, 268; drawing systems 99; models 202; offspring 99; output 99; representation 99; transforming into digital 96, 99
annotations 24, 198, 202, 218
architects 15, 53-4, 186, 197, 202, 212, 225, 230, 247, 254, 264; designing 228; drawing 14; registered 264
architectural 14-15, 18-22, 24-8, 30-2, 52-3, 60-1, 86-8, 110-11, 122-4, 140, 150-1, 167, 202-5, 214-15, 225-6, 245, 247, 249-50, 261-2, 264-5; conditions 14-15, 25, 135, 137, 156, 179, 186, 195, 261; conventions 52-3; discourse 14, 61, 150-1; events 111, 123, 261; filters 256; interventions 31, 140, 205; languages 15, 94, 167, 247; practices 14, 122-3
architecture 14-15, 18-19, 21-2, 24-6, 30-2, 52-4, 86-9, 108, 122-4, 132-3, 135, 137, 150-1, 196-8, 202-5, 228, 247, 254, 261-2, 265; conceptualizing 205; Greek 249; industrial 197; machine 28, 32; new 14; simulated 203; site-anchored 122; speculative 150; theoretical 203, 247; viral 90; visionary 14
artifacts 24, 28, 96, 99, 140, 154, 158, 167, 206, 212, 217, 224-6; architectural 226; designed 224-6; final 30; independent 261
artists 38, 42-3, 267
arts 14, 20, 40, 42, 53, 87, 89, 151, 204, 209, 268
authorship 60, 91, 167, 205; despotic 123; devices 34, 38-9, 198; taxonometric 26, 28, 163

Baldwin, Peter J. 124n18, 161n1
Barthes, Roland 60n5, 60, 137n28, 137, 137n2, 192, 202n38, 202, 228
Baudrillard, Jean. 110n1, 203, 203n40, 209n1, 209
Berger, John. 137n29
bias 24, 40, 53-4; defeating 53; of neatness 54; of purpose 53; racial 53
bodies 59, 123-4, 128, 197-8, 225, 261; all-inclusive 26; calibrated architectural 198; collective 25; dissected 196; human 59; three-dimensional 26; unstable 123; of work 21, 25, 226
books 15, 18-21, 24, 30-1, 35-6, 38, 52-3, 60, 139, 205, 224; archetypal 30; classic 264; holy 140; layout of 224; open 30-1; quality of 225n9

Borrelli, Christopher. 256n32, 259n37
broadcasts 20n1, 24-5, 114, 132, 140, 159, 214
brothels 178-9, 185, 192
Bruner, Jerome 20
buildings 14, 38, 42, 53-4, 86-8, 188, 197-9, 202-3, 245, 247, 254, 265, 268; of Bryan Cantley 198; components 265; interior 265; new 93; sloped-roof 245; small 265; traditional 265
Burrell, Colston 256n31, 256

Camera Noxoculo 228, 232-3, 235
cameras 132, 196, 198-9, 228, 230, 232, 270
campus 43-4, 241-2
Cantley, Bryan 14-15, 57, 86-8, 111, 122-4, 132, 140, 150-1, 161, 197-9, 224-5, 226n15, 226, 228n18, 264-8; architecture 198; and buildings 198; caryatids 87; complexity of 88; iconography 15; influences of 15; machinogenic furballs 89; production processes 122; spatial speculations 124, 151; and treE-hugger device mapping trees 123; works of 19-20, 86-7, 89, 123, 264, 267
Cantley, Kim 97
Carpo, Mario. 202n34, 202, 224n7, 225n12
Carroll, Lewis 18n1, 21n10, 24, 28n10, 30, 36, 37n14
Centers for Disease Control and Prevention 256n35, 256, 259n36, 259
chronologies 24, 135, 164, 182, 185, 266-7; linearity of 27; skewed 167; speculative 182; synthetic 24, 137
churches 128, 132
Churchill, Winston. 188n20, 188
Clapton, Eric 52
Clear, Nic 202
codes 90-1, 94, 102, 196-8, 223, 267; areas 161; behavioral 212; operational 123; phoenix 94; relocation 96; scientific 122
colleges, visual arts 40, 44
communication 25, 31, 161, 164, 167, 202, 209, 212, 215, 218, 225; breakdown 212, 218, 244; devices 43; exposure 221, 223; graphic 218; linear nature of 206, 224; manifesto 209; mass 42, 132, 204; visual devices 44
community 44, 63, 128, 132, 233, 250, 256; inner 245; online 93; rural 265; scientific 196

complexity 18, 54, 57, 86–7, 198, 224, 226; contextual 122; emblematic 245; particular 86; phrasing 218; trusting 87

components 31, 35, 38, 186, 195, 198, 214, 217, 250, 256, 266; architectural 18; building 265; cerebral 31; formal 266; fundamental 30, 247; infectious 94; initial 266; integrated 154, 186, 195; interactive 31, 38; mechanical 264–5; primary dimensional 31; skinned 96; taboo 140

computer viruses 90–1, 94

computers 14, 53–4, 87, 91, 161, 198

congregations 60, 72

connotations 212, 249

consciousness 154, 159, 170, 230, 233; collective 54; explicit 26; human 130; social 262

construction 20, 26, 150, 196, 202, 208, 212, 214, 226, 245, 250; artificial 24; costs 255; environmental 112; pencil 266

consumers 63, 99, 161, 192, 247

containers 161, 224, 226

conventions 52–4, 87–8, 151, 154, 197, 268; operational 61; pairing 198; replication 91

coolness 18, 22, 52, 54, 150

Coronaviruses 259

crash test laboratories 197–9

creation 20, 24, 27–8, 30, 111, 202, 233

Crocker, B. 167n10, 167

CSFU sentinel projects 40

death 228, 230–3, 235

deconstruction 87–8, 123, 265

DeLanda, Manuel. 205n54, 205

Deleuze, Gilles. 123n11, 123, 124n17

Denari, Neil 15, 52, 150, 197n31, 197, 265

denotations 26, 31, 96, 202, 231; see also annotations

denouements 15, 22

design 15, 20–1, 26, 30, 140, 150, 198, 224–6, 228, 250; cinematic set 150; graphic 265; methods 19; new hybrid 202; period set 30; problems 161; processes 15, 202–3, 205, 225, 264; proposals 202

designers 42, 202, 224–5, 266–7

devices 94, 96, 99, 111–12, 114, 122, 124, 128, 132, 182, 184, 186, 198–9; architect's 185; classical 268; filtration 261; iCOn 247; occupant-operated 261; optical 231; recording 162, 234; storytelling 224; transcription 210

diagrams 54, 75, 124, 217, 232, 234–5, 268

dialogue 75, 150, 165, 205, 226; architectural 164; insertions 66; internal 28; organic 212; satellite 208, 214

Dick, Philip K. 204

digital 14, 18, 53, 91, 93–4, 96, 99, 111, 122, 151, 202–3, 224–6, 264, 266–8, 270; concepts 96; Darwinism 93; documents 139; images 99, 203, 230; media 224; techniques 266; theories 99; transformation 93; viruses 94

discipline 18–21, 26, 32, 40, 42, 52–3, 133, 135, 245, 250, 265, 267; architectural 18, 245; expertise 124; techniques 224

drawings 140, 150–1, 154, 167, 182, 184–6, 188, 192, 198, 202–5, 217–18, 230–2, 235, 264, 266–7; action of 154, 186, 195, 214; apparatus 210; architects 14; convention of architectural 52–3; data 182; devices 217; experiments 268; process 264; surface 231; types of 268; typology of 186, 188

drones 37, 59, 61, 63, 74, 94, 132, 258

Eberhardt, Jennifer L. 53n26

engagement 18–19, 44, 86, 88, 111, 151, 161–2; contemporary disciplinary 18; informational 161; intense 88; potential 88; simultaneous 267; social 70, 255; social media 162

entities 25–8, 35, 38, 126, 132, 182, 186, 188, 208, 214, 250; accessible 161; architectural 182; epigenetic 27; government 184; inserted 137; invisible 94; living 93; mapped/drawn 112; physical 140; public 161; segregated 27, 167; semi-autonomous 61; singular 249; social 72

environment 18, 36, 59, 63, 124, 150, 154, 159, 165, 202, 204–5; constructing 165; digital 268; immersive 205; infrastructure 111; natural 24, 111; new social 261; occupiable 205; personal 204; physical 112; urban 94, 178; virtual 202, 204

Evans, Robin 202

events 59, 63, 122, 128, 132, 182, 196–7, 231, 265; background 28; charged 180; coinciding 27; dense 124; flat 235; simultaneous 231; singular 214, 266; un-real 24

exchanges 21, 25, 28, 31, 66, 179–80, 185, 192, 204, 233; fiscal 188; hosted friendly 256; recorded 68

experiments 24, 27–8, 52–4, 69, 108, 150–1, 167, 188, 192, 196, 205; drawing 268; two-space 126; worldwide social 225

explorations 19, 60–1, 63, 212, 224, 238–9, 262, 264; conceptual 225; nurture students 265; theoretical 246; traditional media 96; visible 96

expressions 150–1, 179, 264; architectural 25; creative 122; equalized 26; imaginative 267; process of observation and 264

façades 40, 42, 44, 188, 245, 262;

domestic 256; glass 250; membrane 245
Falfa, Bob. 262n42, 262
fantasy 203–4, 225
filtration 242, 256, 262
fiscal mappings 192–3
Foster, Norman 15
Foucault, Michel. 18n4, 18, 19n6, 19
fracking 59, 61, 63

Genotext 137n2
Germann, G. 247n26, 247
Gibson, William 15
Gore, Al. 161n2, 161
graphics 27, 57, 86, 88, 167, 182; information 99, 186, 266; newfound 15; on surfaces 111
ground planes 59, 61, 179
Guattari, Félix. 123n11, 123n14, 123, 124n17
Guy, Buddy 52n22, 52, 54

Harman, Graham. 28n9, 28n11, 88, 128
Hemingway, Ernest 256
Henry County Museum 128n21, 128

identity 40, 46, 132, 167, 180; architectural 262; classification 132; crisis 247; forced 179; gender 179; group 249; proposal 40; spatial 233
images 71, 76, 88–9, 135, 140, 196, 203, 209, 231–2, 234, 264, 267; discursive 123; holographic 38; mirror 35
information 18–19, 21, 25–6, 31, 38, 70, 75, 111, 202–4, 209–10, 224–6, 266; categories of 19, 21; discharge 161; dissemination of 63, 132; distribution 63, 132; embedded 224; factual 61; physical 266; referencing new 203; residual 99, 232; supplemental 21; synthetic contextual 63; transmitted 24; visual 203
infrastructure 18, 111–12, 203
Inhabitable Drawing 205
innovations 53–4, 226
intentions 20, 31, 53, 86, 88, 94, 111, 167, 224, 231, 235; architectural 25, 167; avoiding the dual pitfalls of premature reduction and homogeneity 19; to examine the plane of community collection 63, 188; political 151
interactions 31–2, 38, 67, 70, 86, 111, 130, 204, 212, 215, 261; architectural 255; human 255, 261; identifiable 86; pedestrian 31; physical 18, 30; relational 59; serendipitous 203; social 64, 128
internet 25, 93, 161, 188, 225
interpretations 18–21, 24–5, 30, 38, 63, 132, 225, 268
inventions 14, 140, 197, 202, 226, 267; arbitrary 52; formal 87

Jefferson, T. 188n21, 188
Johnson, Samuel 75n9
Jones, Angela 188
Jones, Geraldine. 167n9, 167
Jones, Wes 15, 86, 197n32, 197

Kahn, Albert 197n33
Kahn, Louis 249n28
Keillor, Garrison. 262n44, 262
Kelly, Kevin. 58n1, 58
Kennicott, Philip. 36n13, 254n30, 254
knowledge 18–19, 25, 44, 62, 67, 72, 114, 225, 250; crowd source 225; direct 226; disciplinary 19; graphic 214; implicit 24; prior 203

laboratories 165, 197–9
landscape 36, 38, 60, 151, 159, 188, 225, 246
language 15, 27–8, 53–4, 88, 135, 197, 209, 224–5; architectural 15, 94, 167, 247; common 124; formal 167; inscribed 54; machinic 267; multivalent 122; programming 225
Latour, Bruno 123
Le Corbusier 40n16, 40, 204n45, 204, 228
light 20, 186, 196, 249, 266; emittance of 262; rays 186; red 188; ultra-violet 262
logic 24–5, 27–8, 42, 123–4, 197, 202, 270; architectural 123; binary 14; exclusionary 123; programmatic 20

machines 57–8, 61, 72, 86, 93, 97, 154, 159, 161, 165, 182, 186, 264–5; building 52, 197; inequity 245; kitbashed 226
mapping 15, 61, 110–12, 150; fiscal 192–3; modes 124; projective 116; records 94; texture 26; transcriptions 121
Marey, Étienne-Jules 196n28, 196n30, 197–9
mass communication 42, 132, 204
Mayne, Thom. 42n18, 42, 167n8, 217
McLuhan, Marshall 52n21, 52, 202, 202n35, 202, 225
mechanisms 27–8, 31, 38, 63, 75, 99, 212, 224, 247
media 18–22, 24–5, 27, 31, 58–60, 63, 132–3, 140, 154, 158–9, 202–3, 217, 225–6; architectural 132, 167; aspiration 132; culture 21, 122; decentralization 130; digital 14; electronic 209; manipulation 225; protocols 25; saturation 156, 162; shifting 96, 225–6; situational 214; sources 203; traditional analogue 96; typology 44, 111
"Media Logic" 18–20, 25, 31, 59, 91, 111, 135, 159, 215, 231
medium 18, 24–5, 154, 158–9, 196, 202, 205, 212, 217, 224–6, 266; interfacial 124; new 196; social 204; synthetic 204; virtual 225
metrics 28, 63, 110, 135, 156, 162, 167, 171, 192, 259, 261–2; architectural 265; chronological 137; shadow-scanning 185; systemic 192; visual MEdia 156

microscopes 64, 72, 196
models 15, 25, 27, 158, 167, 197–8, 215, 217–18, 226, 266, 270; architectural 167, 218; cam 188; digital 99, 270; physical 167, 270; plaster 198; theoretical 19; wind tunnel test 198
Morpheus 36n13, 39n15, 261n38
Moss, Eric Owen 226n15
Muybridge, Eadweard. 196n29, 196–8

networks 111, 122, 128, 156
non-verbal communications 96
notations 14, 26–7, 60, 97, 151, 224, 226; architectural 15, 225; connoted 249; graphical 25, 198; internal annotated 262; live 27; plane of 142, 148; standardized graphic 226; trajectory 193
Novak, Marcos 204

obfuscation 206–7, 209, 226
Object Oriented Ontology 26, 86
objects 25–8, 86–8, 96, 167, 196–8, 214, 218, 224–6, 232, 235, 259, 264, 266; architectural 26, 218; building 268; dual 99; foreground 28; immoveable 263; malleable 140; observed 59; sacred 140; sculptural 268; sources of 225
occupancy 28, 38, 59, 61, 179, 205; cerebral 203; commercial 261; reservoir 245
occupants 25, 38, 72, 75, 111, 124, 154, 196–7, 205, 232–4, 245
Odinson, Loki. 185n17, 185
operators 42, 59, 63
output 140, 150, 202, 214–15; analogue 99; digital 99; functions 140; idiosyncratic 70; residual graphic 214; virtual 224
ozone 156–7, 161–2, 164–5
Ozonic Metric Anomaly Project 122–4, 156, 167

Page, Jimmy 52
palimpsestuous relationships 126, 198
Pallasmaa, Juhani. 264n45, 264
parameters 108, 111, 122–3, 267; contextual 123; fictitious 24; semiotic 122
Parker, Dorothy. 161n3, 161
Peart, Neil 14
phenomena 111, 114, 185–6, 196, 206–7, 209
Phenotext 135, 137
photographers 228, 231
photographs 19, 99, 196, 203, 228, 230–1, 266n5
photography 196, 198
Pichler, Walter 150
pigments 108, 135, 151–2
planes 24, 38, 40, 61, 63, 97, 150, 192, 197–8, 231, 233; abstracted 150; background 233; becoming-construction 124; exposed 38; horizontal 61; mediated mechanical ground 14; mirrored 38; unperceived 26
process 52–4, 59–61, 63, 70, 88, 93, 96, 99, 154, 196, 202–3, 224–6, 266–7; analog 225; computational 54; convergent photographic 228; creative 267; digital 99; generative graphical 202; inking 266; layered 151; new 93; scanning 99; sublimation 124; subverted architectural 268; technical 264, 266; virtual 226
professions 179, 242, 245, 247, 250
programs 38, 90–1, 93, 128, 180, 184
projections 24–5, 42, 119, 140, 162, 165, 198, 214; immersive 75; mental 39; new social 60; speculative 214
projects 19–20, 24–8, 30–2, 35, 38–40, 44, 93–4, 122–4, 162, 167, 186, 198, 202–3, 212, 214–15, 217, 224–6, 239–40, 255, 267; architectural 26, 167, 214, 217; Cantley's 123; design 20; structuring 262; transgressing practices 122; writing 267
prostitution 178–9

readers 14, 18–19, 21, 25, 28, 31–2, 34, 38, 60, 88, 202
references 15, 19–20, 26, 28, 86, 135, 137, 196, 202, 214, 217, 225, 231; artificial 24; circular 225; dualistic 27; missing 225; polemic 150; pop culture 21; visual 231
registrations 15, 198–9
religion 126, 128
reprogrammable holographic representations 38
reprogramming host cells/conditions 91
residues 26, 61, 63, 111, 137, 185–6, 217–18, 233, 245; dark 108, 151–2; derivate 161; Taxonometric 232; Trajectory 192
responses 19, 21–2, 58, 112, 123, 167, 186, 204–5, 255, 259, 267; architectural 20; finite 167; resounding 264; typological 19
responsibility 24, 60; perceived 224; physical 262
Rogers, Richard 15
Roth, Todd 52
Roussel, Raymond 14
rules 18, 31, 53, 86, 94, 198, 240, 265, 267; new 267; original 267; uploading immediacy 234

Sachs 69
scientists 14, 162, 196
segregated entities 27, 167
self 74, 132, 135, 228, 230–4, 237, 242, 262; appointed tasks 15; awareness 88, 233; digital 39;

expression 265; fictitious 234; two-sided 232
self-governed brothels 178–9, 185, 192
selfies 25, 228, 230–1, 234
sensibilities 124, 154, 198–9
sex workers 179, 188
sexual acts 179–80
shadows 54, 179, 182, 184–6, 192, 266
Sheil, Bob 150, 226
shorelines 108, 151–2
Simpson, Homer. 161n5, 161, 178n13, 178
Sinan, Mimar 228
skin 38, 150, 162, 164, 196–8, 243; atmospheric 162; domestic 248; filmic 108, 151–2; human 162; open 262
Snow, Robert 20
social engagement 70, 255
social interactions 64, 128
social media 18, 24, 60–1, 63, 128, 130, 132, 188, 204, 206, 224–5; engagement 162; membranes 165; omnipresence 132; platforms 124, 224; traffic 156
space 27–8, 36, 38, 61, 63, 128, 130, 140, 150, 196–7, 225–6, 256, 259
space: calibrated 196, 198; conceptual 162; confined 254; contemporary 14; digital 225; domestic 254; egalitarian 256; embedded 224–5; indefinite 123; interstitial 36; liminal 226; non-productive 259; open-ended 224; political 24; productive 226; public 254; residual 112; rockets 198; social 226, 255; virtual 224–6
spatial occupancies 234–5
speculations 27, 54, 61, 108, 124, 150–1, 267; developing architectural 151; experimental 151
Spiller, Neil 18n5, 122n6, 150, 202n37, 202n36, 202, 264
strategies 32, 40, 214, 264; multiple recording 25; online content 264; positional 219; relational 230, 240; situational 113; spatial 114
structures 19, 30, 35, 38, 94, 209, 214, 249, 264; class 63; conceptual 240; graphic notation 27–8; internal 204; new mega-parking 40; nomad's 123; relational 93; rhizomatic 124; unexecuted 90; unified 212; visible 249
students 15, 44, 226, 245, 250, 264–5, 267
subjects 69–70, 75, 135, 140, 150, 196, 198, 218, 228, 231, 233; abstract calibrated 197; imaging 231; knotty 151; photographic 231; segregated 185
surface 42, 59, 64, 72, 75, 93, 96, 135, 137, 140, 197, 203, 259; conditions 111; dwellers 96; instructions 111; qualities 63; scanning 218; splicing 63
syntaxonomes 205, 212, 214–15, 217
systems 38, 58, 63, 93, 96, 99, 111–12, 156, 161, 225–6, 262, 264, 267; architectural 63; background 96; coordinate navigation 150; hierarchical 212; interactive 38; mapping 99; mechanical delivery 247; notational 226; orthographic projection 214; remote 94; rule-based 267; tactical 63

Takei, George. 188n19, 188
taxonometric conditions 26, 28, 163
technology 14, 18–21, 24–5, 28, 60–1, 70, 99, 123, 133, 202; advanced 164; destabilizing 25; digital 122, 209; new 226; of religion 126; space 161; synthetic 234; virtual 93; working 264
tombs 228, 230, 232–5
tools 25–6, 52, 150, 203, 218, 266–8; architectural 210; broken 26; communicative 52; malfunctioning 26
traditions 15, 18, 53–4, 96, 167, 186, 192, 226, 233, 255–6, 264–6; architectural 15, 264; new 54; suburban garden 256
translations 26, 43, 111, 124, 151, 224–5
transmission 28, 41–2, 99, 132; diagramming 222; music 159; repair 218
transmission devices 38, 159
treE-huggers 111–12, 123–4
Tree Huggers mappings 205
truth 24, 44, 75, 80, 83, 132, 140, 151, 167, 186, 224–6; on demand 132; founding 108, 110; multiple 68; perception of 204; ultimate 140
Twain, Mark. 132n24, 132
typologies 20, 96, 140, 167, 205, 215

uBro-ssv 179, 186, 192
urban environment 94, 178

Vaughan, Stevie Ray 52
vessels 31, 38, 114, 179; communicative 28; project 28; technological delivery 192
viruses 90–1, 94, 102, 225, 254, 259; computer 90–1, 94; digital 94; non-resident 91
visual arts colleges 40, 44
voyeurs 38, 65, 69, 132, 245

Wachowski, Lana. 36n13, 43n19
Wallace, Barnes 15
Whyte, William H. 209n2, 209
wind tunnels 197–8
workers 179–80, 192, 265
Worthington, Arthur Mason 196n26, 196
writings 60, 135, 224, 267

York, Thomas E. 111n3, 111
Youngman, Henry. 247n25

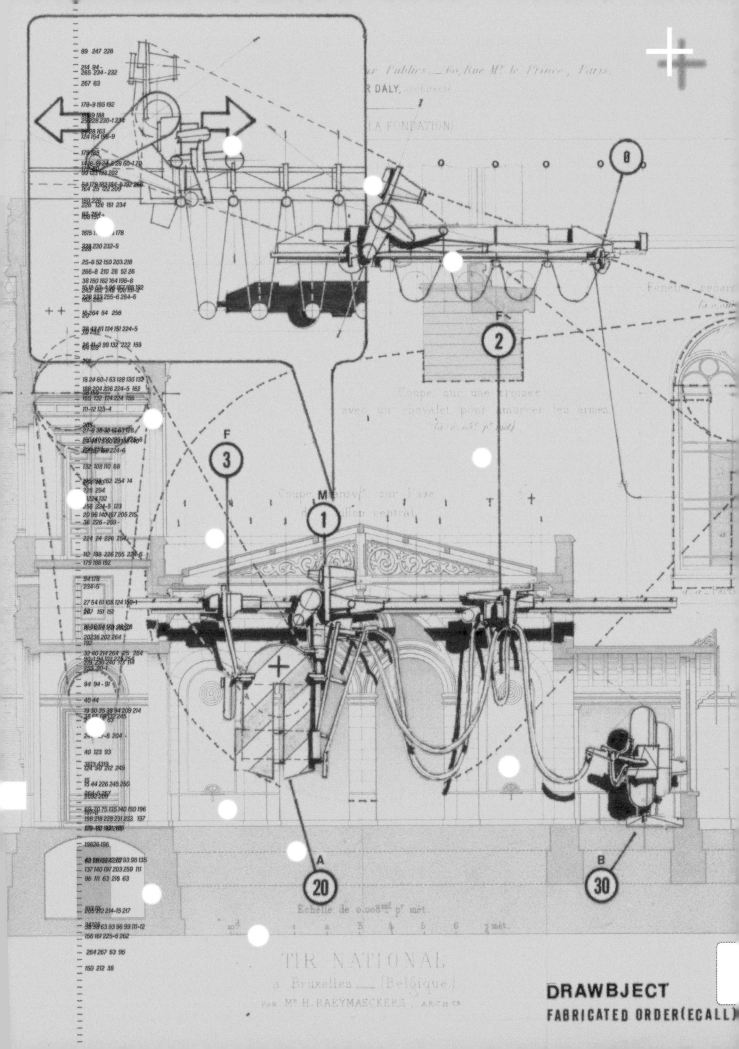

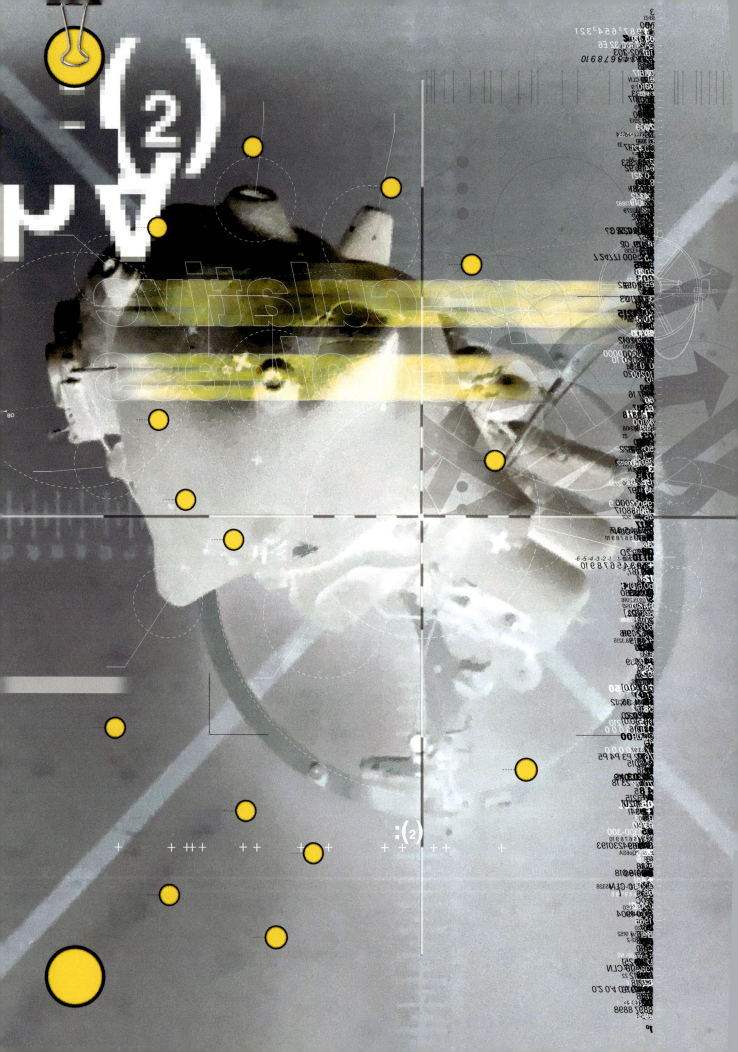